Economics for historians

Economics for historians

G. R. HAWKE
Professor of Economic History
Victoria University of Wellington
New Zealand

CAMBRIDGE UNIVERSITY PRESS

Cambridge
London   New York   New Rochelle
Melbourne   Sydney

Published by the Press Syndicate of the University of Cambridge
The Pitt Building, Trumpington Street, Cambridge CB2 1RP
32 East 57th Street, New York, NY 10022, USA
296 Beaconsfield Parade, Middle Park, Melbourne 3206, Australia

First published 1980

Printed in the United States of America
Typeset by Vail-Ballou Press, Inc., Binghamton, NY
Printed and bound by Vail-Ballou Press, Inc., Binghamton, NY

Library of Congress Cataloging in Publication Data
Hawke, Gary Richard.
Economics for historians.
Includes bibliographical references and index.
1. Economics. I. Title.
HB171.5.H3495   330   79–22127
ISBN 0 521 22734 8 hard covers
ISBN 0 521 29627 7 paperback

Contents

Preface

This book is intended for students of history who realise that their subject demands some understanding of economics. I assume that the main interest of my readers is in some aspects of the past and that the fascination of abstract ideas, while real, is decidedly subordinate. I seek to build on an initial feeling that economics is relevant to understanding important aspects of the past by elucidating the ways in which economics can be important. Readers should eventually be confident that they can recognise when economics is important and what economics is important and that they can go on beyond this book when historical studies make more advanced economics relevant to them.

Within the large class of potential users so defined, I have in mind especially students reading economic history in British universities. They are now more likely than they were in the past to take a course in economics principles, but for most of their studies they will have little contact with economics. They will be taught (and usually well taught) by teachers who give little explicit attention to their reliance on economics. I think it is easy to underestimate the difficulties of relating the first-year economics principles course to the problems encountered in historical studies; practising economic historians forget how much they use the ideas of theoretical economics. So often the student of economic history has memories only of distasteful encounters with things like marginal revenue, which never seemed to occur in historical time, and no one explains how the idea is developed for use in historical studies. I seek in this book to explain economic ideas so that they can be related to historical interests and to persuade students who have done an economics principles course that the subject was not as irrelevant as they thought. (I have not assumed any previous economic background.)

These problems do not exist only in Britain. In Australia, New Zealand, and the United States, for example, it is usual for students of economic history to take more courses in economics, but the difficulty of relating theory to historical studies remains. Even in the United States, training economists with a prime interest in economic history is mostly a graduate activity, although undergraduates also should find this book useful. I have been told that the situation is much the same in Spain and Italy, and it is probably true of other European countries too. Nevertheless, I have kept the historical examples discussed in the book mostly to Britain, partly because of the main readership I have in mind and partly because, as will become clear to the reader, there is a particular merit in having several examples recur throughout the book. I think that readers in other countries will readily find local examples analogous to those used in the text, and I do not think British history is so old-fashioned that it detracts from the interest of the book.

There is a much wider group of people who seek to understand economics so that they can participate in current political and social discussions. They too may find this book useful, especially if they realise that it is an understanding of economic ideas and not a mastery of particular techniques which they want. But my focus is firmly on historical interests (which I think a good route to understanding current issues), and I have not been willing to sacrifice that for a wider immediate appeal.

The main principle by which the content of this book has been chosen is that it should deal with economic analysis that has been used in historical studies. This is at one and the same time the main justification for the book and the main difficulty in its composition. The economics which has been used in historical work is not conveniently organised relative to orthodox introductions to economics; it includes ideas usually included in intermediate rather than elementary texts, it omits material often used as building blocks towards ideas which have been used, and single historical studies usually draw on several aspects of economics, often widely dispersed in an orthodox treatment. An introduction designed for historians is not just the usual text with some reference to events in the past.

I have not used the usual labels of macroeconomics and microeconomics, that is, very roughly, the areas concerned with whole economies and with individual people and firms respectively. The usefulness of these labels is often debated by mainstream economists, but they clearly have little relevance to the way in which economics has been used by historians. I have found it more useful to think in terms of two strands of thought; those economic ideas developed in the course of analysing the level of wealth achieved in a society, and those developed in the context of exchanging one commodity against another. These two strands have frequently intertwined and they do not play a major role in the book itself, but they provide the basis for the order in which ideas are presented.

After Chapter 1, which is designed to bolster the reader's confidence while introducing some fundamental economic ideas in precisely the style used in historical texts, we have a group of chapters which follows the former stream. We begin with the concept of income. I have sometimes speculated that the essential difference between economic historians whose primary allegiance is to economics and those whose primary allegiance is to history is that the former first identify a central process and then analyse it while the latter build up an overall picture from its component parts. Chapter 2 is intended to familiarise the reader with the former means of study, and to set out, by example, the way in which economic concepts are related to empirical reality. Chapters 3 and 4 deal with ideas which have arisen in looking at the determinants of income from various points of view. In Chapter 5 attention is turned to monetary matters but with the focus still on the analysis of wealth.

Chapters 6 to 8 turn to the exchange tradition. The first of these is headed 'Relative Prices' to avoid the usual emphasis on the psychology of individuals and keep attention on the issues associated with individual prices in historical studies. This enables us to go further in topics such as consumers' surplus than many introductory texts without incurring great costs. Similarly, Chapter 7 treats those aspects of international economics used in history while avoiding many of the policy issues found in most textbooks. And contrary to what might be expected, much of the modern development of growth economics lies mostly in the stream of ideas about exchange, and that part which is important to historians is introduced in Chapter 8.

My emphasis is on economic ideas. It would be easy to write

corresponding 'applications' chapters, but I do not wish to write a forbidding tome. Chapter 9 is partly an exception to this self-denying ordinance, and it is included because historians are accustomed to a heavy emphasis on government activities. Examples of the development of economic ideas are otherwise incorporated in the text, using the historical literature. In teaching economics and economic history, I am often aware of a tension between talking about theoretical issues in a particular context (which is often useful for retaining student interest) and isolating a theoretical construct so that it can be recognised in a number of guises. That the shape of the production possibilities curve which is often introduced in some abstract puzzles about international trade has something to do with apparently conflicting measurements of the rate of growth in the Soviet Union in the 1930s often comes as a revelation to undergraduate students. Hence, I have tried to vary the degree to which my references to the historical literature are built into the economic analysis. In most cases (Chapters 3, 5, and 6–9) they are scattered through the text, but the extent to which they are detached or detachable is varied, and in Chapters 2 and 4 they are kept for a separate section at the end of the chapter. This has the additional advantage of showing the different degrees of abstractness of ideas within economics; the study of money has always had a more immediate connection with observation than has discussion of economists' rent.

Chapter 10 draws the book together and returns to some of the themes of the first chapter. Readers who have worked through the book are guided towards an assessment of how it has affected their perception of the part of economics in historical inquiry. I hope there are such readers, but I have been conscious of the likelihood that readers will want to refer to particular topics, and the chapters and even sections within chapters are substantially self-contained.

The intended readership of this book imposes constraints on the way it is written. Given students whose interest does not have to be retained by some device to create 'relevance', I have no doubt that the most efficient way to teach elementary economics is to start with some mathematics (although I do not think that mathematics should be permitted to absorb economics, including the essentially historical processes of relating concepts to reality and interpreting empirical evidence). But the readers of this book are unlikely to tolerate mathematics; indeed, they probably have an active antipathy to it. Consequently, the mathematical demands are very slight. Some equations are introduced in Chapter 4, but the text carefully steers around them. I hope that the treatment shows even the most timid reader that the equations are not incomprehensible and that the few later topics where equations are essential can be digested without undue difficulty.

I have used 'mathematical' here to mean primarily 'algebraic', since that is the sense in which historians usually use the word. The more subtle aspects of 'mathematics' in a sense close to logic are indeed present but expressed in the language used by historians. There is also a frequent use of diagrams. I am aware that history students are often not accustomed to reading diagrams thoroughly, but I do not think that economics can be expounded, or a great deal of economic history literature read, without an understanding of simple diagrams. The necessary skill requires little learning, merely a modicum of persistence and practice. I have, on the other hand, avoided the arithmetic examples usually found in introductory economics texts. My experience is that history students are diverted rather than assisted by such devices, the labour of following the arithmetic taking attention away from the important principle being illustrated. My usual approach is a direct exposition of economic ideas. This makes the text look difficult to those familiar with conventional treatments, but I am convinced that history students can handle more abstract thinking than is usually appreciated. I took a related approach in two earlier books and their reception has permitted me to retain my view [G. R. Hawke, *The Development of the British Economy, 1870–1914* (Auckland: Heinemann, 1970) and *The Evolution of the New Zealand Economy* (Auckland: Heinemann, 1977)]. Indeed, I think the pupils to whom those books were addressed find less difficulty with them than their teachers do! But one of the values of this present book may well be to show conventional British economic historians that they use economic theory a great deal more than they realise and that they can make it easier for their students to gain the necessary knowledge.

A first draft of this book was written while I enjoyed the hospitality extended to a Visiting Fellow at All Souls' College, Oxford. Seminars at the Universities of Cambridge, Edinburgh, Glasgow, Leeds, London, and Sheffield commented generously on some of its ideas. I am even more indebted to friends and colleagues who have favoured me with advice, especially Margaret Arnold, F. Capie, S. L. Engerman, R. C. Floud, J. D. Gould, T. B. Layton, D. N. McCloskey, P. K. O'Brien, and D. C. M. Platt. I should thank too the writers of abstracts for an ANZAAS conference in Auckland in January, 1979. The dullness of the abstracts, which was not justified by the meetings I did attend, contributed greatly to the speed with which the final revision of this book was accomplished.

G. R. Hawke

Wellington, New Zealand
January 1980

1

History and economics

Historical skills in economics

Historians are much too deferential to economics. Economists have an apparent mastery of sophisticated mathematical techniques, and they are able to earn high incomes in public administration or business, presumably because of those skills. For a profession which claims little but trained common sense for its own members, economists appear high powered. Furthermore, unlike most other mysterious disciplines, economics is said to contribute to history itself, to an understanding of the evolution of human societies in the past.

There are indeed claims to be made for the usefulness of economics in a variety of fields, and in the last twenty years or so economic history has benefited from a renewed infusion of economic theory. But in applied work, whether in public policy, business administration, or economic history, the aspects of economics which are most fruitful are not particularly arcane. Rather, applied economics is characterised by the intelligent deployment of some simple concepts, the understanding of which is not beyond anybody who has mastered techniques regarded as commonplace by historians.

Furthermore, those who understand the processes by which knowledge and understanding are derived from the partial and fragmented empirical remains from the past are already halfway to the intellectual equipment needed for applied economics and have, perhaps, gained that equipment in the best possible way. There is a field of study known as decision making under uncertainty which usually occupies a prominent place in the training of economists and which looks mathematically demanding and even frightening to most historians; but in any piece of applied economics it is likely to be much less useful than the process of forming judgment on the basis of incomplete information which, for historians, is the most familiar activity of all. There is yet another comfort for the historian who feels the need to understand economics. Economics is itself becoming a more historical discipline. The recent textbook by Robinson and Eatwell,[1] while generally regarded as idiosyncratic and indeed erroneous in places, is widely approved as having more historical sensitivity than earlier texts such as those by Samuelson.[2] Perhaps even more telling is the extent to which the recent work of some leading economists gives markedly greater attention to history,[3] both the history of the subject and the history of the economies which particular pieces of economic analysis were designed to illuminate. This is partly an incidental byproduct of a desire by economists to improve their analysis of the way in which economies grow. But there is also a more general recognition that the process of intellectual thought itself occurs in historical time and that much can be learned by looking carefully at the sequence of innovations by which analysis is forwarded.[4] As changes over time in both perceived problems and in the responses of disciplines such as economics become more prominent, the skills of historians are likely to be more highly esteemed.

It is not to be expected that the barriers which seem to stand between many historians and economics will easily be swept away. To begin to follow the reasoning of economists, a historian must be prepared to tolerate some differences of style and approach. An economist tends to emphasize the abstract and to be selective in the things to which he devotes his attention. Economic analysis is usually presented as a tentative or conditional answer to a particular set of issues. To the historian advised to include in his ambit all the available evidence and to seek definitiveness in his writing, these characteristics seem simply misguided. The conflict of practice is not nearly so stark. Historians do employ abstraction but mostly in terms and concepts which have come to be part of common language or which were familiar in the society about which they are writing. Historians are selective in their choice of topics or themes, but divisions such as those between politics at Westminster and political organisations in the constituencies are different from the divisions employed by economists. No historian really expects finality in the interpretation of a major historical process, and errors in the handling of evidence are culpable in any study. Differences of degree do remain significant. The usefulness of a selective discussion of an issue and the extent of incompleteness which should be permitted in publication remain matters for individual judgment – about which there is likely to be some difference between economists and historians. But these are hardly matters crucial enough to prevent each discipline from learning from the other.

There is a deeper matter which we have already hinted at. Historians frequently use expressions like 'understanding the past in its own terms', while economists want to employ concepts developed more recently in their studies of past societies. The point might be described as a conflict between 'past centred' and 'present centred' studies. Again, the difference is one of degree. No historian can sensibly restrict himself entirely to the words and concepts of the society which he is studying; nor, even more, can he divest himself of the knowledge and outlook of his own time. Similarly, no economist can hope to explain the motivation of a past action in terms of modern concepts unless he can translate those concepts into notions which might have been present in the mind of the historical actor. But merely narrowing the difference would miss the main force of the point. *Historians and economists do not always ask the same questions.* It makes sense to the latter to ask whether a particular investment was a sensible use of resources, even if the historian knows perfectly well that it was made because the king believed that the well-being of his immortal soul depended on it.[5] There is surely no conflict between these positions, inasmuch as different questions usually have different answers. Historians interested only in the motivations of people may still find it useful to know what economists can tell about the nature of the society in other respects; other historians with less restricted interests may welcome the same gain and more. Economists too may come to understand more of the results of their analyses from what historians with other concerns can tell them; in particular, few economists really have no interest in motivations.

Historians and economists are likely to have overlapping rather than identical interests. Because of the way in which the disciplines have grown, there are always likely to be differences of taste and style between them.[6] Nevertheless, they have a great deal in common.

Economics, academic and practical

'Economic history has been well defined as that part of history which requires a knowledge of economics for its full understanding.'[7] This simple aphorism by a senior British economic historian, who is not normally considered a leader of recent trends in economic historiography, would be acceptable to most historians. It obviously provokes further questions such as how much knowledge is required and what is meant by 'full' understanding. Even more basically, it directs our attention to what economics is.

The most common definition of economics, usually attributed to Robbins[8] and hinted at in the title of Court's book, *Scarcity and Choice in History,* is that economics is the logic of choice, the study of how scarce resources should be allocated among competing ends. It does capture an important part of economics in an interesting way, but it slights some aspects of the subject which are less concerned with sharing out something in short supply such as studies of the incidence of unemployment and the distribution of income. Indeed, the whole field of economic growth is concerned with increasing the total resources of a community as much as with their competing uses and so it does not fit entirely comfortably within such a definition. Against such disadvantages, we can set the way in which the notion of choice provides a cover of respectability for economists who wish to invade areas usually thought to belong to other disciplines (for example, the institution of marriage and the control of crime). Choice of some kind is exercised in nearly all human activities, and economists adopting this definition of their subject have few fetters on their activities.

A definition which neither includes areas thought to lie within the province of economists nor excludes fields of inquiry which belong to other disciplines might not seem to be a good starting point. But other definitions which have been proposed in the history of economics fare no better. Two suggestions of leading economists were the 'study of mankind in the ordinary business

of life'[9] and the study of 'that part of social welfare that can be
brought directly or indirectly into relation with the measuring
rod of money'.[10] Economics does not include the whole of the
ordinary business of living and it does include some extraordi-
nary aspects of life; it includes some things which cannot be valued in cash and excludes some that can. This illustrates only the
difficulty of summing up a varied field of learning within a short
and simple phrase.

It is better to begin in a more empirical frame of mind by noting that the label, 'economist', is attached to people engaged in
very different activities. An economist in the public service, an
economist engaged in private business, and an economist in a
university are likely to be occupied differently with only a small
amount of knowledge or purpose being common to their work.
It is from academic economics that historians hope to learn, and
it is well to begin by emphasizing that academic economists are
justified mostly by their role as educators and only secondarily
by the practical relevance of their subject. Economics, like mathematics, philosophy, or any of the humanities, holds its place in
the university curriculum because it is a suitable vehicle for the
training of minds in honest and consistent thought. It so happens that some of the material contained in economics has been
found useful in fairly direct applications, more so than is true of
pure mathematics, philosophy, or history, but economics would
retain its academic value independently of that feature.

Its academic value is derived from the usual array of intellectual processes found in various balances in any of the humanities. Comprehension of abstract ideas, manipulation of
concepts, collection and verification of empirical material, and
comparison of observations against a priori implications are
common to economics and many other subjects. The context
within which these processes are stimulated can vary widely
while remaining within the subject of economics. There
is little more in common between many courses in econome-
trics and in labour economics than the most general academic
processes just identified.

The point we are approaching indirectly is that the demarca-
tion of subjects relates to university teaching and not to research.
Economics is what it is convenient for a university to teach under
an economics rubric of some kind, while no scholar, in particular,

no economic historian, has to ask whether he is an economist or
something else while he is engaged in research. The content of
economics courses has grown as the preoccupations of teachers
and scholars have changed. Such questions as
Why are some societies richer than others?
Why do prices behave as they do?
Why do periodic fluctuations in prices occur?
What is the relationship of money to the supply of goods?
What is the effect of the introduction of banks?
What is the relationship between agriculture and industrial ac-
    tivity?
How do individuals choose to spend their incomes on a selec-
    tion of goods from those available?
What difference does it make if a significant proportion of the
    total output of a good is under the control of an individual?
What amount of taxation should be raised and in what form?
and a host of others have produced a body of thought and infor-
mation about which courses can be organized and conveniently
labelled 'economics.'

The literature so produced is very rich. It can cater to a taste
for abstract mathematics or to careful sifting of a mass of empirical observation. It is commonly thought that most prestige
attaches to the more abstract and mathematical kind of economics, but while there is some justification for that view, it is
not always so. Even the Nobel Prize in economics, a dubious but
common measure of distinction, has gone to Kuznets who would
normally be regarded as towards the 'empirical' end of the spectrum. More generally, economists prize the originator of a notion on which abstract reasoning is subsequently built, whether
that notion is a striking empirical observation or a simplifying
abstraction. The reputations of two modern economists, Phillips
of the 'Phillips Curve' and Friedman of 'money supply' fame,
conveniently exemplify these possibilities.

Furthermore, the economics used in government or business
is mostly the less abstract kind of reasoning. The cost-benefit
analysis by which the World Bank decides to support a development project or Ford decides to build a new engine plant in
Wales pays scant regard to the complexities known to be involved in valuing time or in interpersonal comparisons. Tariff
negotiations are likely to reflect notions of 'effective protec-

tion',[11] but reveal little concern about the implications of tariff changes for the economy as a whole.

There are two obvious qualifications to be made. First, the arcane reasoning of one generation may become the practical tool of the next. Input–output analysis [12] was a useful way of visualising an economy long before it became the basic tool for economic planning. Second, the simpler concepts are likely to be used better by somebody who is familiar with the more refined qualifications than by somebody not so equipped. There are good and bad practical economists, but the person who refuses to make any decision until all the information required for the most sophisticated version of a concept is available and the 'quack' satisfied that a simple concept is the answer to any question both fall into the latter category. Between these extremes, there is a wide area where the greater the knowledge, the better.

These points apply directly to the way in which economics is used by historians. There is a range of economic ideas on which historians can draw; the relevant ideas depend on the subject matter with which the historian is concerned; it is the relatively simple ideas which historians have found most fruitful; and there are definite advantages for the historian in being familiar with the more sophisticated parts of the literature. Perfection is unattainable, and the intention here is to acquaint historians with some of the ideas found most fruitful, persuade them that economics is not too difficult, and with this confidence enable historians to explore for themselves some of the more refined aspects of any body of economics which they find to be relevant to their own work.

Economics as an engine of analysis

It will already be clear that we perceive economics as a set of tools to be employed rather than a body of knowledge to be known. It was once common to speak of the 'doctrines' or 'laws' of political economy, but the problems and institutional settings of economic discussion now change too quickly for us to have any confidence that today's answer will still be valid tomorrow. Much more attuned to the modern position was Keynes's introduction to a series of Cambridge economics handbooks: 'The Theory of Economics does not furnish a body of settled conclu-

sions immediately applicable to policy. It is a method rather than
a doctrine, an apparatus of the mind, a technique of thinking,
which helps its possessor to draw correct conclusions.'[13]
While most economists would not dissent from this proposition, it is not always honoured. In the literature of economic history as well as in more ephemeral places such as newspapers and
political speeches, we can find the proposition that something
must be wrong because it contradicts a conclusion of economics.
That attitude is clearly inconsistent with our view of economics.

It is true that a piece of analysis in economic history or elsewhere which draws on economic theory can be erroneous in a
number of ways. That is a different matter. Our assertion is that
we cannot detect an error simply by noting that a conclusion differs from one to be found in an economics text. Economics is not
that kind of subject. We might be alerted to the possibility of an
error by noticing that a conclusion runs counter to a presump-
tion created by orthodox economic theory, but then we have to
check whether the assumptions on which that theory is built differ from those used in the passage being scrutinised (and then to
find some reason for preferring one or other set). It is one of the
most cherished maxims of economics that goods are not available free but require the use of some inputs and therefore the
sacrifice of whatever else those inputs could have been used for.
'There ain't no such thing as a free lunch.' But the simplicity of
this maxim disappears if for some reason a society starts from a
position where resources are being wasted, where for example
there is a high level of involuntarily unemployed labour. It
would be foolish to assume uncritically that in the 1920s Britain
could have had more motorcars and electrical goods only at the
expense of building fewer ships – despite the value of the economic literature built on the unavailability of free lunches. For
economic historians, as for applied economists, economics has to
be used. It supplies ideas for historians to build into their explanations, but does not provide ready-made answers which can be
substituted for creative thinking.

We have been thinking of economic theory. The field of economics contains a great variety of propositions, some of which
are simply empirical generalisations. An economics textbook
might, for example, contain the proposition that the share of
governments in economic activity has increased since 1945. That

is derived from observation rather than by deduction from a set of assumptions. It is the kind of generalisation with which all historians are familiar, and it requires exactly the scrutiny which historians are accustomed to make. It gains no special authority from being found in the work of an economist rather than that of a historian.

Rationality, prices, cost, and wealth

Before we proceed to the constructions available in theoretical economics, we can notice some fundamental ideas which are common to a considerable number of them. We in no way wish to detract from our earlier emphasis on the variety of economics, but with sufficient generalisation or abstraction we can find much in common in things which initially appear disparate. There are some central notions which serve as a means of organising the discussion of economic constructions themselves.

We return to our earlier discussion of the idea that the most fundamental concern of economics is choice. Two ideas flow naturally from it. The first is the somewhat peculiar economic notion of *rationality*. In ordinary language and in some other academic disciplines, rationality is asociated with things like conscious consideration or explicit reasoning. It is contrasted with instinct or blind response. But in economics rationality is usually associated with an optimal choice of some kind irrespective of how that choice was arrived at. The rational businessman is one who chooses prices and quantities so as to maximise his profit (or some other objective), and it matters little whether this is the result of careful thought or of 'flying by the seat of the pants' or other habitual or instinctive behaviour. The rational consumer is one who allocates his expenditure so as to maximise his satisfaction, whether he does this by carefully controlled expenditure or by handing his income to a wife who fortuitously expends it in the appropriate way. This use of language (some might say distortion) has disadvantages; in the form of a supposed 'economic man' acting only as a calculating machine, it provides a target for critics of economic theorizing. It is, however, an implication of our view of economics that criticisms should be directed against uses of assumptions in inappropriate contexts rather than

against assumptions as such, and our present concern is only to
note the nature of the concept of rationality common to much
economic theory.[14] Historical discussions often attempt to combine the core ideas of economic and 'ordinary' rationality. The
most obvious example is the extensive discussion of British entrepreneurs in the late nineteenth century. Recent research has
shown that many alleged examples of entrepreneurial failure
did not involve any significant loss of business profits. Businessmen came close to profit maximisation and so can be described
as achieving economic rationality. Any one example might be a
matter of chance or fortuitously offsetting errors, but the
number and consistency of such examples is used to bolster the
argument that businessmen knew what they were doing and
were in conscious control of the position. They can then be described also as rational in the everyday sense.[15] The logic is im-
peccable, but readers need care and a knowledge of the various
'rationalities' involved to avoid confusion.

Secondly, choice leads very directly into a concern with *prices*.
The core idea here is exchange, the coincidence of choices so
that both parties to an exchange are happy to change their positions reciprocally. Under what circumstances can this occur?
Partly because of particular issues in the past, and partly because
of the nationalistic basis on which a great deal of intellectual
work in the social sciences takes place, this line of thought has
developed especially in relation to international trade. The issue
appears also within any country as soon as we ask what determines the price at which a particular commodity is sold. We
might ask why economists emphasize prices more than differences in taste, which might also permit the voluntary exchange of a pair of commodities. The answer is two-fold. A price
enables trading to occur almost continually while coincidence of
'inverse' tastes would permit only spasmodic barter; prices are
more strategic than individual tastes. Also, much thinking was
provoked by particular episodes of inflation or deflation. Prices
have always ranked high in the phenomena which economists
have investigated and thought about.

A preoccupation with prices might at first seem to indicate an
inability to recognise human interest, a concentration on material relics rather than on the people involved. That impression is
just as erroneous as the belief that historians in general cannot

see past documents to the people behind them. Prices are the outcome of thoughts and desires in a particular institutional setting, and the explanation of past prices in the terms of economic theory contributes to an understanding of all those historical concerns.

There is another family of ideas of central importance in economics which flows somewhat less obviously from the notion of choice, although the link is clear enough when it is seen. The first step is the conceptualisation of *cost* which follows from a comprehension of choice. The cost of something is what must be given up to attain it. It is not necessarily the object of an exchange. The holder of a particular object may have two opportunities for exchange at the same time, and the cost of accepting one is the loss of the opportunity for the other. Economists therefore pay a great deal of attention to 'opportunity cost', the value of the next best opportunity which has to be sacrificed.

Opportunity cost arises only if all resources are fully committed and it is therefore closely linked with the idea of efficiency. Again, the terminology of economics differs from that of most ordinary speech, where efficiency has more in common with the language of production supervisors; an efficient machine is one which uses the best available technology and an efficient farmer is one who uses the methods propounded in the most recent manuals of animal husbandry or crop management. In economics efficiency is related to opportunity cost and means only that resources are so allocated as to get as much production as possible from them. There is certainly no guarantee that this will coincide with what we might loosely call 'engineering' efficiency. The most efficient farmers in Britain in an 'engineering' sense are not efficient in an economic sense if food could be obtained more cheaply from New Zealand and the British farmers could be employed in some quite different industry. The farmers of New Zealand who are economically efficient as food suppliers to Britain might be indolent in relation to engineering criteria of efficiency. Again, we might regret that the terminology of economics and ordinary language are in conflict, but our concern is simply to present a particular kind of efficiency as a fundamental economic idea.

The notion of efficiency, of making maximum use of available resources, directs attention to partitioning the growth of output between the growth of available resources and improvements in the effectiveness with which those resources are used. It leads therefore to thoughts about accumulation and productivity. Output per unit of input, or factor productivity, a measure of the effectiveness with which resources are used, is one of the key ideas of economics. It is widely used in history and reappears frequently in the following chapters.

We have introduced such fundamental economic ideas as rationality, prices, opportunity cost, efficiency and productivity as constellations of ideas centred on exchange and the use of resources, both derived ultimately from the central notion of choice.[16] This is necessarily to impose some order on what is really a set of ideas with considerable heterogeneity. We might have taken a quite different starting point. It is possible to assert that the key notion in economics is that of interdependence. An economist is concerned with links, with relationships between variables which might on their surface seem quite disparate. While a common sense approach might treat wages, prices, and consumption patterns as alternative indicators of the standard of living, the instinct of the economist is to investigate the links between them, their interdependence, to build a more unified notion of the standard of living. While a common sense approach might focus on the course of either agriculture or industry in Britain in the late nineteenth century, the natural instinct of the economist is to concentrate immediately on the relationship of agriculture or industry to the rest of the economy. Concentration on interdependence might narrow an economist's vision and exclude discussion of some points which other people find interesting, but the advantages of reducing the possibility of mistaking a part for the whole are real and significant. A relative decline of agriculture or industry looks different if it is seen in a context where resources are being used in more productive activities. From the notion of interdependence, the ideas of relative prices and opportunity cost and their associated concepts can readily be derived.

There are also numerous links between notions which we have assigned respectively to the separate strands of exchange and of wealth creation. International trade theory proceeds from exchange and is allocated accordingly. But there are also international aspects to the accumulation of resources, and so there are links to the growth of income. Indeed, one of the achievements of leading economic theorists in the 1950s and 1960s was a substantial integration of these different aspects of international economics. Conversely, aggregate output must be composed of individual commodities, and thinking that begins with the aggregate must return to the issues of the relative prices which determine how much particular commodities contribute to the total output. Furthermore, there are some issues which do not fit easily into our framework. But the framework itself is not important. It is merely a way of introducing the basic ideas of economics, and it is the basic ideas themselves which are important. We would claim that the framework we have chosen has fewer problems than the more familiar one of dividing the subject between macroeconomics and microeconomics, between a concern with the whole economy and with particular actors within an economy. This is especially so for historians to whom the idea of describing an individual in terms of financial motives only is distasteful. Our presentation introduces the ideas usually given a prominent place in microeconomics without implying that any real individuals are wholly economic calculating machines.

Terminology, abstraction, mathematics, and quantification

There are some matters of style or habits of thought which historians approaching economics are likely to find discouraging. We might classify them under the headings of terminology, the exclusion of complications, the use of mathematics, and the importance attached to quantification.

We have already had occasion to notice the way in which economists attach unfamiliar meanings to words like *rationality* and *efficiency*. These are but examples of a common feature and economics has developed a terminology peculiar to it. Its advantage is that a more precise meaning is likely to be used consistently by an author and to be understood in that precise sense by both author and reader. The use of novel terms, and agreement that a common word should have an unfamiliar meaning, can be thoroughly justified in this way and many attacks on the jargon of economics are simply ill-informed. But not all criticism can be so deflected. Even when it is noted that economists are far from having a monopoly on limited writing skills, it has to be conceded that they sometimes unnecessarily scatter different labels on the same concept, and use the same label with different meanings.

It is usually not difficult to disentangle the variations which occur where one usage has failed to carry the day, and it is mostly mere laziness which makes the terminology of economics a barrier to its understanding.

Recognition that interdependence and interrelationships are central to economic thought explains why many people at first find it oversimplified. It is natural to start with a simple situation in which the relationship is clearly displayed and to see how it is altered by allowing successive complications to enter the picture. To historians or to the applied economists looking for assistance with a particular problem, the simplified case might appear to exclude elements which they cannot regard as insignificant. They are right to advance this objection, but it is an objection only to the appropriateness of the simple analysis for a particular problem. It should lead them to investigate (perhaps by a further search of the economic literature) whether the complication alters the analysis or whether they are wrong in assessing it to be other than irrelevant. Again, it is usually laziness which regards the simplification of theory as making it useless for historians.

The concern of economists with precise terms and the relationships between them makes the subject amenable to mathematical expression. Further, mathematical operations facilitate the drawing of deductions from a set of assumptions so that mathematics is part of the analysis of economics as well as a language in which some of its results can be expressed succinctly. There is no doubt that the learning of economics is greatly facilitated by a knowledge of mathematics and, perhaps even more important, by a willingness to tolerate mathematical expressions. This is really to say no more than that mathematics is an important part of an education, especially one preparing students for abstract thought. But the mathematics of elementary economics is not difficult. An ability to envisage simple equations as graphs, and an understanding of the simpler algebraic manipulations is all that is required.[17]

When we turn from pure theory to applied economics (and occasionally even before that), we find that economics is a quantitative subject. The size of a change in prices, the amount by which the labour supply has grown, and similar quantities play a key role in many pieces of applied economics. The same is necessarily true of economic history. Long before recent trends towards more quantification in economic history, Clapham's famous advice that economic historians should constantly ask questions such as 'how much?', 'how large?', 'how long?', 'how often?', and 'how representative?', that is, that they should cultivate a quantitative sensitivity, was thoroughly good advice.[18] Historians who are not confident that they can follow such a precept have available to them a good guide in Floud's recent book, which should also help persuade them that the intellectual demands of elementary mathematics are not excessive.[19]

Economic history, old and new

We have had occasion to refer in passing to the increased reliance on quantification and on an explicit use of economic theory in some recent economic historiography. It should be made quite clear that the economic theory with which we are concerned, while it is found in so-called econometric history, is also important to the writing and understanding of economic history that is much more traditional in its approach. If we go through a book recently written to form a guide to more recent writings on British economic history,[20] we find only a little reliance on economic theory beyond that which we have identified previously as central. Few authors go much further than the concept of productivity and the supply and demand apparatus for analysing price movements. The last book which could be characterised as traditional in approach to have fallen into my hands before beginning to draft this book, Aldcroft's account of the interwar years,[21] has as much employment of the same pieces of economic theory. A critical reading of it requires at least as much understanding of the theory as does the Floud and McCloskey volume. It may require more, inasmuch as the authors of the latter take some care to expound the theory in an endeavour to make the book self-contained. This reflects its textbook nature and perhaps also the missionary intent of the authors. The general conclusion is that both new and old economic history require an understanding of the simple economic theory which follows.

2

Income

Productive capacity and welfare

Because interdependence is so central in economic thinking, special importance is attached to concepts which encompass the whole of economic activity. Chief among them is income. Its explicit and precise definition dates only from this century. Nineteenth-century economists were usually content to take the meaning of something like the 'wealth of nations' as self-evident once it was distinguished from the stock of gold, although they were very subtle in their understanding of some aspects of it. As the range of statistical techniques and resources expanded, attention was given to various national aggregates, especially in countries of European settlement overseas where 'development' was much more prominent in economic and political debate. Even so, and although Pigou's writings in the 1920s reintroduced concern with the 'social dividend', the statistical measures did not have a large or immediate impact on most economic theorists. It was the importance attached to total economic activity by Keynes and some other writers in the interwar years which brought forth a careful definition of income. Even they would probably have been surprised by the importance which measurements of income have attained in economic discussion since the Second World War.

Historians are usually concerned with the income of a single economy. Its simplest definition is the sum of all goods and services which are produced and used within a given period of time. We can always ensure that the total value of goods and services produced is equal to the sum of incomes earned in their production by a suitable choice of accounting conventions. The most important one is that business income or total profit is simply the residual between the value of output and what is counted as some other form of income. National income accounts adopt such a set of assumptions, so that for most purposes aggregate income and aggregate output can be used interchangeably.[1] There are many loose ends in this simple notion which we must take further, but we note first that there are two threads in the economic conception of income which do not always fit together easily. Emphasis can be on either production possibilities or on welfare. We may be interested in the capacity of an economy to produce goods and services for many reasons and income is used as a measure of that capacity. The obvious example for historians is the literature on the extent to which a particular innovation such as railways increased an economy's potential to supply commodities in general.

There are some complications to this use of income but they are small compared with the welfare thread in the concept. To consider the ability of an economy to provide welfare, it is again natural to begin with a measure of income. There are questions to be raised about such a material conception of welfare, but we might postpone them by noticing that a larger income is likely to be accompanied by a greater degree of choice – and we have already seen the significance of that in economic thinking. The more immediately worrying question is whether we should relate welfare to all production. Commodities may be used for the satisfaction of wants and these we label *consumption*, or they may be reserved and used for the production of more commodities and these are called *investment*. Should welfare be related to production or to consumption?

The enduring eighteenth-century edict of Adam Smith that the purpose of production is consumption might suggest that welfare should be related to consumption rather than to income. We could respond that his dictum was a good slogan in the eighteenth century when there was a strong case for promoting the interests of the consumer rather than of the producer, but that we should now be more willing to acknowledge the role of motivations other than consumption. The importance of the dignity of being wanted is often acknowledged in modern employment policies. But that is not the response which comes most naturally from the economic literature. Emphasis there is placed on the role of investment in increasing consumption in later periods. Otherwise, why delay consumption? The division of income between consumption and investment is itself part of the aggregate choice to be made in an economy, one of the welfare considerations associated with income. Income is then the appropriate aggregate for welfare questions, but we have to note that important questions of the timing of the benefits to be derived from income can be buried if an analyst is not sufficiently aware of how they are built into the concept itself.

Although economists are taught to be sceptical of arguments which proceed quickly from an individual case to the aggregate, and historians are taught to be sceptical of argument by analogy (and both lessons are correct, provided they are framed as cautions rather than prohibitions), a small-scale parallel may illuminate this issue. It is common in many countries to scrutinise the distribution of income among several broad groups such as farmers, wage and salary earners, the self-employed, and business income. (It is only too possible to erect an erroneous argument on such a division, but that is not our immediate concern.) Should the last category include all the income earned by businesses or only that part distributed as dividends? From the viewpoint of immediate consumption, dividends to shareholders are more analogous to a wage. But the retained profits are likely to lead to greater business income and so to enhanced dividends later. It is therefore common to use all business income for comparison with other kinds of income. The analogy with the division of total income is not complete. Retained profits can be expected to influence share prices and a shareholder might sell his shares and, in a sense, consume his portion of undistributed profits. There is no market in capital rights to future national income which an individual can use in a parallel way. But the analogy does enhance the plausibility of using income as a welfare measure despite the supremacy of consumption as the purpose of production. There are, however, many more objections to a simple concept of income yet to be countered.

Conceptual issues

1. The first such objection is that the simple definition of income is too inclusive. Even if the emphasis is on production possibilities, it can be argued that some incomes such as those earned in

the armed forces or the police, should not be equated with the provision of a service. They are costs necessarily incurred in the production of other commodities, and unless they are deducted from the profits earned from those commodities, total income will include double-counting. This line of argument appealed to one of the foremost of the early students of national income accounting, Kuznets, and his variant of the concept will sometimes be encountered by historians. But it has not prevailed. The difficulty is that there is no element of disposability built into the concept of income. That is, the concept ignores the extent of control over disposition of income. If we excluded defence, we could go on to any other essential service. Incomes earned in food production might be regarded as an essential cost in the production of whatever the consumers of food produced. Such an argument is more tenable for basic foodstuffs than for gourmet delights, and similar refinements are possible in other contexts. The argument reflects the impossibility of drawing a single line through what is essentially a sequential process. Some goods and services help to produce others and are called *intermediate outputs*, other goods and services satisfy consumers' wants and are called *final outputs*. Wants may be immediate gratification or steps on the way to an ultimate desire. It is not always clear into which category a particular commodity falls.

Welfare considerations might be expected to lead to some exclusions, but an analogous argument applies there too. Some individual judgments could be that ministers of religion produce no useful service and their stipends should therefore be excluded; others could argue the same of academics, but these judgments might be mutually exclusive rather than held in common. It is to some extent the line of least resistance not to permit any exclusions, but there is no obvious feasible alternative.

2. If income can be thought too inclusive, it can also be charged with being damagingly restrictive. Our initial definition was vague in that it left undefined what constitutes a good or a service or, equivalently, what should count as an income. For the most part, the crucial criterion is that a market is involved. Goods and services are bought and sold, or people are paid for their work in providing them. Most cases are clear-cut. A book purchased from a bookseller is clearly a good, a barber paid for cutting hair clearly provides a service. A person who cooks a

meal and delivers it to an old-age pensioner without any wage or charge transfers income to the recipient but does not provide a service in the sense used here and earns no income. A schoolteacher earns an income and provides a service even though the pupils as such pay no fees. There are many cases where a fine judgment has to be made and inevitably there are some puzzling implications. Economists referred to the paradox of including wages paid to housekeepers while making no allowance for housewives' services (so making it literally possible to increase national income by employing each other's wife) long before feminism became a recognised movement. It is only one example of a more general phenomenon. If you paint your own house, the recorded national income is lower than if you employ a professional housepainter; the unmarketed service provided by the houseowner is excluded.

These problems are tolerated simply because of the difficulty of doing anything else. When it becomes too obviously silly to value statistical convenience above economic sense, an adjustment is made. In modern poorer countries, the omission of subsistence agriculture would be ridiculous and so the definition of income is adjusted. Even in advanced countries, the inclusion in official accounts of an imputed rent to owner-occupied houses can be interpreted as such an adjustment (although another interpretation is possible as we shall see). We should not assume too readily that all necessary adjustments have been made; while the desirable additions in the case of any of the richer countries might be expected to change only slowly – so that these additions are seldom needed for studies restricted to short periods – there is no such assurance for a historian who is interested in a long period nor for international comparisons which might be between countries with different propensities for do-it-yourself activity.

This might be thought to be an oddity of conventional measurement, but it is really quite a deep conceptual point. Fundamentally, what we want is an aggregation of those things which a community values, but what we can get most easily is a measure of what that community produces or distributes through some kind of market. A community might value things which are not marketed; the environmental movement has merely emphasized what was long recognised in the literature of economic theory. Academic economists were used to the idea that their salaries were lower than those of business economists because of the nonpecuniary rewards of university life. Choice includes the possibility of retiring from paid employment as well as selecting among marketed commodities. (The do-it-yourself example is less frivolous than it might appear since many of what are conventionally called leisure activities involve some marketed goods whether it be footballs, books, boats, or walking boots.) Economic theory can be applied to such choices too, but they are necessarily taken separately from the usual definition of income.

There is a related issue more reasonably regarded as a statistical oddity. In many economies, some services are provided free of charge by governments. The incomes earned in such activities are apparently only the wages and salaries of those employed in providing them. If they were supplied by private enterprise, we would expect profits to be earned (to provide capital finance even if the dividends paid to shareholders were negligible). Consequently, an increasing proportion of government activity can be expected to impart a downward bias to measurements of national income.

3. This leads us to a more general scrutiny of valuation procedures. We have so far proceeded on the assumption that the total value of goods and services produced can readily be computed. They must therefore be expressed in some common denominator; that can only be money and therefore the relative prices of goods must be embodied in the measure of income. (This is equally true of computing the sum of incomes earned, but incomes are more directly a monetary expression.) Can we be sure that market prices are an appropriate measure of the relative contribution of two commodities to aggregate income?

We have here one of the most contentious issues in modern economics and also one of the key links, within the concept of income, between what Chapter 1 introduced as the two main strands in economic thought. For income to be related to the production possibilities of an economy, we must have the relative prices of two goods equalling the relative cost which their production imposes on the resources available. In certain theoretical constructions, such as the system of perfect competition which is described in Chapter 6, this can be guaranteed. However, in many of the world's economies we are well aware that for various reasons there is no guarantee that this is true. The concept of income may have to be adjusted before it can be employed in an empirical analysis.

A very similar problem faces the use of income in assessing welfare. In this case we should have to be sure that the relative prices of individual commodities accurately measure the relative contributions they make to the welfare of the community as a whole. Difficulties arise as soon as we ask how valuations are to be made by the community as a whole. Even if the preferences of every individual are entirely separate, it is not easy to aggregate them in any sensible fashion. Interdependence between individuals, so that the valuation of a good by one person is affected by the reaction to it of another, makes the task even more formidable. Furthermore, a person's tastes may vary within a year or for whatever period income is calculated. It is possible to build theoretical constructions which guarantee that prices are appropriate for using income as a measure of welfare, but in practice we have to accept that some approximation is involved.

These valuation problems occur in the context of estimating and interpreting national income estimates for any one economy in a particular year. There are related but distinct problems involved in the change of prices over time. In comparing two periods, our treatment of income as a measure of either production possibilities or welfare implies that we are interested in the volume of goods and services available. If all prices double while all else remains unchanged, we would want to say that income was unchanged; that is, we would want to eliminate the effect of price changes and consider what economists call *real* income. There are no problems if all prices change equally but that does not occur in practice. When prices change unequally, there is no single measure of the change in real incomes; an 'index number problem' is incurred.

To see this, consider an economy producing only two commodities for which there is an unambiguous measure in physical terms. (Notice how we consider a simplified, abstracted problem.) In the first period 10 units of one commodity A and 20 of the second commodity B are produced. Their prices are respectively £2 and £1 per unit so that total income is £40. In the second period 15 units of A and 25 of B are produced, but their prices have changed to £3 and £4 respectively. Total income is then £145 but some part of the difference between that and £40 is clearly the result of the general increase in prices. By how much has real income changed? If we use the first-period prices, then the real income of the second year is £30 + 25 = £55 and comparing that to the £40 of the first period, we might say that real income has grown by three-eighths. If we use the second-period prices, then the first-period income is £30 + 80 = £110, and comparison of that with £145 indicates a growth of a little less than one-third. There is no way in which the 50 percent growth in A and the 25 percent growth in B can be summarised unambiguously into a single number.[2] This is disconcerting for those who like simple answers but it is necessary to look closely at the way in which income series are 'deflated' or corrected for price changes. We consider this point further in Chapter 3,[3] but it may be clear from the example that the issue is essentially one of the relative weight given to good A and B respectively.

4. From the complexities of valuation we return to more everyday problems of place and timing. Our simple definition of income evaded any distinction between the timing of production and consumption. The carry-over of stocks from one year to another raises the problem in one regard but is easily overcome by regarding stock accumulation as investment (and stock decumulation as negative investment), merely another way in which one period's income may be devoted to increasing income in future years. Stock changes are therefore included directly in income.

But the issue is not thereby resolved. Many goods can be bought in one transaction but used over a long period. Houses are the obvious example, and the alternative interpretation of the customary imputed rents for owner-occupied houses in official accounts to which we alluded earlier is that houses are so important that some spreading out of their purchase is required to bring the accounts into line with the services provided. Houses are however only an extreme example of the general class of consumer durables. Should the services of privately owned consumer durables also be spread over a number of years? In logic they should be, but the bother is universally judged to outweigh the attractions of consistency.

What then of producers' equipment? In any modern economy part of the stock of machinery and buildings held at the beginning of a year is used up during it in the course of producing income. The distinction between the timing of production and consumption cannot be entirely ignored.

We have already explained why investment is invariably included within income, and so we cannot exclude producers' equipment entirely. Some allowance must therefore be made for the use of the stock of buildings, plant and machinery, and so on. The difficulty is in estimating the amount of income to be regarded as so devoted. In practice, the depreciation allowances of business accounts are determined mostly by taxation laws and may be far from the appropriate economic concept. Therefore, national income statisticians tend to adjust them as much as possible to a 'capital consumption' basis but still present the estimate in a form which enables the reader of the statistic to use it as he wishes. Net output incorporates the best available, but admittedly shaky, estimate of depreciation; gross output is the estimate before allowing for depreciation. In the form of gross national product, or GNP, the latter has passed into everyday use, but it is a mistake not to realise that depreciation uses resources even if we refrain as far as possible from relying heavily on measurements of it.

Production and consumption can also differ in place. The residents of one country (and a country can be equated with an economy for present purposes) may have ownership rights to part of the production of another country. The issue can become complicated by the exact legal meaning of 'residents', but a simple case is an international loan. Part of the income earned in one country must be passed as interest to a resident of another country. The solution to the accounting problem involved is to refine income into two concepts: *domestic* is the label attached to production within a country, and *national* to production accruing to its residents.[4] Thus, in our example, the interest belongs to the domestic production of the debtor country and to the national production of the creditor. Despite all the attention given to multinational economic activity, gross national product and gross domestic product seldom differ by much; one of the biggest gaps occurred in Britain in the early twentieth century when GNP exceeded GDP by about 7 per cent.

5. There are some points about the welfare conception of income which are implied in what we have said already but which deserve an explicit statement too. Much early economics was associated with Benthamite philosophy and an individualistic em-

phasis can be discerned within the concept of income. The approach allows no judgment on the net effect of a gain to one person at the expense of a loss to another. Questions about the distribution of income have to be introduced quite separately. This is not a criticism of the welfare concept but a caution against accepting too readily the belief that a growth in income must necessarily be desirable; other value judgments are possible.

Secondly, there are occasions on which we want to break the implied connection between prices and welfare. The clearest is in centralised economies, where welfare is more naturally defined in terms of the choices of the planners rather than those of individual consumers. At the very least, this introduces a subtle change into the nature of income. It occurs, too, in other countries in wartime.

6. While points 1 to 4 cover the main cautions required for income as a production capacity measure, it must be remembered that our interest is often in production possibility rather than in achieved levels of output. Income produced by an economy which is not at full employment is obviously a dubious indicator of production possibilities. The meaning of full employment is less than obvious and frequently intermingled with social and political judgments. We are all familiar with discussion of just what percentage of the labour force is unavoidably unemployed, that is, at what percentage unemployment is full employment of labour judged to be attained, and technical analyses and political prejudices are combined in various mixes. Similar issues arise in considering specific pieces of equipment. Is an engineering norm that in practice a machine should achieve, say, 80 percent of its theoretical output a suitable measure of economic full employment? If that seems somewhat niggling, what view should be taken about the possibility of running plant and machinery through night shifts or even continuously? Social considerations pervade even the production possibilities conception of income.

In many situations movements towards the limit of what income is possible may be more significant than movement of the limit itself. This is obviously more true of a short than a long period since a movement towards a fixed limit must eventually become infinitely slow. But even historians have to concern themselves with what is possible in a brief interval and the point is most conveniently explored with the aid of Fig. 2.1.

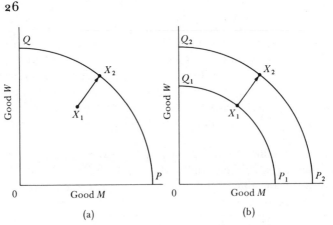

2.1 Towards the frontier versus shifting the frontier

If we visualise an economy producing only two outputs (and this is purely for diagrammatic convenience), we can construct a production possibility frontier. In part (a) of Fig. 2.1, by devoting all its resources to the production of good M, the economy can secure total production of $0P$; by using all resources for good W, total production is $0Q$. By dividing resources between M and W, it can produce any combination of them shown by the curve QP.[5] Curve QP is therefore the visual representation of a key economic concept, the production possibility frontier. But the economy may not use all its resources efficiently. Its output will then be less than it could be and will be represented by a point such as X_1, inside the production possibility curve. A gain in income can be the 'correction' of such a situation, a move such as that from X_1 to X_2 in the diagram. For an economy which is operating on its frontier, gains in income can come only from additional resources or improved technology, so that the production frontier is itself shifted; this is illustrated in part (b) of the diagram, where Q_1P_1 is the first production possibility curve and Q_2P_2 the second. It is now commonly argued that gains of the kind illustrated in part (a) may be at least as important as those illustrated in part (b), and this points to the need to retain a distinction between income and income possibilities.[6]

For these and other reasons income must not be regarded as one of those conceptions which have become so familiar and obvious as to be treated as a simple empirical observation. Income is a valuable concept, but there are sufficient doubts and ambiguities that cannot be resolved and are built into the concept itself as to require some caution in its handling. This has been more generally recognised in recent years in issues such as ensuring that proper regard is taken of the community's valuation of a pollution-free atmosphere or of a historic building, but it has long been familiar to economic theorists. Environmentalist pressures have not affected economic theory; they have properly been directed to ensuring that qualifications recognised in economic theory were genuinely included in practical decisions involving use of the concept of income.

Measurement procedures and problems

There is necessarily a substantial quantitative element in the concept of income. In the preceding discussion we have attempted to confine ourselves to the more conceptual issues that surround the overall notion, although the line between conceptual and measurement problems is far from clear-cut. It is worth pursuing a little further some of the distinctions which statisticians use in compiling income estimates.

We have already referred to the convention by which it is ensured that incomes and output are equal. We have also noted the way in which consumption can be distinguished from investment. There are many different ways in which incomes and output can be subdivided and there are variations among countries' accounts before the level of fine detail is reached. But there is broad agreement on the most important conventions and a generalised typical set of accounts looks something like Table 1.[7] It must be remembered that each column of the table is an approach to the same concept, so that in the absence of measurement error the totals would be equal. Statisticians use the different approaches because they provide checks on each other, and the components of the columns may themselves be of some significance.

The approach labelled 'income' consists essentially of adding different kinds of income, separating out that received from activities located outside the United Kingdom to distinguish gross domestic product from gross national product. It is, of course, incomes in the sense defined earlier which are relevant; such

Table 1. *Estimation of national income, U.K., 1907 (£ million, current prices)*

Income		Expenditure		Output	
Income from employment	1008	Consumers' expenditure	1811	Value added in agriculture	140
+Income from self-employment	348	+Public authority current expenditure on goods & services	163	+Value added in industry	760
+Trading profits of companies	271	+Gross domestic fixed capital formation	150		
+Public authority trading surplus	15	+Stock building	10	+Value added in services	1060
+Rent	233	=Total domestic expenditure at market prices	2134		
		+Exports of goods & services	671		
		−Imports of goods & services	649		
		=Expenditure on gross domestic product at market prices	2156		

		1960
− Indirect taxes		155
+ Subsidies		0
= Expenditure on gross domestic product at factor cost		2001
+ Net property income from abroad		144
= Gross national product at factor cost		2145
− Depreciation		98
= Net national product		2047

	1875
= Gross domestic product at factor cost	
+ Net property income from abroad	144
= Gross national product	2019
− Depreciation	98
= Net national product	1921

	1960
= Gross domestic product	
+ Net property income from abroad	144
= Gross national product	2104
− Depreciation	98
= Net national product	2006

Source: The figures are from C. H. Feinstein, *National Income, Expenditure and Output of the United Kingdom, 1855–1965* (Cambridge: Cambridge University Press, 1972), Tables 1–4, and W. P. Kennedy, 'Economic Growth and Structural Change in the U.K. 1870–1914', *Univ. of Essex Discussion Paper No. 112* (May 1978). The estimates are not entirely independent, but they do illustrate the kind of measurement error to be expected in historical work.

receipts as pensions look like income to the individual but they
represent payments not matched by contemporaneous contributions to production. (This says nothing at all about their justification.) Such *transfer payments,* as they are often termed, are sometimes included to provide a subheading such as *private income,*
but they must then be deducted before the social aggregate is estimated.

The 'expenditure' approach sums different kinds of goods
and services, notably consumption, investment (separated in the
table between fixed assets and stock building), exports, and imports. We have already discussed the place of consumption and
investment within the concept of income. Exports constitute a
final demand for the national economy with which we are concerned, whatever foreigners choose to do with the goods and
services supplied to them. Imports are deducted since they are
already included in expenditures on consumption and investment (and exports in the case of imported goods and services
which are exported after some processing).

The expenditure approach also requires us to introduce the
distinction between valuation at market prices and at factor cost.
Indirect taxes (those levied on particular goods rather than on
income) add to market prices as they are passed on to the consumer while subsidies reduce market prices. To get to expenditures on goods separated from the activities of government,[8] the
net effect of indirect taxes and subsidies has to be counteracted.
A term such as *at factor cost* is used to indicate that such an adjustment has been made.

The approach labelled 'output' draws attention to the concept
of 'value added'. The production of most commodities requires
the use of components of various kinds which are themselves
commodities. Clearly, the summation of the total value of all
commodities would overstate the goods and services available in
an economy; some commodities would be double counted. The
income and expenditure approaches avoid this issue by looking
at final uses such as consumption and investment.[9] In principle
we could add up only the outputs of each sector of the economy
destined for final uses, but in practice this would be difficult.
Therefore, for each productive activity, the sum of commodities
used is deducted from the gross value of output, and the difference, called 'value added', is summed to estimate gross domestic output.

This point is conventionally, but usefully, explained by the example of an agricultural product. Farmers grow wheat, but (for simplicity) all of this is sold to millers rather than destined for some final use, so their product is 'intermediate'. Millers sell some flour for household use and the rest to bakers who use it to bake bread which is sold for consumption. These transactions can be set out in the following accounts.

Farmers:	Sales		
	Intermediate	100	
	Final	0	
	Total		100
	− Purchases		0
	= Value added		100
Millers:	Sales		
	Intermediate	110	
	Final	10	
	Total		120
	− Purchases		100
	= Value added		20
Bakers:	Sales		
	Intermediate	0	
	Final	130	
	Total		130
	− Purchases		110
	= Value added		20

Total consumption is 10 of flour and 130 of bread, totalling 140, and as we have abstracted from investment or any other final demand, income is also 140. Total value added is 100 by farmers, 20 by millers and 20 by bakers, equalling income at 140. Total sales, however, are 350, much greater than income.

The significance of value added can be reinforced by a mental experiment. In our example farmers, millers, and bakers are separate entities. Consider the implications of a bakery absorbing the milling activity and also the farm. This is what is called vertical integration in business history (the opposite, horizontal integration, is the merger of different firms making the same product – the merger of two or more bakers or two or more millers for example). Then the intermediate transactions became absorbed in the firm's internal acccounts, and all that we see is the sale of flour and bread. Consumption is unaltered, but the total of sales is markedly reduced. Sales depend on industrial

Table 2. A simplified input–output table for U.K., 1907 (£ million, current prices)

Sales to or purchases from:	Agriculture	Industry	Services	Total, intermediate	Final demand Consumption	Investment	Exports	Total, final	Total
Agriculture	16	39	11	66	156	0	4	160	226
Industries	17	527	103	648	525	229	388	1142	1790
Services	16	220	34	270	805	23	310	1138	1408
Total, intermediate	49	786	148	983				2440	
Imports	—	290	42	332	219	3	92	646	
Wages, rents, profits, etc.	177	714	1219					1794	
	226	1790	1409						

Notes: 1. This is a simplification of probably the earliest input–output table to be used for an historical study of Britain, that of J. R. Meyer, 'An Input–Output Approach to Evaluating British Industrial Production in the Late Nineteenth

Century', *Explorations in Entrepreneurial History*, 8 (1955), reprinted in A. H. Conrad and J. R. Meyer, *Studies in Econometric History* (London: Chapman & Hall, 1964), pp. 186–7. Some of the figures would be slightly altered by later work as can be seen by comparing Tables 1 and 2.

2. The upper left-hand bloc shows the transactions between the individual economic activities. Thus agriculture, for example, sold £16 million to itself, £39 million to industry, and £11 million to services. The right-hand columns show the composition of final demand. Thus industry, for example, provided £525 million for consumption, £229 million for investment, and £388 million for exports, a total final demand of £1142 million.

Reading down the left-hand columns shows the resources used by a particular activity. Industry, for example, used inputs of £39 million, £527 million and £220 million from agriculture, industry, and services, a total of £786 million of intermediate inputs. It also used £290 million of imports and paid £714 million in incomes to the people and businesses involved. Its total purchases of £1790 million equals the total of its intermediate and final demand sales.

3. Gross domestic product is the total of final demands satisfied minus imports (£2240–646 million). It is also, but for rounding errors, the total of incomes earned in the separate activities (£ million 177 + 714 + 1219) minus the total of imports used directly for final demands (£314 million).

4. The simplification of this table should be appreciated. For example, we have suppressed all problems concerned with government actions.

organisation as well as on income produced. The practical significance of this for historians is most readily seen by comparing
a ranking of nineteenth century American industries by total
sales with a ranking by a modern inquiry using value added. The
apparent size of the agricultural processing industries is markedly reduced.[10] The concept of value added was developed
only recently. It is the absence of anything more than a dim hint
of the idea which makes it a major exercise to use the relatively
abundant data on total sales to produce estimates of national income for any year much before the Second World War.

For statisticians, value added leads naturally to the concepts of
input – output accounting. Its simplest form is illustrated in
Table 2. The basic input – output account is simply a tableau
whereby the accounts of the economic activities in an economy
are amalgamated, distinguishing the intermediate transactions
among activities from those whereby primary resources such as
wages and imports are acquired and those whereby goods and
services are delivered to such final uses as consumption, investment, and exports. The immediate value of such an account is
the picture it gives of transactions in an economy within the
overall concept of income creation. For modern economics even
more important are the uses which can be made of tables
derived from the basic one for various planning purposes. From
an input–output account we can calculate what demands an expansion of one activity will make on other activities and on labour and imports including the labour and imports used in the
consequential expansion of the other activities.

Because of the enormous data collection problems, input –
output analysis has not yet been widely used in historical studies, but the basic apparatus provides a useful framework as
much for historical as for contemporary thinking. For recent
history direct applications are becoming more frequent. G. N.
von Tunzelmann has used early input – output accounts to lay
to rest any simple notion that in interwar Britain the 'new industries' formed a group of activities closely linked together and
isolated from the older, staple industries.[11]

The input – output framework permits us to explain a little
further what was previously presented as a matter of accounting
convention only, the equality of output and income. The input –
output table illustrates how inputs to an economy are rewarded
(by wages and salaries, rents, interest, or profits) from revenues

earned by satisfying final demands such as consumption, investment, and exports – after allowing for imports. The definitions of output and income are such that they must be equal, and we see how this is a conceptual matter, an implication of how an economy is visualised, rather than a mere convention. We see too some matters which remain to be discussed and some which have been introduced more directly; how are incomes to be divided between wages and other forms of reward such as rent or profit, and how are the relative prices of goods produced in the various sectors to be compared? It is worth repeating that they appear within the first step of defining the concept of income.

Historical uses

There are at least five ways in which the ideas presented here contribute to historical analysis. The first is the simple but essential recognition of income as a scaling device, the measure of total economic activity against which any particular sector can be seen in perspective. The immediate impact on a community of even a doubling of productivity in an activity which constitutes only a small percentage of national income is not likely to be dramatic, a reflection which is important in many historical reassessments such as that of industrial growth in nineteenth-century Russia. Care is necessary in using income as a scaling device, because the low figures that result when setting an activity against the total of all activities can be misleading; however, the utility of this use of income is significant in historical as well as in contemporary studies.[12]

Secondly, it is important to have some overall conception of aggregate economic activities into which studies of parts of an economy can be fitted. The obvious historical example of this is the literature dealing with Britain in the late nineteenth century. An apparent decline in Britain's industry relative to her competitors takes on a different significance when that industrial record is placed in the context of an income which was growing under the stimulus of nonindustrial activities. Even more, the absolute decline of British agriculture looks different when it is seen as part of an international mechanism whereby income grew in both Britain and other parts of the world through Britain's acceptance of agricultural imports in exchange for her provision of services.[13] Examples can be found in other countries too. Attention to income rather than accepting international trade as a measure of economic activity may lead to a reappraisal of New Zealand's development in the nineteenth century. Important insights come from incorporation of the concept of income in standard historical reflections.

Thirdly, measurements of national income are important in the description of changes in an economy over time. Central to many historical concerns is the way in which productive capacity and welfare have changed, and a great deal of useful effort, notably by Kuznets in the United States, Feinstein in Britain, and Butlin in Australia, has been given to the construction of long-term series of national income.[14] Official series prepared with all the resources of modern statistical services rarely go back before the Second World War, and although unofficial series usually extend no earlier than the middle of the nineteenth century, they add enormously to the material available to historians.

Fourthly, historical studies make much use of the sectoral division of national income. The writings of A. G. B. Fisher and Colin Clark, influenced by their experiences in Australia and New Zealand, drew attention to an apparent tendency for the share of national income originating in agriculture to decline as income grew. This was extended and refined in many ways by development economists in the 1950s, and national income estimates have enabled historians to extend the studies backwards in time. Discussion of the theoretical links between sectors and description of the process by which growth occurred in a number of countries has thereby been enriched.[15]

Fifthly, historians have used the concepts of which national income is a summation. The share of wages in national income once occupied many theoreticians and historians and threw new light on some aspects of labour history. The division of income between consumption and investment gave a new thrust to discussion of the standard of living of wage earners during the industrial revolution in England.[16] These and other examples from the historical literature used little more than the classificatory schemes employed in the definition and measurement of national income. But historians have also used the additional ideas which economists have woven around such concepts as consumption and investment, and it is to these that we turn in the next chapter.

3

Factors of production

Land, labour, and capital

Once we understand the meaning of income, we can ask what determines its size. As is so often the case in economic affairs, an apparently simple question can be resolved into several facets. The two most important are an explanation of a difference in levels of income between two economies (or one economy at two dates) and an explanation of the path by which an economy moves from one income level to another. (Economists describe this distinction as that between 'comparative statics' and 'dynamics'.) The two questions are obviously related, but the second is more complex. It involves a greater knowledge of interconnections within an economy and falls naturally into more advanced areas of economic theory which are introduced in Chapter 8.

In view of the discussion in Chapter 1 readers will not expect economic theory alone to provide a clear answer to even the simpler question. Rather, theorising about the question provides a set of ideas which can usefully be drawn on for an attempt to explain the level of income found in any particular economy. This set of ideas is conveniently expounded in the traditional classification of factors of production, the reasons for comparative income levels classified as land, labour, and capital. It is, indeed, tautological[1] to think of a country's income level as being limited by its supply of natural resources, the quantity and quality of manpower which it is able to bring to bear on those resources, and the quantity and quality of man-made equipment with which it is able to facilitate that labour. The traditional trilogy of land, labour, and capital does no more than identify the elements of that tautology. It is nevertheless useful as a framework of analysis.

Classifications are seldom unique and we could create a different set of income determinants. In particular, labour concerned with the direction of resources can be separated to create a fourth factor of production, entrepreneurship. That is sometimes useful, but so are further or different subdivisions, and the traditional three enable us to capture the theoretical ideas which are most valuable.

Land

The supply of natural resources is an obvious starting point for analysis of income levels. Countries generously endowed by nature will have at least a potential for higher income levels than less fortunate ones. It is natural resources which economists have usually had in mind in this connection even though they use the heading, land. In the eighteenth and nineteenth centuries, as the analysis was developed, the most important natural resource was land. The terminology also reflects the urban background of the early economists since although they knew that land in a farmer's sense was far from being entirely a natural resource, they hardly gave the point the importance which would come naturally to one with a rural background. The economist who contributed most to understanding the difference between natural and man-made resources was Ricardo, and he defined 'land' as the 'original and indestructible powers of the soil'; a farmer would have been more impressed by his knowledge that the origin was a long way behind him and that that there is very little about soil which is indestructible. A different conception of natural resources would have led economic theory more quickly into a problem which is recognisable in the modern world, the pattern over time by which a natural resource should be depleted. But that is a problem of dynamics, and there are things of value to be learned from traditional theorising.

Much the most important is the idea of the *margin*. The economics of land soon becomes the economics of differential fertility and the margin. Consider the supply of land in a particular economy. Some of it is more fertile than the rest. In producing output of various levels, the more fertile sections are used first and others brought into use successively in the order of their fertility. Now distinguish the ownership of the land from the labour with which the product is obtained, and assume that all labour is identical. Then we can distinguish the product of the labour from the product of the land (in the economists' sense) simply by observing the difference between the product of any piece of land and that of the last land (of equal area) brought into use. Economists' land, the natural resource, is really fertility, and the return to be attributed to it is simply the differential between the product from any area and that of land at the margin of cultivation. The device of the margin enables us to partition the total product between labour and (economists') land.

We are still excluding any problems associated with improvements to the land or other man-made assistance to labour. If it is natural to call the part of the produce attributed to labour, wages, it is then equally natural to call that part attributed to land, rent. To make quite clear the difference between rent and payments for land and buildings (and, especially in America, other assets), it is often called *economic rent*. If we assume that landlords supply the natural resource only, we can deduce immediately that economic rent is the maximum which landlords can extract from tenant farmers before those farmers would be able to increase their own incomes by moving to land which lies outside the frontier of cultivation, the margin.

So far, labour has had little more than a passive role in this analysis. Let us introduce another element of choice for it. Suppose that additional labour on a given piece of land increases its output but that successive increments of labour produce smaller and smaller increases. Such a situation, where only diminishing additions to income can be attained by combining more and more of one factor to a fixed amount of another, is called a case of *diminishing returns*. Here the variable factor is labour and the fixed one is land, and we have 'diminishing returns to labour'. This gives us another margin. An additional unit of labour might be the second on one piece of land or the tenth on another. To secure maximum output, the last unit of labour used on each unit of land must result in the same increase in output. Otherwise, a unit of labour should be transferred from the relatively unproductive use to a more productive one and total output will be increased. The second margin is called the *intensive* margin. It is less easy to visualise than the 'extensive margin', as the physical frontier of cultivation is called, but it is again an equality which must be satisfied if maximum income is to be attained.

If there are both diminishing returns to labour and a stock of unused land, then the same thought process in which labour is shifted from one possible use to another will convince the reader that when income is being maximised the produce of a unit of labour at both margins must be equal. That is, the return to labour at the intensive margin must equal that at the extensive margin. The two margins will therefore provide the same partitioning of the product between wages and (economic) rent.

As an analysis of agriculture, this will strike historians as thin in the extreme. It rests on the use of land in order of fertility and evades any questions about how knowledge of fertility is gained. In some formulations people arrive in a new country and immediately begin using the most fertile land before spreading into areas of lower fertility. This is even more unrealistic since a greater amount of new knowledge is needed in such circumstances. Notice, however, that it is the best use of known land which is at issue and the discovery of new land such as the American prairies is readily accommodated as a new ordering of relative fertilities. On the other hand, 'fertility' is often stretched; it may even include location – land being more 'fertile' only in that it is closer to a market. (The reader should check that the argument is unaffected by this change of meaning.) The analysis presented here deals only with the maximum rent which can be extracted by landlords and says nothing about the complexity of motives with which landlords might fix actual rent levels. Nor could any agriculturalist treat improvements so cavalierly. But the analysis is concerned with economists' land and not with historical (or contemporary) agriculture.

Even on its own terms, the analysis is primitive and those with a knowledge of elementary calculus will recognise it as an application of the simplest maximisation theory. But it does introduce the important notions of the margin and diminishing returns. (The latter is usually called the law of diminishing returns, which reflects only the staying power of an old-fashioned terminology and has no methodological or epistemological significance in itself.)

A great deal of theorising can be built on this simple foundation and some of it is important for historians. First, we should note the subtle interplay of fertility and differential fertility in our exposition of economic rent. If all of the relevant natural resource were equally productive and it were really unlimited in supply, then rent would be zero. If it is all equally productive but the supply is limited, then an intensive margin exists and rent will be positive. If the resource is varied in fertility, then there may be a recognisable extensive margin, depending on whether or not the resource is in excess supply. We might fudge the various possibilities by dividing land into categories of fertility so that we could speak only of the supply of each category, but in the case of natural resources, it is easier to think of rent as derived from both limited supply and differential fertility.

The element of fixity of supply does, however, direct our attention to the possibility of generalising beyond natural resources. A man-made object such as a building or machine might be available only in limited quantities, at least in the short run, that is, for a period in which an economy as a whole has insufficient time to respond to the value placed on it and increase its supply. In the short run the owner of such an object can obtain a rent exactly as if he were the owner of economists' land. Thus, to the extent that he could retain control of all of a particular kind of machine, Watt could secure rents from his eighteenth-century steam engine, rents which in legal language were called patent royalties. When the use of computers outran the supply of trained operators in the 1950s and 1960s, the owners of the skills in temporary short supply could secure rents which were normally seen only as unusually high salaries. Such rents differ from economic rent in that the supply shortage is amenable to human control, at least eventually, and for that reason they are termed *quasi rents*. As is usually the case, a conceptual distinction loses much of its clarity in empirical inquiry; natural resources can, after all, be increased by new discoveries or even, in effect, by human inventions. Economic and labour historians of interwar Britain are well aware that when oil replaced coal as a source of energy, the rents attainable from coalfields were reduced. (The reference here is to the rents attached to skilled mining labour as well as royalties on coal deposits.)

Second, historians will notice that economics is not, as often alleged, necessarily concerned only with harmony. If a system of property rights requires that rent should go to one group in the community while labour is supplied by a different group, then the simple analysis of rent shows that the interests of these groups may be opposed. Early in the development of economics, Ricardo demonstrated that rent will increase relative to wages as production is expanded by using land of progressively lower fertility.[2] This is obviously incompatible with many notions of what is harmonious.

The ideas of the margin, rent, and quasi rent are deeply embedded in economic theory and are therefore found, usually in a subordinate place, in many pieces of historical analysis. We shall encounter some in the context of international trade later, but the easiest example to introduce immediately comes from studies of the effect of railways. Building a railway in an agricultural district changes the differential 'fertility' of individual pieces of land, since the extent to which a farm gains from the cheaper transport varies with its distance from a point at which produce can be shifted on to a railway. Consequently, if it is appropriate to believe that market rents move to the same extent as economic rents (something which may be more true in some countries than in others), the effect of the railways on incomes derived from land can be measured by the change in total rent which follows the building of the railway. Similarly, if we want to know how much agricultural land would have fallen outside the extensive margin if an economy were deprived of its railways, we can compare the effect of proximity to railways on rent levels with the additional transport costs which would necessarily have been incurred in the absence of railways. The locus of points where increased rents just equals the additional transport costs is the new extensive margin after the removal of railways. Both of these lines of inquiry have been used in historical studies of railways.[3]

Labour

It might at first seem obvious that the larger the amount of labour available in an economy, the larger its income will be. But the most casual of glances around the world, or even at the United States and India alone, would engender caution. A more careful statement that given equal endowments of land and capital, a larger supply of labour is likely to be associated with a larger income is much more acceptable. More labour, other things being equal (or *ceteris paribus* as economists often say), surely permits more output. Even so, this hardly answers an interesting question. More labour is likely to be associated also with more consumers, so that the income produced has to be shared by more people. We needed some caution in linking more land to more income, but it is the dual character of people as producers and consumers which makes the link of labour to income even more complicated and interesting. It is not obvious, and empirically untrue, that more labour is necessarily associated with more income per capita. The connections between labour and income therefore require more investigation.

We begin by noting that labour is usually best conceived as a flow of services rather than as a stock of resources. Land, in the sense of natural resources, is a stock; but it is the capacity of labour to be employed in income production over time, which provides one of its interests to an economist, and this is a flow of services rather than the existence of a stock. As usual, there are some exceptions. The obvious one for historians in the importance of a stock of labour in studies of slavery in the United States and of indentured labour in Queensland, Australia.

It is from people that this flow of services must come and few economists have forgotten that. The common charge against economists of being entirely heartless comes from a misreading of economic literature; that people are involved and that people have interests and attributes other than those connected with production is too obvious to need constant restatement. In any case the flow of labour services must begin with people and therefore with the study of population.

Demography has become a discipline in its own right and historians are accustomed to drawing on its terminology and analysis. (It is a minor puzzle why birthrates, death rates, net reproduction rates, and so on seem to be less forbidding than the concepts of economics, even if we suspect that the terms are sometimes used by historians, and others, without any deep understanding of their meanings and limitations.) But its concerns have never ceased to be involved in economics. Although in many short-period problems, the possibility of population adjustment is nil or negligible, immigration and emigration may be responsive in periods that are not very great, and in the longer run population changes generally must necessarily be considered.

Net immigration and emigration responds to the relative opportunities for and rewards of employment in different countries although it responds to other influences too. So does the natural increase of population. In the case of mortality a higher income implies at least the opportunity for a more nutritious diet and so a greater resistance to disease. A higher income also implies that more resources can be used for things like the provision of better housing, sewage systems, and clear water supplies as well as the removal of disease traps such as pools of stagnant water. Indeed, higher income at least facilitates such technological influences on disease as the use of chemicals to combat malaria. Thus we would expect income to be associated with population growth through its influence on mortality. There may, however, be countervailing tendencies. If income growth leads to overcrowding or other insanitary conditions, it may involve more deaths. The overcrowding might be temporary as when the building industry is unable to cope with an increased population in an area of strong economic growth, or it might be more permanent if the growth is accompanied by an increasingly unequal distribution of income, and the higher mortality of those made poorer outweighs the beneficial effect of higher incomes among other groups. Another way in which higher income may induce more deaths is through introducing processes which are not entirely understood, as in the case of asbestos poisoning among construction workers. The relative balance of these various links between income and mortality may vary from time to time and place to place.

Similarly, we can distinguish conflicting influences of income on fertility. On the one hand, rising income and confidently held expectations of further increases might lead to increases in fertility since all members of larger families could be expected to have no difficulty in securing adequate livings. On the other hand, rising income is likely to be associated with a wider variety of goods and services, and some of the newer opportunities might be incompatible with the care of children.

Our concern here has been to establish reasons for thinking that population will itself be influenced by income and not to give an exhaustive treatment of the subject. Nor do we contend that all changes in population can be traced to these influences; most analysts have found it necessary to appeal to some other reasons to explain the widespread increase in fertility in the richer countries of the 1950s.[4] We do note that although the points we have made owe as much to studies of economic history as they do to economists,[5] they follow directly from relating the concept of income as the total of goods and services available to a community to influences on births and deaths.

Influences on population are not the same as influences on the supply of labour services. There are two distinct gaps to be crossed; individuals may or may not be involved in supplying labour services, and the quantity of labour services supplied by a member of the labour force may vary.

The participation rate, the ratio of the labour force to total population, is most obviously related to social customs, perhaps embodied in law. It is social custom which dictates that people under a certain age should be fully involved in education and so ineligible for the labour force. Similarly, social custom dictates that people over a certain age should retire although most societies allow a greater flexibility in this requirement. Social custom may also impose limitations on the ability of married women to be employed, and quite dramatic changes in this custom have been observed in many countries in recent decades. Customs may also bar women from particular jobs, and these customs may operate effectively on the participation rate as a whole. When we widen our horizon from Western advanced economies, many other influences on the participation rate may be observed.

But there are economic influences too. To begin with, the concept of the labour force is one of being engaged in producing income and is subject to all the nuances of the definition of income discussed in the preceding chapter. Just as (measured) income would rise by the general employment of wives as housemaids, so would the labour force and the participation rate. Secondly, while participation in labour does have intrinsic worth in giving us the satisfaction of being useful and wanted, it has disadvantages too in that it requires some loss of control over our own activities. It is therefore undertaken with an eye on the rewards to be gained. In the language of Chapter 1 participation in the

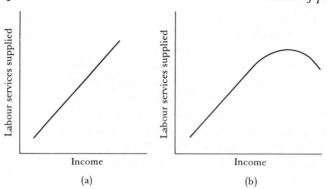

3.1 The supply of labour services

labour force has an opportunity cost. While for one member of a household, the opportunity cost of not being employed[6] may be so great as to foreclose the choice involved, other members of the household may have more freedom of choice.

Even the major wage earner in a household may have some discretion over the extent to which he is employed, over the hours which he works. Again, institutional features circumscribe the choice for many people but there may be some flexibility in the form of negotiated changes in hours, optional overtime, or secondary employment. Flexibility is even greater in some circumstances and is worth exploring for the light it can throw on the constrained choices more usual in modern advanced economies and for its direct historical relevance.

We can conceive of a society involved in little other than subsistence living. An opportunity is created for employment in the production of a new commodity, and the output of that commodity adds to the low income of the community. The new commodity is attractive, and people offer labour services to produce it. Income and the supply of labour services therefore both increase and are associated in a curve of the kind drawn in part (a) of Fig. 3.1. Even a new commodity can pall, and eventually the supply of labour services responds less to the increase of its output. We may even eventually reach a backward bending supply curve of labour services as in part (b) of the diagram;[7] labour supply is reduced as incomes grow beyond the point at which desires for available commodities are satisfied.

These relations have been found in almost exactly the simple circumstances described. In Papua the willingness of people to engage in introduced agriculture declined when the rewards were kept in too homogeneous (and primitive) a form.[8] In Russia in the 1920s the supply of peasant labour services for the production of marketable foodstuff declined once a given level of industrial goods could be purchased. It seems likely that in the Industrial Revolution period in Britain hours of work generally increased,[9] although there are obvious difficulties in measuring the hours of work put into agriculture. Consideration of the link between income and labour supplied shows that the empirical observation of increased hours is insufficient for us to distinguish betweeen the possibilities that capitalist masters intensified exploitation of their workers or that the greater incomes made available by industrialisation led people to increase their supply of labour services along a curve such as that of part (a) of Fig. 3.1.

We have concentrated here on the way in which changes in the participation ratio and in hours of work enable the labour supply to be responsive to changes in economic rewards. The points made do not exhaust the possible influences and responses. The degree of effort of a worker may vary, whether his labour be manual or intellectual, although in any particular case it is very difficult to tell whether there have been real changes in effort or merely political rhetoric from trade unionists or employers. The important point is that labour services can be expected to respond to economic incentives.

This should be distinguished from a wrong formulation. It can be said that people want leisure as well as income; that is merely substituting a particular term for the opportunity cost of labour supply. But leisure should not be equated with mere absence of work without investigating whether that absence is in accordance with a deliberate choice. Being unemployed when we want work is completely different from being leisured; the latter requires a measure of security not associated with involuntary inactivity. Historians who find an identification of unemployment and leisure distasteful should direct their justified protest at individual writers rather than at economic thinking in general.

So far we have treated labour as homogeneous, but in at least

some respects we would want to differentiate among particular
skills and abilities. Much of the previous analysis is readily sub-
divisible. There can be no doubt that custom and a loosely
formed sense of fairness contribute a great deal to the relative
rewards of different kinds of labour. So do individual interests
and various kinds of satisfaction to the choice of occupation. But
the acquisition of many skills has an opportunity cost in that ac-
quiring them requires time which could otherwise have been
used in immediate income creation. (It is because this is so similar to reserving goods from current consumption to provide a
greater income later that it is termed *investment in human resources*
and the stock of such attributes, *human capital,* topics which now
have a substantial literature.) Similarly, skills acquired through
on-the-job experience enable a worker to make a more substantial addition to output in the kind of production for which the
experience is relevant, and there would therefore be an opportunity cost incurred if he should transfer to a different activity.
There are sound economic reasons for differentiating between
the wages of kinds of labour.

Capital

The nature of capital and its place in economic theory are even
more complex than are the cases of land and labour. There are
several distinct notions bound up in the general concept.

Much the most common sense of capital is that of fixed capital,
the stock of man-made implements of various kinds used for income creation. Statisticians compile series of the total of buildings (often finding it impossible to disentangle land) and plant
and machinery in the confident expectation that a higher level
of capital so conceived will be associated with a higher level of income. The intuitive appeal of such a procedure is overwhelming, and historians have found it useful in a wide array of inves-
tigations.

This *materialist* approach, as it has been christened by Hicks,[10]
hides a large number of difficulties. Buildings and plant and machinery take a wide variety of forms even in a primitive economy, and they have somehow to be aggregated in a single measure of capital. In general, prices must be used to value each
building or piece of the plant and machinery and a value of capi-

tal can then be computed. But what determines the price of capital goods? This is an important question in itself, but is especially so to us as it is a major example of an interdependence which historians and others often ignore. The price of a factory (and perhaps the chance of a capital gain to its present owner) must be related to the expected profitability of its operations, unless indeed the factory site might be used for suburban development, in which case the price of the factory may be determined by the valuation which is placed on housing services. The value of the capital stock depends on the expected course of the prices of a number of components of income, an interdependence which is not as obvious intuitively as economists often assume, especially to somebody nurtured on an undefined notion of 'speculation.' The implication of most immediate concern to us is the conceptual difficulty this poses for the measurement of capital. We need to know the prices of future goods, but what goods are produced and their relative prices depends on what capital formation is undertaken now. There is a circular relationship between capital and income. Capital is, in some sense, necessarily a dynamic concept, while we are seeking an instantaneous measurement.

A second line of approach, to which Hicks has given the name, *fundist*, does not avoid the same conclusion. The fundist approach derives from an accounting view of a single enterprise. There it is usual to use balance sheets to show the state of the enterprise at a given time. A simplified and formalised balance sheet lists the current assets (that is the cash held, sums due from debtors and stocks of raw materials and finished goods) and the fixed assets (land and buildings, plant and machinery, as before) to derive the total assets of the enterprise. From these are deducted the current liabilities (bank advances and amounts due to creditors) and any long-term liabilities such as mortgages. The difference is the capital, or net worth, or proprietary interest in the enterprise. That is, capital is conceived as a fund representing the interest of the owners in the enterprise. If we ignore deficiencies in the balance sheets prepared by accountants, it is the value of the firm as a going concern rather than the value of its buildings and machinery, the amount for which the owners would expect to sell the entire business rather than what could be raised by a separate sale of its various assets.

As is obvious from the debates over inflation accounting around the world, such an approach will not evade problems in valuing assets and liabilities. In particular, capital will still depend crucially on the valuation of the fixed assets.

The materialist and fundist approaches have some features in common. Both permit the intuitive conclusion that capital and income will be positively associated – will vary directly or in the same direction – but whereas the materialist view is naturally of assets producing income, the fundist view follows the accounting notion of profits feeding capital, that is, of income producing capital. Similarly, both link income concerns to ownership conventions, but whereas the materialist emphasis is on the direct ownership of assets, the fundist view links more immediately to the financial markets where shares in the proprietary interest are valued, bought, and sold. A fundist view of capital points towards the valuation of firms by the price of their shares on the stock exchange rather than by the prices of their assets.[11]

Whether in a materialist or fundist view, capital is a conceptual construct and there is no possibility of deciding immediately that one or the other is the only correct way of approaching the subject. We simply record the different ways of conceiving capital, note that a valuation problem has to be resolved at some time, and explore the usefulness of the general concepts and the further ideas to which they lead.

Two such ideas are *depreciation* and *competition*. The first of these has already been encountered in the national income accounts of Chapter 2. It will be recalled that assets are 'used up' in the course of producing output, so that net output must be output minus the extent to which such using up occurs. In measuring the capital stock, we want to allow for this using up. To measure the change in the capital stock in a given year, we have to know what deduction to make for that year. It is sensible to link the asset as closely as possible to any available external measure of its using up; there might be some engineering criterion for a machine capable of producing an exact number of machine hours of work which can be used. But few assets have such a convenient characteristic and even if one exists, the invention of a new machine may render an old one obsolete while it has some machine hours left in it. (The incursion need not be a new machine; a loss of demand for the product of a particular machine may accelerate the depreciation which is appropriate for it.) The inadequacies of accountants' rule of thumb and tax laws for depreciation within the concept of income apply also to the measurement of capital, but such inadequacies may have to be tolerated there too.

Depreciation might seem to be linked most directly to assets and so to the materialist conception of capital. But it has to be known before the size of the profits which feed proprietors' funds can be calculated, and so it is equally involved in the fundist conception.

The idea of competition is deeply embedded in economic theory, and it is only too easy to employ it uncritically. It has been refined and formalised in the concept of perfect competition which we shall come to in Chapter 6, but the original notion still has an independent existence. It is an immediate consequence of the importance attached by economists since Adam Smith to self-interest, and specifically to the idea that in a community there will be sufficient people with a strong desire to improve their material position to ensure that any opportunities for gain will be exploited. This fits easily into the fundist conception of capital. If there are some people keen to exploit opportunities for gain, and if there are institutions able to spread knowledge about them and willing to finance entrepreneurs, then funds will be shifted from less profitable to more profitable pursuits until the rate of return is equal in all activities, exactly as in our discussion of margins. Unless knowledge is kept secret, or investment activity is restricted (not only within an individual firm but in that entry by new firms is prevented), competition ensures that the return on capital funds is equalised throughout an economy. The assumptions of the argument built around a general rather than a refined sense of competition are not negligible – the implication of a ready transferability of capital reflecting the fundist conception is perhaps the most demanding – but neither are they especially stringent.

The notions of capital and equalisation of returns on it can be carried over to a materialist conception. With the same conditions of self-interest, freedom of knowledge, appropriate institutions, and investment funds, decisions to add to the stock of one kind of asset rather than another will be such as to ensure that the rate of return on each will be equal. There are conflicting aspects of an assessment of the likely restrictiveness of the conditions under which this result is obtained. Knowledge is now needed about the profitability of assets rather than enterprises; that seems to increase the restrictiveness of the assumptions, and so does the notion that small additions can be made to the stock of individual assets (which is needed to ensure equalisation of the returns to them), although what is to be counted as a separate 'asset' is a question for each particular case rather than a subject for general discussion. On the other hand, much investment is financed out of the profits of an enterprise retained within it rather than distributed to shareholders. Managers controlling those funds may have better knowledge of the returns to groups of assets used by the firm than is available to outsiders seeking to influence the flow of funds among firms. What we are seeing in this particular context of competition is the general tension between materialist and fundist conceptions of capital on the relative emphasis to be given to two aspects of investment, its financing by contacts between an enterprise and outsiders and its embodiment in specific assets within the enterprise.

This simple group of ideas about capital is usually used by historians in conjunction with others yet to be introduced. But we can notice the use of capital and competition more or less in isolation in some historical studies. A great deal of attention has been given to the way in which in the late nineteenth century firms in different regions of the United States increasingly competed with one another, so equalising rates of return more or less throughout the country, and it is debated whether the main change was new institutions competing with old or the reduction of legislative barriers to new entrants in the financial markets.[12] Similar questions explain much of the interest in country banks in England during the Industrial Revolution.[13] The implication of competition that large profits are earned by the first to take advantage of an opportunity, but that the trade affected then experiences a narrowing of profit opportunities as the rate of return is returned to the economy-wide average is well documented in many historical contexts such as the Industrial Revolution cotton industry and modern synthetics.[14] Alternatively, even in what most English readers will regard as distant places, resources were so allocated as to earn roughly equal returns in a variety of uses. This was so for the land of Serbian peasants which found a new possible use in plum orchards before the First World War,[15] so showing that competition operated in what is often regarded as an area of stagnation. Naturally, good historians will not rely directly on the notion of competition in places where knowledge is confined or where, for some reason, the opportunity to use knowledge is restricted.

Production functions

We have followed the traditional approach in which land, labour, and capital are the factors of production which explain the level of income. It is easy, especially with a materialist conception of capital, to take this one step further and form a production function. To do so requires no more than a shift from the literary tradition of identifying 'factors' to the mathematical one of focusing on relationships by writing that income depends on[16] the supplies of land, labour, and capital as

$$Y = f(N, L, K)$$

where Y = income, N = land, L = labour, and K = capital. Furthermore, if we think of an individual activity, it is easy to see such a relationship as almost an engineering truism.

The production function has indeed proved a fruitful (although still controversial) approach to many problems in economic theory and in applied economics, including historical problems. But to the extent that it is a small rearrangement of the connections between income, land, labour, and capital which we have already encountered, it cannot evade any of the previously discussed difficulties. Writing a symbol Y in place of the word *income* does not remove any of the outstanding issues raised by the concept of income. The same is true of the other variables or concepts involved. In particular, the valuation of capital and its immediate interdependence with income remain problematical. And as the production function approach directs attention to the assets used to produce output, that is, to the materialist conception of capital, it offers some slight danger of forgetting the capital funds aspect of an economy. The danger is slight, because a theory should be assessed in the hands of its skilled users rather than as it is employed by weaker minds. For some problems the financing issues might not be important and for others we should be able to remember and counter the dangers implicit in a production function approach. We have to remember in any case that the notion of capital depends on valuation procedures and that any problem involving other than a short period might encounter changes in the relative price of capital goods.

Of the many ideas which have grown around the central notion of production function, three are especially important for historical studies. These are substitutability, returns to scale, and productivity. All of them can be expounded independently of the idea of a production function, but they find there a natural framework.

The expression $Y = f(L, K)$ is a general statement that income depends on labour and capital (so saying that the distinction between natural resources and capital is unimportant for the topic in hand, something about which economists have recently become more cautious). It is too general a statement for many purposes where it is intended to use the expression in mathematical manipulations so as to show other relationships in the economy. The choice of specific functions by which to represent a given economy (or sector or other part of an economy) immediately raises the question of the extent to which labour and capital can be substituted for one another. By analogy with an individual production line in a factory, this is often referred to as the 'technology' of the economy. It is not an entirely happy terminology since much more than technical considerations may be involved, especially for an economy but also for an industry. It does capture the role which technical knowledge plays in limiting the available choices. For example, the function,[17]

$$Y = L^{\alpha}K^{1-\alpha} \qquad \alpha < 1$$

which is referred to as a Cobb–Douglas production function, after the two authors who first used it, implies that labour and capital are readily interchangeable. The interchangeability is not complete; only if $\alpha = 0.5$ will a given percentage change in labour have the same effect on income as an equal percentage change in capital. But the economy has a very wide range of possible combinations of L and K with which it can produce a given Y.[18]

This is, however, an implication of the particular form of the production function rather than of production functions in general. For example, it may take the form (the somewhat fearsome form, some may think, and we will not take the matter further)

$$Y = (aK^{-\beta} + bL^{-\beta})^{-1/\beta}$$

which is known as a constant elasticity of substitution or CES production function because the elasticity of substitution [19] can take values implying a restricted ability to interchange capital and labour but remains the same for all levels of L and K.

We can remark too that the input–output analysis introduced in the preceding chapter is characterised by an assumption that substitutability is very limited indeed, at least in the period for which an input–output analysis is deemed appropriate. The analysis assumes that the output of a particular commodity requires fixed inputs of other commodities and labour; the coefficients or entries in the input–output table are fixed and there is therefore no possibility of substituting one for another. It is possible to relax this restriction somewhat, but substitutability remains less than that implied by a Cobb–Douglas assumption. Theorising can proceed on a number of assumptions about substitutability, and the choice among them depends on the problem under consideration.

The Cobb–Douglas production function also serves to introduce the idea of economies of scale. [20] We can observe first that the form used earlier,

$$Y = L^{\alpha}K^{1-\alpha} \qquad \alpha < 1$$

can be said, in terms introduced earlier in the context of Ricardian land, to exhibit diminishing returns to each of the factors, labour and capital. That is, if either labour or capital is increased by a given percentage while the other factor is held constant, output will increase but by less than that percentage. Given the Cobb–Douglas form, this is simply a consequence of each of the exponents in the function, α and $1 - \alpha$, being less than one. But what happens if labour and capital are simultaneously increased by the same percentage? With the particular function given here, income will also increase by that percentage. With the Cobb–Douglas function, this is simply an implication of the exponents summing to unity. More generally, if we have

$$Y = L^{\alpha}K^{\beta} \qquad \alpha, \beta < 1$$

and we increase both L and K by a given percentage, then

If $\alpha+\beta=1$ income increases by the same percentage and the function is said to show constant returns to scale.

If $\alpha+\beta>1$ income increases by a larger percentage and the function is said to show increasing returns to scale, or economies of scale.

If $\alpha+\beta<1$ income increases by a smaller percentage and the function is said to show diminishing returns to scale.

This does no more than establish the names for a scheme of possibilities and is readily generalisable to any form of production function.

It is only too easy to use the concept of increasing returns to scale inappropriately. Economic historians are used to dealing with economies where output has grown over time. That is by no means sufficient to establish that increasing returns to scale have been experienced. Consider an economy whose production function is the constant return to scale kind, $Y=L^{\alpha}K^{1-\alpha}$. In comparing two years we find that income in the second year Y_2 is greater than that of the first year Y_1. One possible explanation is that the economy has somehow been able to gather greater supplies of labour and capital so that we have simply

$$Y_2=L_2^{\alpha}K_2^{1-\alpha} \quad \text{exceeding} \quad Y_1=L_1^{\alpha}K_1^{1-\alpha}$$

(Notice that depending on the increase in labour and capital, this change may also imply an increase in output per head, Y/L.) Even if we cannot attribute the increase in income to an increase in resources, we may find that the form of the production function is unchanged. That is, we may find

$$Y_1=L_1^{\alpha}K_1^{1-\alpha} \quad \text{and} \quad Y_2=c \cdot L_1^{\alpha}K_1^{1-\alpha}$$

where c is a constant greater than 1. Progress has occurred so that inputs produce more output in the second year than they did in the first, but the economy is characterised by constant returns to scale throughout. The essential point is that return to scale is an instantaneous concept and should not be confused with an increase of income over time.

Growth of output in excess of that in inputs leads naturally to the concept of productivity. It too is a term commonly used in everyday speech and a concept which is capable of misuse.

The essence of productivity is that it is a quotient, a ratio of outputs to inputs. In many contexts, especially among engineers and increasingly in public discussion of incomes policies, it is labour productivity which is involved, measured by something like output per man-hour. Farmers still use land productivity, output per acre for example, and occasional uses are found for capital productivity. But economic theorists usually use productivity, unless especially qualified as labour or some such, to mean total factor productivity, the ratio of output to the sum of the inputs used to produce that output. In terms of the production function as we have been writing it so far, it is the change in the function resulting in a growth of output by more than the growth in inputs. In a particular simple case already encountered, productivity might be represented by A in the expression

$$Y_t = A_t f(L_t, K_t)$$

that is, output in any period is determined by the labour supplies and capital supplies at that time together with an index changing over time of how effectively resources are used. We can now emphasize the close link between economies of scale and productivity by noting the converse of an earlier conclusion; if an economy which is really characterised by increasing returns is assumed to have constant returns to scale, the effect of the scale gains will be counted as productivity gains.

Productivity is not necessarily tied to the notion of a production function. We can develop it directly from the production possibility curve as indeed we did with Fig. 2.1. We can think of productivity gains as the extent to which greater output can be obtained from a given supply of the relevant resources. This shows that productivity is not necessarily burdened with the problems of capital valuation, although in practice the concept is used more often with capital of some kind as one of the relevant resources.

Measurement problems remain in any case. They occur in both the output and input components of a productivity measure. If we consider an economy with just two outputs, then we can draw a production possibility curve for a unit of input as in Fig. 3.2. In part (a), the proportionate shift between periods is the same whatever combination of the two outputs is produced, and there is no difficulty knowing what rate of growth to use as the numerator in a measure of productivity. But if the change is

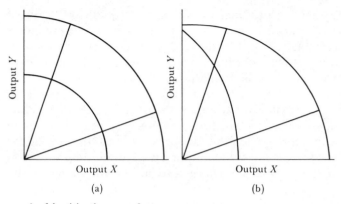

3.2 Ambiguities in growth measurement

as in part (b), the percentage change in output obviously depends on the combination of outputs along which the gain is measured. It is much greater in a combination which has more of X and less of Y than in a combination in which these proportions are reversed. There is no single number which can sum up the two-dimensioned change in output. We have the index number problem which was introduced in a different way in Chapter 2.

Even if we can measure the gain in output, we might have an analogous problem in measuring the extent to which the inputs have changed. If we can be sure that output has grown by 10 percent, and that labour supplies have grown by 5 percent and capital supplies by 15 percent, then productivity will have increased, remained constant, or declined depending on the relative importance of labour and capital in the measure of inputs. And the relative use of labour and capital may change between the two points in time which are under consideration. These measurement problems are by no means obscure curiosities; debate over the growth record of the Soviet economy in the 1930s and the 1950s rests on just such issues in the measurement of outputs and inputs.[21] Index number problems are widespread.

More generally, productivity can be written as the ratio of a weighted sum of outputs to a weighted sum of inputs,[22]

$$P = \frac{\Sigma_i z_i \, \Delta Z_i}{\Sigma_j w_j \, \Delta I_j}$$

where P is productivity, the Z_i are the various kinds of output, the z_i measures of their relative importance so that $\Sigma z_i = 1$, the I_j are the various kinds of input, and the w_j their respective weights so that $\Sigma w_j = 1$. In some cases such as an economy with a Cobb–Douglas production function with constant returns to scale and with sufficient competition to guarantee equalised rates of return everywhere, it is possible to argue that particular weights are correct. Those for output, the z_i, are the relative shares of each output in the total using market prices for relative values, and those for inputs, the w_j, are the exponents of the production function which we have previously written as α and $1 - \alpha$, and which under these assumptions are equal to the relative rewards of the factors in total output.[23] In these circumstances, mathematical manipulation enables us to write the formula for productivity in the form of rates of growth as

$$\dot{p} = \dot{g} - \alpha\dot{L} - (1 - \alpha)\dot{K}$$

where $\dot{p}$ is the rate of growth of productivity
$\dot{g}$ is the rate of growth of output calculated as described
$\dot{L}$ is the rate of growth of labour
$\dot{K}$ is the rate of growth of capital
α is the share of wages in total income

But in many cases the z_i and w_j have to be taken as more or less arbitrary solutions to index number problems.

Even when we have some confidence in a measurement of productivity, there being grounds for preferring some particular measures of the z_i and w_j and for thinking the Z_i and I_j to be measured appropriately, not too much should be claimed for the result. It is interesting to know that productivity has increased if only because obtaining more output from a given level of inputs does establish that an economy is somehow 'better off'. But it is only a start to understanding how and why that happy outcome was achieved. Productivity can easily be a measure of ignorance, a statement of what gains in output did not come from increased inputs, rather than an understanding of why inputs became more productive. Giving a particular name to an area of ignorance does not remove that ignorance. And the attempts which have been made to partition productivity gains among specific factors such as the spread of literacy and education are not very convincing in general, although they may be in specific cases.

   While the concept of productivity is not the solution to all economic issues, the studies for which it does provide a convenient framework include historical ones. Indeed, the concept came to prominence in a historical study of the United States.[24] and one of the reasons for its continuing attractiveness is that in this particular case, while increases in the available factors of production explain most of the growth of the output in the nineteenth century, productivity gains are much more prominent in the twentieth century.[25] Productivity studies provide a means of incorporating gains in knowledge into the analysis of changes in income even if we cannot analyse much further just what gains in knowledge are important and how they are related to output. Similarly, the study of comparative growth in the United States and the Soviet Union was given a powerful thrust by studies which suggested that while Soviet output has grown faster in at least some periods, productivity cannot be shown to have changed at significantly different rates in the two countries.[26] And the study of productivity has become a natural accompaniment to the historical reconstructions of income levels cited in the preceding chapter.

Conclusion

We began this chapter with the question, 'Why do income levels vary between one economy and another?' and although we could not avoid some skirmishes with the way in which income changes with time, our focus remained unchanged. We cannot answer the question if only because we do not believe economics provides universal answers. But in introducing the theorising which has been provoked by our question, we encountered taxonomic structures such as land, labour, and capital, and theoretical ideas such as rent, the margin and diminishing returns, influences on population growth and the participation rate, materialist and fundist conceptions of capital, the production function and substitutability, returns to scale and productivity. These are drawn on in historical studies, albeit often buried in apparently straightforward narrative and description. Depth of understanding depends on familiarity with the underlying theorising. Readers of the Floud and McCloskey volume, for example, should notice both the implicit and explicit uses of the production function in the chapters by Crafts, Jones, McCloskey, Hueckel, Floud, and von Tunzelmann;[27] virtually every chapter draws on some of the ideas discussed in this chapter. There is also the opportunity to seek and to evaluate the mostly implicit use of the same ideas in a book such as that by Aldcroft referred to earlier.[28]

4

Income determination

Keynes

Chapter 3 dealt with long-run or fundamental influences on income levels. We were concerned with the resources available for income creation and the skill with which those resources were used. A different line of thinking begins by asking what determines whether the resources will in fact be used, although again the theory so provoked has many points of contact with other questions.

The maximum use of resources immediately or at least without significant delay gained urgency in the interwar years when unemployment of labour was so obvious in many countries. Together with more purely theoretical puzzles of consistency in economic thinking, this condition inspired the writing of the book with most impact on modern economics, Keynes's *General Theory of Employment, Interest and Money*.[1] Although other writers were working on related lines, the ideas of Keynes had the most influence and led to a different approach to the formulation and criticism of government economic policies in many countries. Keynes must not be credited with, or blamed for, too much. The problems of government policies are diverse and much of the Keynesian economics with which they are approached is far from its origins; experience and further thought have simplified and reassessed the relative importance of many of his ideas. It is with a much simplified version that we are concerned here. The basic theoretical ideas are those which are involved as soon as we ask what determined the course of income in Britain in the 1850s[2] (or any other decade) just as much as if we were concerned with competing hypotheses about the way in which government policy affected the British economy in the 1960s and 1970s.[3]

Multipliers

We begin with the ex post equality of savings and investment.[4] If we simply divide income receipts into the amount spent on consumption goods and the amount saved, and we divide output into consumption and investment, then it follows from the definitional equality of output and income that savings must always equal investment. It is usual to write this in mathematical form as

$$Y = C + S \qquad (Y = \text{income}, \ C = \text{consumption}, \ S = \text{savings})$$
$$Z = C + I \qquad (Z = \text{output}, \ I = \text{investment})$$
$$Y = Z \quad \text{by definition}$$

therefore $S = I$

but it really requires no such formality. There are some points to be noted in identifying the words or symbols used with economic concepts. Consumption goods and spending on consumption must be the same, and so an accumulation of stocks of consumption goods must be included in investment; but we have seen that this is the usual procedure of economists. It is only when we know that before Keynes it was usual to define savings and investment in other ways which did not guarantee their equality that we can understand why the ex post equality of savings and investment should ever have provoked any dissent.

The equality is of no interest until we notice that what happens is not always what was intended. The desired additions to savings and the desired level of investment need not coincide. In particular, we might assume that savings intentions are determined by income levels while investment decisions are quite independent of income (which is conveniently described as 'autonomous'). Savings increases with income because higher incomes permit satisfaction of current desires and some provision for the future while investment depends only on the wit to see opportunities for profit or the 'animal spirits' of entrepreneurs. (Remember that we are setting up a particular combination of assumptions, not offering these statements as descriptive of an actual economy. There are alternative sets of assumptions which lead to different theories.) Then it is immediately apparent that for any level of 'animal spirits' savings and investment

intentions are attainable simultaneously only for a particular
level óf income.

Furthermore, should there be a change in the level of investment, savings would have to change equally; the ex post equality
must be satisfied. But intended savings are related to income
and therefore to reach a new position where savings intentions
are realised, income levels will have to change too. As savings are
only a fraction of income, the change in income will have to be
greater than that in investment. This is the famous *multiplier*
principle.

It too can be expressed mathematically. That savings depend
on income can be written

$$S = a + sY$$
or equivalently $C = a' + cY$ where $s = 1 - c$

The a, a' are merely constants equal and opposite in sign, and s
and c represent the disposition of a marginal increment to income between savings and investment; (that is, for an increase of
one unit in income, the fraction s is added to saving, and $c = 1 - s$
is the fraction added to consumption). They are called the
'marginal propensity to save' and the 'marginal propensity to
consume' respectively.[5] Now an increase in investment leads to
an increase in income and therefore to an increase in planned
savings of

$$\Delta S = s \, \Delta Y$$

For planned savings to be achieved, the increase in planned savings must equal the increase in investment;

$$\Delta S = \Delta I$$

therefore $s \, \Delta Y = \Delta I$

and $\qquad \Delta Y = \frac{1}{s} \, \Delta I \quad$ or $\quad \frac{1}{1-c} \, \Delta I$

In this very simple system, income increases by a multiple of the
increase in investment, the multiplier being $1/(1-c)$.

This simple analysis can be presented diagrammatically as in
Fig. 4.1. The curve for C is a straight line. As investment is independent of income, the curve for $C + I$ is a straight line parallel to that for C. Where $C + I$ cuts the 45° line (which of course
ensures that vertical lines to the horizontal axis are equal in

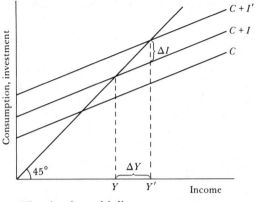

4.1 The simple multiplier

length to the distance from the intersection with the latter to the origin, that is to income), the sum of $C + I$ equals income so that planned investment equals planned saving. If investment is increased to I', the equality of planned investment and planned savings can occur only at Y'. The increase in investment is shown by the distance between $C + I$ and $C + I'$; the increase in income is $Y' - Y$; and the size of the multiplier is determined entirely by c, the slope of the C line.

All of this is simple mathematical manipulation, but it is sufficient to establish the point that given certain conditions about the behaviour of savings and investment, income *may* settle at any level and there is no guarantee that it will be at such a level that all of the available labour force is employed. Some change of the original conditions such as intervention by government to change the level of planned investment is needed if full employment of labour is an objective of policy. That was the political message that was so important in the 1930s and later.

The analysis rests only on the identification of consumption and investment and of the relationship of both to income. The notion that consumption spending depends on the level of income is intuitively plausible, although it is less acceptable that it depends on nothing but current income. We are interested here in aggregate consumption and aggregate income, so that random divergences of individuals from governing their consumption spending by their incomes need be of no concern to us. But systematic divergences would require amendments to the consumption function. It would no longer be merely $C = f(Y)$. The most important such divergences which have been examined concern permanent income and wealth. Consumption plans may be based on the level of income which is expected to be maintained rather than on what the current level of income happens to be; windfall gains would be divided among consumption and savings differently from changes which are expected to be permanent. Changes in the value of an individual's total assets, and not only in his current income, may affect spending plans; consumption would then be affected by things like interest rates and the relative value of different assets. These points can be described as substituting a more complicated function for $C = f(Y)$, but their implications are far-reaching. The simple analysis is appropriate only when consumption is at least dominated by current income levels, as it seems to have been, for example, in Britain in the interwar years.[6]

We can use the simple consumption function to develop some other important points. We can, for example, derive the multiplier in a different manner. We think of an increase in investment beginning a chain reaction. It becomes immediate income to some group within the community. That group increases its consumption spending by an amount determined by its marginal propensity to consume and the size of the increase in its income, the increase in investment. Its spending, $c \, \Delta I$, is income for another group. Its spending increases in the same way but by $c(c \, \Delta I)$. And so on. Eventually,

$$\Delta Y = \Delta I + c \, \Delta I + c^2 \, \Delta I + c^3 \, \Delta I \cdots$$

and the geometric progression[7] sums to give the same expression as before, $\Delta Y = (1/1 - c) \, \Delta I$. This formulation forces on us a consideration of time; the sequence of receipts and spending of additional income cannot be instantaneous, and so the process must take some time. But the geometric progression which we sum to the standard multiplier formula is an infinite one and after the three or four rounds of spending which could occur within a calendar year, the usual period in which politicians and others are interested, the multiplier may have reached only a fraction of its eventual value.

Deriving the multiplier from a sequence of consumption expenditures has another advantage too. Each of the rounds of the

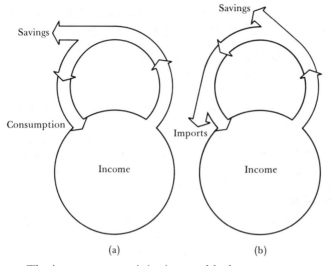

Savings

Savings

Consumption

Imports

Income

Income

(a)   (b)

4.2 The income stream: injections and leakages

process is seen to be adding to income. If it is real rather than monetary income with which we are dealing, additional resources must be being brought into use. We must therefore be concerned with a situation with unemployed resources. This underlines the origin of the theory in a period of widespread unemployment and the limitation of its direct appropriateness to such a situation. We can observe the same point by noting that it is assumed that there are no effective limits on new investment; resources are readily available.

It will be noticed that the important characteristic of investment in this simple theory is merely that it should be independent of income. The mathematical manipulations can be repeated for any division of income into autonomous and income-related components. What we really have is a conception of an income stream with leakages and the analysis is readily extended to any classification of this kind. So long as income leads via expenditures to further income within the economy, increases in autonomous components will be multiplied, the size of the multiplier being determined by the extent of leakages from the income stream (remembering that to interpret this as real income, resources must be available). The simple analysis we started with is represented in part (a) of Fig. 4.2. If we think of both exports and investment as autonomous, and imports as well as savings as income related with propensity to import of m, then we reach the situation portrayed in part (b) of Fig. 4.2. It is easy to show that the multiplier is then given by

$$\Delta Y = [1/(s + m)] \Delta A$$

where ΔA is an increase in either, or both, of the autonomous elements, exports and investment, and m is the marginal propensity to import. Similarly, if we conceive government spending as autonomous and tax receipts as leakages from the income stream, it is easy to develop a multiplier in these terms too. As it is then more natural to relate consumption plans to tax paid, or disposable income, the multiplier has a slightly different algebraic form.[8] The important point is that the key elements in this analysis are unemployed resources and leakages from the income stream.

Accelerators

Several developments of this analysis are available. One is to distinguish the consumption functions of different groups of income recipients. If, for example, we separate wages and profits and assume that the recipients of these kinds of income have different marginal propensities to save, s_w and s_p respectively, then the multiplier is given by

$$\Delta Y = [1/(s_w \cdot w + s_p \cdot p)] \Delta I$$

where w and p are the shares of wages and profits in income. That is, the multiplier is the reciprocal of a weighted average of the two separate marginal propensities to save. Numerous other divisions could be made equally easily.

This example, however, leads into a different kind of extension. It can be noted that if all wages are spent on consumption and all profits are saved, $s_w = 0$ and $s_p = 1$ and the multiplier is determined by the share of profits in income. What is surprising to those not entirely familiar with the elementary theory is that the smaller the share of profits, the greater the multiplier. This is clearly counterintuitive, but can easily be checked perhaps by inserting some numbers into the equation. It is readily understood by referring back to Fig. 4.2. Savings are leakages from the income stream. We obtained our paradoxical result by slipping in words so that the leakage all came from profits. The more profits relative to income, the more leakage. We did this to establish the significance of the assumption that investment is autonomous; it is very natural to associate the word *profits* with investment and so to expect an increase in its share to lead to more investment. But that is not what is being assumed here.

We could go on to change our assumptions and consider profits as a determinant of investment but it is more convenient to think of investment as responding to changes in income, returning to the simpler case where income is not divided between classes of recipients. We can write this as

$$I_t = v(Y_t - Y_{t-1})$$

Investment in a period is a constant fraction of the change in income between that period and the preceding one. The constant v is known as the acceleration coefficient. It is so known because changes in the level of investment will be a magnified or accelerated reflection of changes in the rate of growth. While income changes by a constant amount between successive periods, investment will be unchanged; if income grows more rapidly, the proportionate change in investment is even more pronounced so as to maintain the relationship between the *level* of investment and *changes* in the level of income.

When the accelerator is combined with the simple analysis of the preceding section, we have a direct feedback relationship between income and investment. The two equations

$$\Delta Y = [1/(1-c)] \, \Delta I$$
$$I = v(Y_t - Y_{t-1})$$

imply that from any starting point, the paths of Y and I in later periods are completely determined, and their shapes depend on the values of v and c. Different combinations of values for v and c can produce explosive growth in Y and I, continuous cycles, damped cycles, or explosive cycles. These possibilities are shown in Fig. 4.3.

Historians and economists have found it worthwhile to pursue this analysis in only one context, that of the trade cycle. From the nineteenth century onwards, many commentators and economists have thought they detected cyclical movements in output

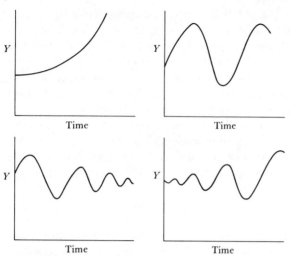

4.3 Income paths which may be determined by the multiplier and accelerator

series and have offered various explanations for them. Particular values of v and c could provide an explanation, but those values of v and c are not among the most plausible, and the chance of an economy being characterised by them and by the simple consumption function and accelerator are slight.

An analysis we owe to Hicks[9] shows that explosive growth from the multiplier-accelerator mechanism and two additional elements can provide a more acceptable explanation. The two additional elements are a full employment ceiling and the presence of some investment not connected to income changes by the accelerator but autonomous as in our earlier analysis. (That determined by the accelerator relationship is called *induced* investment.) It is plausible to think of an economy being limited by supply constraints at which it runs out of the unemployed resources we have been assuming so far. The limit itself grows over time as the result of productivity change. That gives us the full employment income line of Fig. 4.4. It is equally plausible to think of some investment being tied to the 'animal spirits' of entrepreneurs while some is related to changes in income. We assume that autonomous investment is rising over time, to give us the line so labelled in the diagram. We can then deduce the income path shown in the diagram.

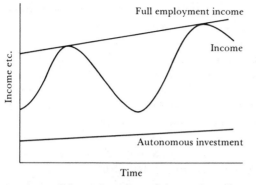

4.4 A possible explanation of the trade cycle

We begin, arbitrarily, with income at less than a full employment level so that resources are readily available. By assumption the multiplier-accelerator relationship produces explosive
growth, and income approaches the full employment ceiling.
Resources cannot then be obtained to continue the process, and
income necessarily grows more slowly. The accelerator relationship therefore produces an even more rapid deceleration of
investment. The multiplier then converts that into a further
deceleration of income, and we have the multiplier-accelerator
relationship in reverse. Income starts to plummet, but this does
not continue indefinitely since the autonomous investment provides a floor. Sooner or later the positive multiplier attached to
autonomous investment outweighs the negative one applied to
induced investment. The course of income is then reversed and
the whole process starts again.

Nobody would advance this, not even in a more rigorous exposition, as an explanation of any historical trade cycle. It is,
again, economic thinking as a source of ideas for incorporation
in historical analysis that we see here. The same applies to all of
the full employment ceiling, autonomous investment, and the
multiplier and accelerator relationships. Historians of all kinds
have noticed the greater instability of industries producing investment goods in a period such as the 1930s and have therefore
incorporated some kind of accelerator into their explanations.
The emphasis on government expenditure and road building in
accounts of Germany in the 1930s is much clearer when the multiplier mechanism is understood. And so on. The ideas as ex-

pounded so far are appropriate for fluctuations or incomplete cycles, but only if the movements are in income levels; even then historians will be aware of certain monetary features such as bank failures and 'panics' which have no place in the analysis so far, although they can be built in. For those nineteenth-century crises in both Britain and the United States (and in other countries) which historical research has shown to be fluctuations in confidence and in monetary areas but not in real output, analysis must proceed in quite different terms.

What we have done here is to take the simple analysis with which we started, add some further relationships to it, and follow the creation of new links between variables which have been found useful in historical analysis. We have clearly started what could be a very lengthy chain of thought. It is how the large-scale econometric models which are used for planning policy measures and for guiding critiques of policies have been evolved. We have linked only investment and income. By bringing in explicit relationships for money, prices, interest rates, wages, and employment levels, we would be well on the way to even the largest of the econometric models. Such steps must await the next and subsequent chapters. Even then, as the large scale models have not as yet been much used in historical analysis,[10] we shall be interested in the links themselves rather than in the complete systems to which they lead.

Other kinds of extension are possible too. We could explore further the way in which the accelerator appears in economic terms instead of leaving it as a mathematical expression only. Why should investment be linked to changes in income? We might think of a technical requirement for more machines to maintain a growing level of income. Or we might see income growth as fostering confidence in the profitability of future economic activity, so that entrepreneurs accumulate the assets needed to take advantage of those opportunities. This more economic line of thinking sits more easily beside our earlier emphasis on the assumed existence of unemployed resources. It directs our attention to expectations, and it also suggests that perhaps investment should be linked to changes in profits rather than income. We would then have ex ante investment related to profitability, and reverse the paradoxical result we constructed earlier when investment was entirely autonomous while the leakages from the income stream were determined by the ratio of profits to income. The valuable lesson here is the crucial importance of looking closely at exactly what combination of assumptions about investment and savings behaviour is being made. It is the combination and interconnection of variables which is important. For any empirical analysis it is essential that an appropriate choice be made from the sets which are available.

Our focus has been on income determination in particular sets of circumstances. We have included some consideration of changes over time but our focus cannot yet be said to be on the process by which the income of an economy grows. That requires the basic concepts of several other areas of economic enquiry.

Historical applications

Although the ideas of this chapter are most useful when they are joined with others yet to be introduced, some further pointers can be given.

First, for historians dealing with the years since the Second World War, the simple Keynesian ideas have become part of their materials. Analyses of economies in terms of full employment and the multiplier have become commonplace. Although we can wonder just how deep was the understanding of some of the politicians who used the concepts in their statements, the public service advisers guiding government policies have comprehended at least the simple ideas expounded here. (Their judgment might, of course, have been wrong or overridden by political considerations.) This may be obvious, but it is worth emphasizing that it was the Keynesian approach to economics that brought theory into a much more prominent place in the concerns of political historians.

Second, we can refer again to the subject of trade cycle history. It became less fashionable in the 1950s and 1960s, but trade and other cycles have been revived by the events of the 1970s. Many episodes in the past have been analysed usefully by drawing on the multiplier analysis.[11]

Third, the more general notions of a division between autonomous and dependent elements within the income stream have been found useful in historical cases where exports are of special importance. Many rest also on the concepts to be treated in Chapter 7, but some turn almost entirely on the multiplier to be associated with exports. Meyer's famous article is an example of this in the case of Britain.[12] In economies that were even more open to international trade such as Australia and New Zealand, the point is still more obvious; the notion of exports as an autonomous engine of growth and of imports as the major leakage from the income stream is indeed the central theme in the economic history of such countries.[13]

And yet none of the uses by historians listed so far is the most pervasive employment of the simple ideas with which we are concerned here. Rather, that is the simple employment of a framework such as [14]

$$Y = C + I + G + X - M$$

along with full employment and the multiplier as the framework within which the economic ideas remain implicit. Thus an historian seeking to account for the rapid economic growth of France and Italy in the first half of the 1920s turns naturally to a sequence in which he establishes that unemployed labour existed, that there were no institutional barriers to investment, and that export markets were buoyant. The implicit notion that the autonomous items were attractive to entrepreneurs is really the core of the analysis. Similarly, when it is argued that in the 1930s X could no longer lead growth but that in France real wages grew to produce a home-demand growth (via C), while in Italy only government expenditure and import substitution were available for this role, the same set of ideas is implied.[15]

Although it might seem that the argument is purely 'literary', the kind of argument familiar to any historian, an understanding of exactly what is being assumed depends on knowledge of the economic ideas presented here. For example, what connection is there between real wages and income growth? What does this imply about investment decisions? What does it imply about unemployed resources?

5

Money

Monetary history

Many historians find monetary topics tedious, and many more must have experienced the 'switching-off' effect which the introduction of money or banking has on an audience of students. There is a widespread belief that the important economic component of any historical discussion is necessarily real[1] rather than monetary, and that treatment of the latter is merely tedious detail. There is some justification for such beliefs; we have defined income in terms of real goods and services and it is natural to go on to conceive the growth of an economy, the topic which most easily arouses the interest of historians, as the use of real resources to produce real income. It would be foolish ever to lose sight of that conception. But it would be equally foolish not to recognise the market transactions which must lie behind such a process. These transactions involve money; they may be frustrated by monetary phenomena, and they might be forced into particular paths by monetary considerations. Even historians whose economic interests are confined to growth should be equipped with the basic ideas needed to understand the role of money.

Other historians should need no such persuasion. Institutions intimately concerned with money such as banks and discount houses are important in their own right as bases of power and influence within a community. They can be complex organisations within which people interact to produce a unified policy. For these and other reasons historians might be interested in them; and there are many such 'institutional' histories. The understanding of any institution is greatly facilitated by a clear sense of what it does, and monetary economics cannot fail to be helpful in this respect.

Historians' prejudice against monetary economics sits oddly beside its nature relative to other parts of the subject. Because money and even banking are much more observable than something like income, monetary economics has always been one of the more empirical fields within the subject. Bankers keep good accounts, and central governments have always been interested in the management of money, so that in most periods, from ancient times to the present, statistical information is more readily available for monetary matters than it is for most economic concepts. Furthermore, the monetary arrangements of different countries vary in ways that are not mere detail. More subtly, the monetary institutions and arrangements of a single country can change over time in ways that react with other aspects of the economy. Economists interested in explaining the role of money have therefore had to keep closer to empirical events than their colleagues concerned with somewhat more universal phenomena.

Monetary economics is not a clearly defined and distinct branch of economics. The old subject of 'money, banking, and credit' concentrated on describing monetary institutions and their immediate impact, and could indeed be treated as substantially self-contained. It had links to other parts of economics, but it is those links themselves which occupy the central place in 'monetary economics', a subject which has proliferated in several directions. Both the old and the new provide elements of what has proved most useful in historical studies.

The two triads

Money can be defined only by its function. Starting from the intuition that money is anything which is generally acceptable in settlement of debts, we can distinguish several functions of money and several related reasons why money is held. It is usual to divide both the functions of money and the reasons for holding money into three, and they are known as the 'two triads' of monetary theory.

The three functions of money are acting as a unit of account, as a means of exchange, and as a store of value. The first refers to the need to establish some common denominator in which the prices of two commodities can be compared. In a market in

which a number of commodities are exchanged by direct barter-
ing, any one of them might be taken as a numeraire so that the
statement of relative prices is simplified. If the market were
slightly more sophisticated and accounts were kept on paper
and successive barterings offset, or 'cleared' to use the terminology associated historically with banks, the accounts would be
kept in the chosen unit. (There is a clear analogy with the accounts kept in friendly games of chance.)

Anything which was a unit of account only would not be recognisable as money. The means of exchange brings us much
closer. Something which is a means of exchange permits exchange to take place even when the two parties do not each have
a commodity which will satisfy a want of the other. The exchange is of commodity against money instead of commodity
against commodity. For money to be 'generally acceptable' as a
means of making exchanges, there must be confidence that its
possession will permit a later acquisition of commodities. Almost
anything could be used. Although a means of exchange could
conceivably be limited to a particular market in the sense of a
medieval fair, such moneys are not of historical significance, and
it is reasonable to think of money as requiring durability. That
was probably the major reason why gold and silver were often
used. (Their ability to be divided into various amounts and to be
recombined were also convenient characteristics of the precious
metals.) When confidence extended beyond gold and silver to
the trustworthiness of certain groups of merchants, gold and
silver were supplemented by bank notes and eventually by bank
deposits. Coins themselves came to be based on the same kind of
trust as amounts of precious metals were replaced by mere to-
kens.

The economic criterion of confidence differs from the law-
yers' concept of legal tender, something which must by law be
accepted in payment of a debt. The status of legal tender obviously confers confidence except in the unlikely event of doubts
about the survival of the authority by which it is conferred, but
the economic concept of money is much wider. Indeed, because
everyday language confuses money and currency – the coin and
bank notes of which legal tender is usually composed – it is
worth emphasizing that a monetary economy could operate
without currency at all. Consider again a particular market, but

no longer one of barter only. There is a banker in whom all
buyers and sellers have confidence. Exchanges take place, not
commodity against commodity, but by each pairing of a buyer
and seller notifying the banker. The bank's accounts now
operate as a means of exchange and not merely as a unit of account. This simplified construct is much closer to the kind of
money used in advanced economies, cheques being the agreed
notification to the banker, than is the conceptualisation of
money in terms of gold or even banknotes.

The store of value function, also known as the asset function,
carries the element of durability much further. Its essence is
widening the range of choice by enabling an individual to defer
the purchase of commodities in the hope or expectation that a
better bargain will be available at a later time. A money which
was a means of payment at a particular fair but not acceptable
anywhere else whould have a very limited store of value function. A full money could be retained in the knowledge that it
would be equally acceptable at a later date. Two elements are involved here. One is the semilegal consideration that the money
will still be acceptable in payment of debts. The other is that a
given amount of it will still command about the same amount of
goods in general. The second of these is the more important in
most circumstances and is the reason for the very close link between money and inflation. It will be noticed that it is storage
over time which is involved; like so much else in economics,
monetary theory has proceeded on a national basis, and although we shall later explore some monetary aspects of international economics, the usual definition of money does not require
that it should be a store of value across national boundaries.

The second triad is of reasons why money is held. Transactions balances refer to money which happens to be held when a
count of assets is taken simply because the date of that count is in
the middle of a planned sequence of purchases. A household example is simplest. If income is received in money weekly, it is
natural to dispose of that part of it not required for household
operations, holding enough to finance the week's requirements
so that the balance gradually diminishes to zero when the next
instalment of income is received. If a count of assets is taken at
any time during the week, a certain 'transactions balance' of
money will be revealed. In a business with continual cash re-

ceipts as well as cash payments, the matter is slightly more complex, but the idea of a transactions balance as the net result of the flows is still apparent.

We have deliberately spoken of transactions balances rather than the transactions demand for money or the transactions motive for holding money since no positive desire to hold money is involved. The economic literature in general is less concerned with the linguistic appropriateness of words and does use the alternative terms. By an accident of the way in which the theory evolved, transactions balances are sometimes referred to as 'active' balances, an unfortunate terminology now too well-known to be displaced.

Transactions balances are linked closely to the means of payment function of money. The other two elements of our second triad are linked more to the store of value function, and are known as the precautionary and the speculative demand for money. If we return to our household example, it would be only a household with complete certainty about its expenses which would deliberately plan to hold no money at all just before the next instalment of income was due. Households of a more familiar kind are aware that they sometimes incur unexpected calls on the available money. Such households plan to hold some money which in a normal week would be undisturbed but which would be available for any emergency. A midweek count of assets would then reveal the sum of a transactions and a precautionary balance. Similarly, any business might know what the usual demands for money are but retain in addition some money in case of unexpected expense or in case an opportunity for additional profitable business should occur. Precautionary demands are found in both households and businesses and are connected with the store of value function of money.

The speculative demand for money differs because while it too is related to uncertainty about the future, it concerns what is expected to happen rather than the unexpected. Continuing our household example, we began by holding money to meet expected expenses and added a second sum for possible emergencies. We thought of the remainder being devoted to something outside the household, some form of saving which would not be counted as household money. It might, for example, be the purchase of a security giving some interest. But if the household thought that the price of a security was likely to fall, then it may decide to defer its purchase. If the price does fall, more of the security can be obtained for the available cash, so that over some period there is a greater return despite the sacrifice of interest for the time when the saving is held in cash. In the meantime, there is a speculative money balance.

A simple example may clarify this point. Consider a household which, after making allowance for its transactions and precautionary balances, has £100 left from each weekly instalment of income. With this it normally purchases a bond which entitles it to receive interest of £5 weekly but which cannot be converted to cash again for three weeks. The household thinks that it is likely that new bonds will soon be available, still paying interest of £5 weekly but costing only £50. By electing not to buy a bond this week, it sacrifices £5, but if its expectation proves correct two bonds can be bought in its place one week later and over the following two weeks it will receive £20 rather than £10. The increased income is more than enough to justify the sacrifice of a week's return. The numbers here are extreme, but the idea of holding cash while speculating on the probability that a better bargain will become available is clear. This time, the example can be put in terms of a household or a firm with no change at all. During the delay, a count of assets will reveal a speculative balance of money.

The example can be developed in two important directions. The first is the link between money and interest. Our example employed an unexplained fall in the price of bonds paying a fixed return. We note that a payment of £5 on £100 represents an interest rate of 5 percent (per 'week' but it would be in the interests of realism to think of a 'week' much longer than a calendar one), while £5 on £50 represents 10 percent. Speculation on a fall in bond prices is equivalent to speculation on a rise in the interest rate. Money and interest are intertwined. If we rest content for the moment with the notion that the interest rate depends on the productivity of capital (in the sense of Chapter 3) we begin to see the speculative demand for money as one of the links between money and the real economy.

The second point to notice in our example is that purchasing bonds involved a commitment of funds for three 'weeks'. If, when the price of a bond changed from £100 to £50, it were possible to redeem those held and make a new purchase, there would be no point in holding a speculative balance of money. It would confer no advantage. This leads us to the concept of liquidity, essentially the flexibility to reconsider and rearrange the disposition of assets in the light of changed circumstances.

Money has liquidity in that it can be used for a variety of purchases. The bond has no liquidity at all for a fixed term; it is illiquid because it deprives the owner of control over the funds invested in it. In practice there is a gradation of assets which have varying degrees of liquidity. Money is necessarily fully liquid; a fixed deposit with a banker who will permit it to be withdrawn with little penalty is almost fully liquid; a bond which can be resold at any time but without certainty as to its price is more or less liquid; and a machine which is confined to a particular use is virtually illiquid. The spectrum of liquidity is dependent on the institutional development of the relevant economy.

Banking

Even when the spectrum of liquidity is very finely subdivided, the banking system occupies a unique position. Because the debts owed by bankers – which is how the deposits placed with them look from the other side – enjoy the confidence of the public and are acceptable as a means of payment, banks are able to create money. The precise meaning of this can best be explained by an example.

Consider for the moment a bank without competitors, or a unified banking system. Its bank notes are accepted as the means of payment for small amounts and balances at the bank are regarded as a safe store of value as well as the means for larger payments. However, there is a quite distinct currency used in a neighbouring economy. Let us begin examination of the system when the bank has just received payment of the equivalent of £100 from the neighbouring economy. There is no shortage of entrepreneurs wanting bank finance in the economy with which we are concerned, and the bank selects one and makes a loan of £100.

The entrepreneur promptly spends it on an investment project. Most of the spending goes to local people but some, say one-tenth, is used to purchase imports from the neighbouring econ-

Table 3. *The simple bank money multiplier*

Round	Increase in loans	Increase in deposits or note issue	Foreign currency
0			£100.0
1	£100	£90.0	90.0
2	90	81.0	81.0
3	81	72.9	72.9
Eventually sum to:	£1000	£900	0

omy. The recipients of the nine-tenths spent locally deposit the funds in their own bank accounts, while the other tenth disappears from our view. As this stage the bank still holds £90 of the original inflow of foreign funds, its loans have increased by £100, and its deposits have increased by £90. It now makes a further loan of £90 and in the same process the increase in its loans rises to £190, the increase in its deposits to £171 (£90 + $^9/_{10}$ of £90) and its holding of the foreign inflow falls to £81 (£90 − $^1/_{10}$ of £90). Further rounds produce the figures shown in Table 3.

Eventually, the original inflow of £100 produces an increase in bank deposits of £900. As bank deposits are part of the money supply, the inflow of funds is multipled in the resulting increase in the money supply. The increase in money is the original inflow, plus a much larger portion created by the banking system.

The mathematical parallel between this multiplier and the multiplier of the preceding chapter is obvious. There are some economic parallels as well. We again have a closed circle of transactions except for a specific leakage, this time of funds going outside the economy altogether. The size of the multiplier is again determined by the size of the leakage; in our numerical example, the leakage is one-tenth and the multiplier is therefore 10 (counting the original inflow as a deposit). But the economic process is really quite different. We are concerned this time only with monetary amounts, not with income creation. Availability of unemployed resources is not so important this time; confidence in the banking system is. If people were not willing to hold their funds as bank deposits, the process would break down. In the example the only alternative people have is the holding of the foreign currency, and if at any stage foreign currency were demanded for holding outside the bank, the multiplier process would be terminated much more quickly and at lower levels. We can create an alternative mechanism by postulating a governmental body which issues notes and which is willing to hold foreign currency but not the notes issued by the bank nor to keep deposits at the bank. Then a loss of confidence in the bank could lead to a greater holding of government notes, purchased with bank notes or bank deposits which the government then insists that the bank should settle in foreign currency. The circular process of loans and deposits within the bank is then subjected to a greater leakage and the money multiplier is reduced in size. This multiplier process then is determined by a circular flow of loans and deposits dependent on a supply of willing and acceptable borrowers and confidence in bank deposits subject to some leakage.

We have chosen for illustrative purposes the particular leakage of foreign transactions. We choose this presentation to make clear immediately that the determinate multiplier process is in no way dependent on a monetary role for gold, as might appear in the more conventional presentation that economists use in a misguided nod to history. In England and some other countries banks did indeed grow in economies where gold coins already provided a money supply. People could hold coin rather than the deposits or notes of the banking system, and the greater convenience of the latter would be outweighed if there were any doubt about the security of the banks. Banks had to hold at least a fraction of their assets in gold (or something readily convertible into gold such as the securities of a trusted government) either to meet actual demands for gold or, even more important at an early stage, to give the appearance of being able to do so and thus to maintain public confidence in the banks. This 'reserve requirement' constituted a leakage from the circular process and so provided a determinate multiplier process. But it is the leakage rather than its particular form which is important and our presentation avoids possible confusion.

The role of gold has now been attenuated almost to extinction, but that of governments has increased. We can best show the significance of government by returning to our example. We introduce a government which has secure control of the country and enjoys complete confidence. It runs its own bank outside the banking system with which our first example was concerned. There is a requirement, established by law or unchallenged convention, that the banking system maintains balances of a fixed percentage of the deposits placed with it in the government bank which does no business for customers other than the government.[2] Consider now the process of government expenditure. The government acquires the resources it wants simply by writing a cheque on its bank. The recipient, however, deposits it with the private banking system. There is therefore a transfer of funds into the private banking system and the multiplier begins as before. But with each increase in its deposits, the private banking system has to increase its own deposit with the government bank and this provides a leakage which ensures that the multiplier process converges. Government expenditure therefore has a determinate multiplied effect on (private) bank deposits and so on the money supply. Tax collections have the same multiplied effect in reverse.

Again notice that this can take place entirely with bank money in the sense of bank deposits accepted as money. The phrase in which a government is said to 'print notes' is metaphorical.

Unlike a leakage into gold or foreign currency, that into a separate government collection immediately raises the possibility that the banking system can be manipulated directly for certain policy ends. So it can, and this is the basis of monetary policy. Government might, for example, want to restrain the availability of finance. In the light of our example, the simplest way to do so is to raise the proportion of deposits[3] which the banking system must hold with the government's bank. Such changes in *reserve ratios* have been used in many countries including the United States, Australia, and New Zealand, and to a limited extent, Britain. Another method is for the government to compete with the banking system for deposits. This could be done by offering private accounts at the government's bank, but such a mechanism would be cumbersome. It is simpler to sell government securities to the public. Individuals and companies use cheques to purchase the securities, and the government collects the aggregate of the cheques from the banking system. The balance of the latter at the government's bank is therefore reduced. To maintain it as the (unchanged) required ratio to deposits, the banking system has to reduce its deposits by more than the amount of cheques written by individuals, or to acquire new reserves. It might, for example, not allow the money multiplier to operate on government expenditure. By any of these methods the government can restrain the availability of private bank finance.

Repurchase by the government of its own existing securities has the opposite effect; it expands the money supply to the private sector. Government's transactions in its own securities are known as open market operations and are a major instrument of monetary policy in many countries. To influence private credit conditions is often the main purpose of government's internal borrowing, and it is wise not to think that government and private borrowing always have the same motivation.

We have been expounding the power of a banking system to create money subject only to leakages to alternative currencies, foreign transactions, and government requirements, perhaps modified by deliberate government policy. It will have occurred to many readers that despite our attention to leakages and government controls, this attributes much more power to banks than the rhetoric of most bankers acknowledges. So it does. We have been concerned with the banking system as a whole; bankers are usually concerned with an individual bank. One bank among many has much less freedom of movement simply because by far the most important constraint is that it will lose funds to its competitors. If one bank seeks to expand loans faster than the average for the banking system as a whole, it will find that it is receiving a smaller amount from cheques drawn on other banks than those banks are receiving in cheques drawn by its own customers. It will therefore have to clear balances due to the other banks. If it has received an injection of funds (from abroad or from government transactions) it can meet the balances due to other banks without difficulty. Otherwise, it has to restrain its lending so as to come back into line with the banking system as a whole.

Furthermore, while in most countries loss of confidence in the banking system as a whole is now a remote possibility, loss of confidence in one bank is by no means so unlikely, especially in countries unlike the United Kingdom where the banking system remains composed of a large number of separate banks. The bankers' power to control the money supply, already limited by such things as external transactions and government, is available only for coordinated use. To the individual banker his business looks much more like collecting deposits to finance loans, a kind of money pawnshop or cloakroom, than like part of a process of money creation. But in aggregate, it is the latter which is the correct characterisation of banking.

These points are directly relevant to historians concerned with banks, but perhaps even more important are the interrelationships revealed between banking and the government or foreign trade. The direct significance to historians concerned with banks is that they should not be treated as simple channels between savers and investors, depositors and borrowers. A bank which is entrusted with providing means of payment increases the supply of money. Thus the country banks of the Industrial Revolution in England were not merely channels in which savings flowed; their creation expanded the supply of finance in the economy. Because of the availability of alternative forms of money, gold, and Bank of England currency, and because country banks were confined to particular localities and could not build a national reputation for security, the reserves which they needed were high and the multiplier attached to their activities therefore low. But it would be misleading to ignore the multiplier entirely. Similarly, the spread of banks in other countries does more than permit the transmission of savings; a potential for credit creation is introduced. It is only in the light of the theory expounded here, and with a knowledge of the actual reserves of banks, that we can follow Temin's argument that the financial trends of the 1830s in the United States were not caused by 'wildcat' banking. The important developments were in the flow of bank reserves, not a change in banking practices to tolerate a marked lowering of reserve requirements.[4]

It is convenient to illustrate the links of money to government and to foreign transactions from New Zealand history. Until 1934 there was no separate government bank and the government maintained its balances with the private banking system. Flows of funds to and from the government did not act as leakages from and injections to the banking system as a whole although they did affect the position of the particular bank holding the government account relative to the system as a whole. It was the government's inability to affect the funds of the banking system, not any antidemocratic conspiracy of bankers, which was changed by the establishment of the Reserve Bank of New Zealand. Furthermore, as gold was never of great significance within the New Zealand economy, external transactions provided the source of injections to and withdrawals from the banking system. It was this relationship, not a vague 'colonial dependency' which made the course of foreign trade so important to the economy.

It is noteworthy too that these points could not be derived from contemporary comment which was directed almost exclusively to the position of an individual bank rather than to banks as a whole. Historical understanding is entirely dependent on a knowledge of the economic theory of banking.

Nonbank financial institutions

There is much less of theoretical interest to be said about the wide range of business known collectively as nonbank financial institutions, NFI. They do act as channels whereby funds are moved between those who have a surplus of some kind to those who wish to borrow. In a rich society there is room for a good deal of specialisation, different kinds of NFI each having their own sources of deposits and making loans for varying purposes. The precise pattern of NFI specialisation found in any economy often depends most on the historical path of evolution, something which historians are well equipped to trace and not an area where they can expect to learn from economists. Thus the discount houses in Britain and the stock and station agencies of Australia and New Zealand are somewhat peculiar institutions traceable to particular features of the history of those countries. That Post Office Savings Banks and Trustee Savings Banks are found in Britain, Australia, and New Zealand while building societies or savings and loan associations are found in all those countries and in the United States must be traced to suitably general or local historical events. In no case does economic theory provide much assistance.

It is worthwhile noticing that the NFI and the banking system can be arranged in an ordering according to their distance from the financial centre. In any modern economy the focus is the central bank, and it is surrounded by the banking system. The central bank deals only with the banking system; the banks deal with the central bank and also with some NFI outside them. These are the NFI known as intermediaries which connect different parts of the financial system. Outside them are those NFI which deal directly with members of the public. And outside them are household and businesses concerned with the production and consumption of real commodities, using the financial system but not being part of it. The significance of this conceptualisation is that it reinforces the concept of liquidity introduced earlier, and reveals that policy changes at the central bank may take some time to affect the real economy sitting on the outside of the concentric rings. But the pattern of evolution of the NFI in any economy means that institutions tend to cross the boundaries of neat conceptualisations and an understanding of their particular functions gains little from it.

When we notice that the concentric circles can be straddled, we might wonder whether the line between banks and NFI is clear-cut either. It is not. The previous section makes clear that the crucial characteristic of a bank is that its debts are accepted as money, being used not only as a store of value (as deposits with the NFI may be) but also as a means of payment. Can any debt of a bank be so used? Clearly not since banks like any other business can borrow in a form such as a mortgage. It is their deposits which are relevant. But all deposits? A deposit which the depositor guarantees to leave undisturbed for a fixed term in return for interest is not available as a means of payment. But some banks pay interest on deposits which are not made for a fixed term but are not subject to withdrawal by cheque. On the one hand, we may say that such deposits must be turned into a cheque account or notes before they can be used for payments and so they are not money. On the other, we may say that conversion is so quick and simple that the deposits are effectively available as a means of payment. And then there are fixed-term deposits documented by something like a 'transferable certificate of deposit' whose ownership can be changed; they too might be regarded as available for payments. Money is sometimes defined as something which is 'readily available' as well as generally acceptable as a means of payment, but that really does no more than evade the question (and provoke wry comments about the availability of money). It is better to leave the issue for determination in particular circumstances, recognising that much depends on the precise institutional practices of the banks.

The same difficulties apply to some deposits with NFI. Accounts with trustee savings banks may be judged effectively available as means of payment, and if they are subject to withdrawal by cheques cleared in the same way as bank cheques, the case is overwhelming, even if it blurs the bank/NFI distinction. It is a point like this which explains the variants of measures of the money supply in most modern economies. One finds a measure consisting of notes and coin in circulation and noninterest-bearing deposits at the commercial banks, usually labelled M1. When the definition of money is widened to include interest-bearing deposits at the commercial banks, a series labelled M2 is produced. A still more inclusive series M3 includes demand deposits with NFI. (To avoid double counting, as more forms of deposits are included, the deposits held by one included institution with another are usually eliminated.) Much confusion can result from regarding the series as alternative measures of the money supply without due regard to at least the broad outlines of their construction. The appropriate series depends on the particular question at hand. In making this choice, the key part of the distinction between banks and the NFI, the ability to create credit, will often be important.[5]

There is one NFI which deserves a further word because the significance with which it is treated in much popular discussion may mislead historians. This is the stock exchange. It is an NFI with several functions although it is clearly towards the outside of our set of concentric circles. First, it is a market for buying and selling shares of various kinds of companies. Simplifying only a little, we can say that for every buyer there must be a seller and transactions on the stock exchange have no effect on the supply of funds to business. The market is one in titles to ownership of shares. In many countries the average trend of prices on the exchange is taken as some kind of barometer of the future course of real income in the economy. That might be so if people trading on the exchange were able to foresee the income stream of particular firms with accuracy. At the other extreme some people regard the stock exchange as no more than a respectable casino; there is a good deal of evidence in their favour, although changes in average prices could still be significant if they affected expectations about the future. (The relevance of this to the valuation of capital, in a fundist conception, is apparent.)

A second function of the stock exchange is important more directly. It is the new issues section of the market where new securities are sold to NFI and directly or indirectly to members of the public. New issues do raise finance for business activities and remembering that the purchase must set up a chain reaction in the banking system as cheques are cleared, the new issues section of the stock exchange is one of the most important links between the financial system and the real economy. A new issue of a particular firm will be more or less attractive to members of the public, depending on what is happening to the price of previous issues by the same firm, perhaps by the course of prices of shares in similar firms, and perhaps, but more remotely, by an index of average share prices. The two functions of the exchange are related, but it is new issues activity which has the more immediate economic significance.

Monetary economics

We have so far concentrated on elucidating the nature of financial institutions and mechanisms, following the focus of money, credit, and banking. We turn now to follow for a short distance the links between money and such things as incomes, prices, and interest rates, the focus of the more modern monetary economics.

The simplest such link is the *quantity theory* or *Fisher's equation of exchange*.[6] Writing M for the quantity of money, V for the velocity of circulation or the number of times on average money is used in a given period, P for the average price level, and T for the number of transactions that occur in the same period, we have

$$MV = PT$$

The left-hand side can be interpreted as the total payments made in the period; that follows directly from multiplying the stock of money by the average number of times each unit of money is used. Similarly, the right-hand side can be interpreted as the total of receipts. Payments must equal receipts and therefore the equality follows directly from the definitions of the variables. Tautologies can be useful, but they do not themselves constitute explanations. Those who recognise this one as underlying many journalists' and politicians' statements about 'money chasing goods' will rightly regret the lack of any convincing analysis.

There is nothing in the equation itself to suggest a stronger link between M and P than between any other pair of the four variables. Why should M not affect T, the variable nearest to a measure of real goods marketed? Some additional consideration such as the unavailability of additional resources and the distinction in Chapter 2 between final and intermediate goods has to be introduced. And what is the nature of V? It is introduced here simply as a means of converting a stock variable M into a flow equal to the total value of transactions. At the very least we would have to have reason for believing that changes in M and V were not simply offsetting before we could.expect M to affect either P or T. To obtain an immediate link between M and P, we need a set of assumptions such as that T is determined by real resources available while V is constant.

Even the earliest economists writing about the quantity theory thought of the equation as an equilibrium condition rather than as a tautology. They did not think that V was entirely invariant when M changed, but they thought that V could be expected to settle to a value determined by the monetary institutions and by customary habits. They thought of a gold currency meeting an expected pattern of transactions with no frenzied spending to beat anticipated price rises and no hoarding of currency against other contingencies. Then a change in M greater than the contemporary change in T can indeed be expected eventually to produce a proportionate change in P.

This theory possibly originated in, and has certainly been much discussed in the context of, the historical inflation of the sixteenth century. The inflow of American silver and the rise of prices in Europe seemed explicable in terms of the quantity theory. Historians have vastly elaborated on and improved the explanation, noting, for example, that American silver was not the only possible source of an increased money supply, explaining how the increased money supply reached individual countries such as Britain, and so on. Indeed, in exploring the real limitations on T, and in shifting the emphasis from the average price level to the differential rises in agricultural and industrial prices, they created something close to a different explanation. But the rise in M and appropriate limitations on V and T remain essential parts of the explanation of a general rise in prices.[7]

In the hands of an intelligent historian the simple quantity theory can be used to good purpose. But it leaves too much to be brought in as specific considerations to really rate as a theory of money or prices. It does not, in this initial form, even relate money to income, let alone to savings, investment, and interest rates.

It might be thought that the first point can easily be taken care of by writing

$$MV = PY$$

where Y is income and the V is the income velocity of circulation rather than the transactions velocity used until now. This has been done frequently. If there were a clear connection between transactions in final-demand goods and transactions in intermediate goods, there would be a simple relationship between the two velocities. Otherwise, there would not, and the meaning of income velocity is much less immediately obvious.

This defect can be repaired by moving from the Fisher equation to what is known as the *Cambridge equation*,[8]

$$M = kPY \quad \text{or} \quad M/P = kY$$

There is an algebraic equivalence between k and the reciprocal of income velocity, but the economic interpretation is likely to be different. The first formulation $M = kPY$ suggests only that people's holding of money is likely to be related to their current monetary income. We might think of this as a reflection of the transactions balances discussed earlier, although this is not the only possible interpretation. It has been useful for historical studies because it provides a means of estimating income, data on money supply being abundant relative to that on income. Given information on M and k, we can estimate monetary income PY and it may not be fanciful to suggest that some such idea underlay the common nineteenth-century habit of judging the 'progress' of an economy by the course of its bank deposits.[9] The determinants of k and its constancy must still be found in the institutional features of the relevant economy.

The second formulation of the Cambridge equation $M/P = kY$ suggests a different line of thought. M/P can be interpreted as *real balances;* it is the amount of money deflated for price changes so that 'real' has the meaning usually given it in econmics. The equation can be regarded as a behavioural relationship, an expression of people's desires that the amount of their balances should vary proportionately with their income. Such desires might be explained in terms of the precautionary and speculative motives for holding money discussed earlier in this chapter.

Once this step is taken, it is easy to go further and think of a demand for money, a desire for real balances, being related not only to income but to other economic variables such as interest rates. This too relates closely to our earlier discussion of the speculative motive for holding money. We would then have

$$M/P = f(Y, i)$$

real balances desired are a function of income and interest rates. We could marry this with the money creation process discussed in the second section of this chapter, whereby the money supply is determined by injections and withdrawals because of international transactions and government operations. We would then have a system relating incomes, prices, interest rates, bank reserve ratios, and flows of funds which constitute injections and withdrawals (and are known as *high-powered money*).

This system has been used directly in the writing of history; indeed its construction and its use for analysing history have always been closely related.[10] Once they have got this far, historians will find nothing unusual needed for the customary historical appraisal of such works.

Understanding the key notion of a demand for money, especially of a demand for real balances, needs some care. It should not be interpreted as a miserly desire to hoard; it is an indirect representation of consumers' choices of how to dispose of their income among consumption goods and savings, in which a desired level of cash is implied. Still, a great deal hangs on simple relationships between cash holdings and the important behavioural decisions.

There is an alternative line of thought which has the advantage of being more clearly concerned with willingness to tolerate

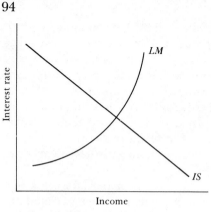

5.1 The Hicksian cross

certain money balances rather than suggesting a positive desire for money balances. We assume, as seems reasonable, that at higher levels of income people are more willing to hold money for speculative purposes, and that both the transactions and precautionary balances are higher. Furthermore, we assume that people will hold more for speculative purposes when interest rates are low than when they are high. It will be recalled from our example that interest rates vary inversely with the price of bonds. We assume that the money supply is controlled by, for example, government controls on the reserves of the banking system. (The money supply may be affected directly by such things as external transactions but suitable manipulations of reserve ratios or open market operations can offset them.)

The supply of money is controlled, but will be what people are willing to tolerate only at certain income or interest rate levels. A given money supply M, which is tolerable at one pairing of income and interest rates, will remain tolerable only if both income and interest rates rise or if both fall (so that their effects are offsetting). Otherwise, the same level of money supply will not be acceptable. In this way we deduce a curve such as *LM* in Fig. 5.1; it is called the *liquidity-preference function* and it shows pairs of income and interest rates at which the balances tolerated are equal to a given supply of money (and there is a different *LM* curve for each level of the money supply).

The *IS* curve of the diagram follows quickly from the multiplier analysis of the preceding chapter. We assume that I is related to interest rates; we could say that entrepreneurs are governed not by animal spirits but by the cost of borrowing so that lower interest rates result in higher ex ante investment and higher interest rates produce lower ex ante investment. Only at certain combinations of Y and i will ex ante investment then equal ex ante savings and these pairings are those of the *IS* curve. Increased income produces increased ex ante savings; there must therefore be higher ex ante investment if equality is to be maintained; interest rates must therefore be lowered at the same time that income is increased, and conversely. That is sufficient to establish the downward-to-the-right shape of the *IS* curve.

Again, we have a simple system linking money, income, interest, investment, and savings behaviour. The shape of the *IS* and *LM* curves ensure that they intersect or cross; [11] that is, there is a unique pairing of income and interest associated with any (controlled) level of the money supply such that both desired saving and desired investment can be realised, and the stock of money is just sufficient for the level of money balances which people are happy to maintain. (We have simplified and left out prices; the simplest way to bring them in is to assume that the government controls the money supply at the level at which monetary spending is just sufficient to keep all resources employed; more spending produces inflation since output can no longer respond.)

This apparatus has proved useful in a number of contexts. Consider for example the *liquidity trap*. We start with an economy where resources are unemployed. Government chooses to use monetary policy to stimulate the economy. It increases the money supply. This appears in the diagram as a shift of the liquidity preference function such as that from LM_1 to LM_2 in part (a) of Fig. 5.2; higher incomes or lower interest rates are needed for the increased money balances to be tolerable. Equilibrium of savings and investment is now possible only at a lower interest rate and an increased income (Y_2). Assuming that equilibrium is reached, monetary policy secures higher income and so a reduction in unemployed resources. But in part (b) of Fig. 5.2, the left-hand side of the *LM* curve is horizontal. Interest rates have a minimum which may be the result of a number of administrative or institutional features. For example, there may be a conventional difference between long- and short-term rates

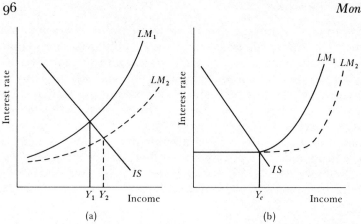

5.2 The liquidity trap

and even short-term rates are always positive; then the average rate will have a floor above zero. It follows then that monetary policy of the kind we discussed earlier may be powerless to change the equilibrium level of income; the extra money supply is simply soaked up in money balances, but equilibrium income remains unchanged. This is the liquidity trap. It can be regarded as originating in Britain in the 1930s; it is needed to understand the policy debate in that period and to evaluate the validity of various positions on what interest rate changes could be expected to do then, and it is transferable to any analysis of the use of monetary policy in depression conditions.

A stable *LM* curve implies a clear idea of what are tolerable money balances and a willingness to engage in transactions to dispose of unwanted balances. (The difference from a demand for money is of degree and presentation only.) The notions of liquidity and of concentric circles spreading from the central bank to industrial firms which we discussed earlier suggests that there may be more flexibility in an economic system. If an increase in the money supply results in a reappraisal of just what balances are tolerable so that there is also a change in liquidity preference, then again income may be undisturbed. In Fig. 5.3, we draw the result of such a reappraisal by itself as a movement of the *LM* curve from LM_1 to LM'. It is however accompanied by an increase in the money supply which, by itself, would have shifted the curve to the right of LM_1. The net effect of both the

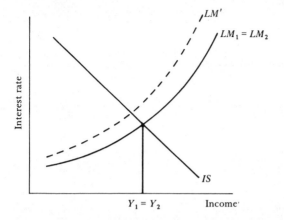

5.3 Compensating variations in liquidity preference

increased money supply and the reappraisal of tolerable balances is that the LM curve is unchanged, LM_1 and LM_2 coincide. And the intentions of policy makers are frustrated. Whereas the liquidity trap is the beginning of an analysis appropriate to the 1930s, offsetting changes (in the context of official measures to reduce the money supply) may help towards an understanding of the 1970s.

The *Hicksian cross* is merely a starting point for a body of economic theory. It is directly useful for questions such as the power of a central bank at any time to influence equilibrium income and interest levels. Its inventor has himself used and extended it in exploring historical events,[12] reinforcing the general point that monetary theory has a larger historical component than many other branches of economic theory. Nevertheless, its main value for historians is a pedagogic one; it shows the interdependence of monetary and real aspects of an economy. Historians frequently have to construct a narrative on the basis of partial information, and some may be monetary and some real. The combination is likely to be much more satisfactory if the historian understands how the real and monetary are linked together and to the course of the economy as a whole.

Relative prices

Prices and income

So far, we have followed various lines of thought concerned with
the aggregate income of an economy. Nevertheless, readers with
any previous acquaintance with economics will have noticed several references to supply and demand, and we had occasion to
notice the role of prices at the core of the concept of income. We
begin an alternative path of thought by thinking of the disposition of income. The outlay on any particular good or service is
equal to the amount of it purchased multiplied by its price;
counting savings as a good, income must be equal to the total of
such dispositions.

$$Y = p_1 q_1 + p_2 q_2 + \cdots + p_n q_n = \sum_{i=1}^{n} p_i q_i$$

What are the relations between each p and q within a pairing?
What connections might there be between one q and the p's associated with other goods?

Demand curves

Our starting point is a demand curve, which is nothing more
than a representation of the notion that the quantity of a good
which people want to buy depends on its price. It also depends
on other things; on incomes, tastes (the economists' word for attitudes or inclinations in general), and on the prices of other
goods. That is simply another way of saying that all the terms in
the equation just given are interrelated. A demand curve for a
good simply separates out the influence of its own price. There

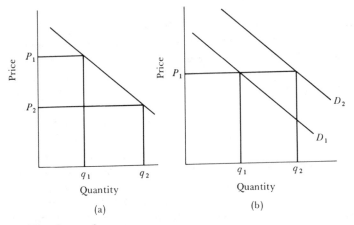

6.1 The demand curve

is no implication that prices alone govern people's lives and
changes in other determinants result in a shift of the curve as a
whole. We draw some demand curves in Fig. 6.1 although we
defer discussion of their shape for the time being. Part (a) shows
that when the price of the good changes from p_1 to p_2, all else
remaining unchanged, the amount which people wish to buy
changes from q_1 to q_2. Part (b) shows that if incomes increase or
the taste for the relevant good increases, the curve itself shifts
from D_1 to D_2, and the amount which people wish to buy increases from q_1 to q_2 while the price remains at p_1. Notice that this
may be a change of tastes, that is, of neither prices nor incomes.
The standard demand analysis requires no assumption that
things usually regarded as 'noneconomic' are necessarily unimportant.

The usefulness of representing behaviour in curves such as
those of Fig. 6.1 depends on several things. First, we need to
know the good to which each curve refers. This is less a question
of theory than of the problem under discussion. We might, for
example, be interested in wheat, or in hard wheat, or in some
still finer subdivision of the grain. Some goods are easier to
handle in isolation than others. The curve will be more useful if
we can expect it to remain stable while we investigate the conse-
quences of changes in the price of the good to which it refers.
Continuing the same example, we might think that the price of

wheat will move more independently from other prices (remembering that changes in them will shift the position of the demand curve for wheat) than is the case with a specific brand of wheat. (A change in the price for one brand may well be accompanied by changes in price of other brands too.) This is a matter of degree, since the price of wheat and potatoes may be interrelated.

We can extend this line of thought by recalling that income is the sum of expenditures on various goods and that we are using a demand curve to consider changes in the price and quantity of one good while holding income constant. At the elementary level (since advanced theory has more options), we must be dealing with a good which is not sufficiently large in total expenditure for a change in its price to be itself a significant influence on the total income of the person or group with whom we are concerned. Economists often refer to this distinction as demarcating situations where *partial equilibrium* and *general equilibrium* methods are appropriate. For partial equilibrium, we can deal with one good in isolation; general equilibrium methods allow for things like a change transmitted through income changes and are appropriate when the wider or 'second round' effects cannot be regarded as insignificant. Partial and general equilibrium have quite specific meanings and do not denote any hierarchy of approval; each is relevant in particular situations. The elementary demand curve is most easily employed when partial equilibrium is appropriate.[1]

Second, we have drawn the demand curve as continuous. This implies that small adjustments of price and quantity are possible. We might be thinking of one individual's demand for a commodity which is physically divisible into small parts, seldom admittedly of infinitely small parts but at least to an approximation comparable to the practical monetary divisions of 1p or 1¢ into which prices can be divided; we think of purchases of sugar in prepackaging days contrasted with the purchase of a house. Alternatively, we might be thinking of the demand for a good by the community as a whole. Even one house might then be a small difference in quantity relative to the thousands purchased by the community as a whole.

Third, we have drawn the curve sloping downwards to the right.[2] It is intuitively acceptable that people, or an individual, will usually want to buy more of a good if it is cheap than if it is dear, and that is enough to establish the downward-to-the-right shape.[3] There are possible exceptions. The notion of people wanting more of a fashion good if it is known to their friends to have a high price is perhaps frivolous and belongs more to the realm of legend than of observation. A thought known as the *Giffen paradox,* after a nineteenth-century statistician of that name, may seem to be a more significant exception. As recounted by the famous economist, Marshall, the suggestion is that a rise in the price of bread makes 'so large a drain on the resources of the poorer labouring families' that 'they are forced to curtail their consumption of meat and the more expensive farinaceous foods: and, bread being still the cheapest food which they can get and will take, they consume more, and not less of it.' But this clearly envisages a movement in income as well as in price, and it does not postulate an upward-sloping demand curve. Nor has it been well supported by empirical study, although those who are most sceptical of its possibility have perhaps taken too little account of Marshall's emphasis on the poorer labouring families rather than the community as a whole.[4]

For most historical purposes it is sufficient to accept the still intuitive notion that most demand curves will be of the usual shape. It can be derived from other assumptions in a rigorous manner. It was once common to start from some psychological notion of utility which itself was subject to some conditions forcing the utility of a good to decline as more of it was bought. Historians will not encounter more than terminological relics of this in other than specific contexts. A much more interesting derivation starts from the notion that people make expenditure choices that are consistent in the sense that if one collection of goods *a* is preferred to another *b*, and *b* is itself preferred to *c*, then *a* will be preferred to *c*. This line of reasoning has its own attractions but is not likely to be important to historians and can, if required, be found in any standard intermediate or advanced economics text. It does show rigorously that the condition for a Giffen's paradox to arise is that changes in the price of one good have a marked impact on the real income of the community or individual in question.

We can give the flavour of this analysis, and in so doing in-

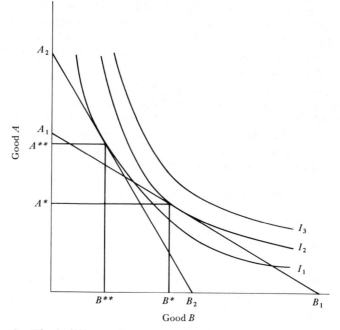

6.2 The indifference curve

troduce a concept which will be significant to us later, the indifference curve. Consider a consumer judging the relative merits to him of various combinations of two goods. Sometimes he will be able to say that one combination is preferable to another, but some combinations will be equally acceptable; the consumer will be indifferent between them. An indifference curve is simply a line joining combinations of the goods between which the consumer is indifferent. For any pair of combinations on an indifference curve concerned with only two commodites, we would expect that if one has more of a good *A* than the other, it must also have less of the good *B;* a combination of more of both goods would be preferred to one with less. That explains the downward-to-the-right character of the curves. The curvature incorporates the notion that as the combination contains an increasing proportion of one good *A*, it takes a bigger and bigger increase in *A* to compensate for the removal of a given amount of the other good *B*, where 'compensate' means leaving the

consumer indifferent to the combinations of A and B so constituted. We thus reach curves shaped as in Fig. 6.2, where I_1, I_2,
and I_3 each shows combinations of A and B among which the
consumer is indifferent and all those combinations on I_2 are
preferred to those on I_1.[5] There is an infinite number of such
curves, each representing a different level of satisfaction.

Figure 6.2 also has some straight lines, and these represent
budget constraints. For a given income they show the combinations of A and B which are available to the consumer, and they
are therefore determined by the prices of A and B. They are
analogous to the production possibilities curves introduced earlier but are concerned with what is available to a consumer. Thus
for an income Y_1, the consumer can gain A_1 of good A by spending all his income on it; he can gain B_1 of good B by using all his
income on that good, or he can buy some combination of the
goods[6] along the line A_1B_1. With that income he will choose the
combination $A*B*$; no indifference curve giving a greater degree of satisfaction is available to him.

A change in the relative price of the two goods is shown by a
change in the budget constraint. A fall in the price of A relative
to that of B shifts the budget constraint to A_2B_2. The consumer's
greatest satisfaction is then given by the combination $A**B**$.
We notice that a fall in the price of A results in an increase in the
quantity of A purchased; a rise in the price of B results in a fall in
the quantity of B purchased. Hence, we have shown, at least in a
preliminary way, how consistency of consumer choices results in
a demand curve of the shape previously illustrated.

It is worth emphasizing that the concept of a demand curve
does not rest at all on an outdated notion that satisfaction can be
measured or that it is assumed to possess an arbitrary relationship to quantity purchased. Even the more acute comment
that it rests on consistent preferences requires the qualification
that it is the assumption of stability in the demand curve which is
so based; changes in the pattern of preferences are changes in
tastes in economists' vocabulary and simply result in a movement
of the whole demand curve.

There are some additional concepts which can be developed
directly from the demand curve. The first of these is *elasticity of
demand*. It is simply a measure of the responsiveness of demand,
given a stable demand curve, to a change in price. It might be

thought that the slope of the curve immediately gives such a measure; indeed, it can, and economists and historians have sometimes used it as such. But for various reasons, of which the most important is that the slope of a curve can be altered arbitrarily by changing the units in which prices or quantities are measured, economists have generally preferred a different measure. This is the ratio of a proportionate change in quantity demanded to the proportionate change in price which induced it. In the usual terminology the proportionate change in quantity is the change in quantity divided by level $\Delta q/q$, and the proportionate change in price is $\Delta p/p$, so that the elasticity of demand e is given by

$$e = -\frac{\Delta q/q}{\Delta p/p}$$

The negative sign is inserted into the definition for convenience. The usual shape of a demand curve means that prices and quantities move in opposite directions and the elasticity of demand would be inconveniently negative but for the adjustment. The formula is incomplete in that it does not specify whether the q and p are to be taken before or after the relevant change. The Δq is obviously $q_2 - q_1$, where q_2 is the amount demanded after and q_1 the amount demanded before the change in price, and similarly with Δp. Should q_1 or q_2 be used to divide the change in quantity? If the change in q is small, it obviously will not matter much; elasticity is a concept associated with small changes and should be used with caution if a change cannot be regarded as small.[7] Historians are often interested in large changes. Thus, it has been noted that the volume of fish consumed in Manchester rose from 3 tons to 80 tons per week when its price fell from 9d per pound to 1¾d per pound on the introduction of rail transport.[8] There is no reason to think that income shifts altered the demand curve for fish, nor that a change in taste for fish occurred; we should therefore be able to deduce the elasticity of demand for fish in Manchester. Here Δq is clearly 77, Δp is $-7¼$. If we use the initial price and quantity figures, we calculate an elasticity of about 32 ($77/3 \div 7¼/9$); if we use the price and quantity figures from after the change, then the calculated elasticity is slightly less than a quarter ($77/80 \div 7¼/1¾$). The formula breaks down. The reason for this can best be explained with a little ge-

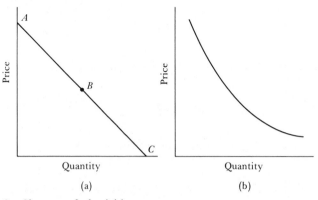

6.3 Slopes and elasticities

ometry which also helps to clarify the distinction between slope and elasticity.

While the slope of a straight line is constant throughout its length, the elasticity is not. In part (a) of Fig. 6.3, B is the mid-point between A and C. It can be shown that in the segment of curve AB the elasticity of demand is greater than 1, while in the segment AC the elasticity of demand is less than 1. (At B it equals 1.) A curve which has the same elasticity throughout its length looks like the one drawn in part (b) of the diagram. The reason for this is that elasticity is defined in terms of proportionate changes, and constant elasticity curves are such that proportionate changes in p and q, not their absolute changes, must be equal and opposite in direction throughout its length. If we believe that the elasticity of demand is the same over all prices, we can use mathematical techniques to fit a constant elasticity curve to the data and then calculate the elasticity of that curve. In the case of Manchester fish the resultant elasticity is approximately 2.[9]

The midpoint B in part (a) of Fig. 6.3 divides the curve into an elastic portion AB, where the elasticity of demand exceeds 1, and an inelastic portion BC, where the elasticity is less than 1. The origin of the terminology is that on an elastic curve total revenue increases with falling prices, and on an inelastic portion total revenue declines as price is reduced. This can be shown rigorously but is probably clear from the reflection that on an elastic curve quantity responds more than proportionately to

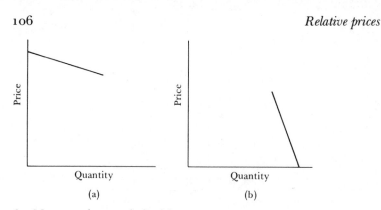

6.4 More on slope and elasticity

price changes, while on an inelastic curve the response of quantity is less than the change in price. Elasticity then relates directly to the way the total market – or more precisely total receipts – responds to price changes. In the case of part (b) of Fig. 6.3 whether the curve is elastic or inelastic depends on whether the value of the elasticity is greater or less than 1, and it is so throughout the whole curve.[10]

It can now be remarked that there is some jusification for the elliptic expressions whereby economists seem to confuse slope and elasticity. If we draw a linear demand curve so that it is nearly horizontal – that is, one with little slope – it is elastic in the sense that the section appearing on a diagram as in part (a) of Fig. 6.4 is likely to be the equivalent of the section *AB* of part (a) of Fig. 6.3. If we draw a curve which is nearly vertical – one with great slope – it is likely to be the equivalent of section *BC* of part (a) of Fig. 6.3. With appropriate care we can identify slope and elasticity in a way which is obvious to the mathematically inclined but often very puzzling to other readers. Where the two need distinction, it is usually elasticity rather than slope which is relevant, and this is because of the relationship between elasticity and total revenue.

This might seem a lengthy path for no purpose, although the notion of elastic and inelastic markets may strike historians as potentially useful. Indeed it should, because it powerfully reinforces the need to think of prices and quantities as interdependent, which is often important in historical and other arguments. Why are falling prices sometimes treated as beneficial and sometimes as adverse? Why are the falling prices of English cotton textiles in the early nineteenth century advantageous to the textile industry, while falling wheat prices in the late nineteenth century are a problem? Part of the answer is that cotton exports in the early nineteenth century faced an elastic market. Why this should be so remains to be explored, and so does the ability of England to increase output and remain profitable despite lower prices, but at least the first step towards clarifying an apparent contradiction has been taken.

Elasticity of demand is a measure of responsiveness of the market to price changes. If the demand for one good is elastic while that for another is inelastic, then the consumers of the first are more responsive to changes in its price than are the consumers of the second. This might be so for a variety of reasons. All individual consumers might be expected to respond more to changes in the price of 'luxuries' than of 'necessities,' and it is in terms of elasticities that economists attempt to define these imprecise terms more closely. Even more important is the availability of other commodities from which additional consumers can be attracted by price reductions or to which consumers will shift in response to price rises. We can think of movements in the price of butter with the price of margarine held constant. Then if the price of butter falls, purchasers are attracted away from margarine, and so we can expect that price reductions will have a large effect on quantity. That effect might be even more pronounced if we are dealing with the demand for Irish butter with Danish butter as an available substitute. On the other hand, if we turn to a country where for some reason margarine is not available, we might expect the demand for butter to be insensitive to price changes. The choice available is only to use more or less butter as its price falls or rises since there is no other similar good from which demand can be readily switched. The change in quantity must be obtained by persuading consumers to make an adjustment of expenditure among all goods purchased.

More formally, two goods X and Y are *substitutes* if when the price of X falls (rises), the quantity of Y demanded falls (rises), while both X and Y separately have normal demand curves. Goods which satisfy this condition are pairs, where an increase in the relative price of one causes demand to shift to the other. It is natural then to ask what goods are such that when the price of one falls, the quantity demanded of the other rises (instead of falling as would be the case for substitutes). That is, we look for goods where the quantity reactions are similar and they are naturally called *complements*. Examples are usually more technical than is the case with substitutes. When the price of petrol falls, one might expect more pleasure motoring and an increased demand for tyres; tyres and petrol are complements.

In defining substitutes we related changes in the quantity of *Y* to the price of *X*, and we can follow the same procedure as before and define a more precise notion of cross-elasticity – the ratio of the proportionate change in the quantity of *Y* demanded to a proportionate change in the price of *X*.[11] This suggests two things. First, we need a more precise name for our earlier elasticity which is obviously a member of a larger family. That chosen is the *own-price elasticity of demand* although when there is no possibility of confusion, this is usually shortened to *price elasticity*. Second, we can identify other members of the family by recalling what variables were held constant in the construction of the demand curve and varying each of them in turn holding all the remaining variables (including price) constant. The only one which historians are likely to meet frequently is the income elasticity of demand, which is obviously the proportionate change in quantity demanded as a ratio of the proportionate change in total income which induced it. The parallel is obvious from the usual symbolic form. Writing p^e for price elasticity and y^e for income elasticity,

$$p^e = -\frac{\Delta q/q}{\Delta p/p}, \quad y^e = \frac{\Delta q/q}{\Delta y/y}$$

Because an increase in income usually results in an increase in quantity demanded, there is no need for an adjustment of sign for income elasticities.[12]

For the most part, this merely establishes a terminology in which the quantity of a good demanded is related to income changes. It is a terminology which enables us to distinguish succinctly between goods like meat and dairy produce for which the income elasticity of demand in the late nineteenth century was high and goods like grain for which the income elasticity was low. This is the single most important key to understanding the course of British agriculture in the late Victorian economy; as

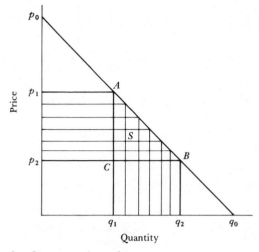

6.5 Consumers' surplus

incomes grew, the demand for meat and dairy products grew much more than the demand for grain.

There is one further concept associated with the demand curve which has been much used by historians, the *consumers' surplus*. It cannot be developed rigorously without more advanced theorising than is appropriate here but the basic notion can be expressed. In Fig. 6.5, we have a demand curve and when the price falls from p_1 to p_2, the quantity demanded rises from q_1 to q_2. We assume that the good in question is too small a part of total expenditure for its change in price to have a significant effect on real income. We then notice that if price had changed from p_1 to p_2 not in a single step but by successive changes, relevant consumers would buy small additional quantities at each stage. When the price arrived at p_2, they would still have increased their purchases by $q_2 - q_1$, but they would have paid a higher price than p_2 at each of the intervening stages. When price changes in one step, the consumers gain a surplus, the sum of the differences between the price paid and the maximum price they would have been prepared to pay for each successive increment of the good. If we can make those increments sufficiently small, the total consumers' surplus associated with the price reduction from p_1 to p_2 is measured by the triangle marked

S.[13] But we can readily extend the concept from a change in price. There is a consumers' surplus associated with the choice of a quantity demanded at any price. In Fig. 6.5 again, the surplus associated with the choice of quantity q_1 in response to price p_1 is the triangle marked out by p_0Ap_1; when the price is p_2, the quantity q_2 is associated with a surplus marked out by p_0Bp_2 and so on. (Notice that the difference between these is the surplus we traced earlier on the increase in quantity from q_1 to q_2 *plus* an additional surplus on all units which would have been demanded at a higher price – the rectangle marked out by p_1ACp_2.) Consumers gain a surplus because they buy a given quantity at less than the maximum which could have been extracted from them by successive sales summing to the given quantity.

The conditions for this construction should be carefully noted; they remain unchanged for a more rigorous development of the notion. The good has to be sufficiently divisible for a continuous demand curve to be an acceptable approximation, and any effect on income of expenditure on the good in question has to be negligible (or perhaps accounted for separately). It might be thought that wealth has to be held constant too; someone's demand for cars might alter radically once one was already possessed and that would prevent the construction of a consumer's surplus. But it is permissible to think of this condition as already embodied in the requirements of divisibility and negligible income effects.

Historians have used this concept directly. The introduction of railways can be conceived as reducing the price of travel. How can we assess the impact of this effect? We might simply compare the total cost of the travel which was purchased after the price change at the new and old prices. This difference is shown by the rectangle $ABCD$ in Fig. 6.6; in the case of railways it is the correct answer to the question, 'How much extra would it have cost to maintain the travel chosen after the price change at the price which existed before the change?' But that is not the question which an economist would ask. He would prefer an answer to the question, 'What is the difference in satisfaction which consumers gain from the change in price?' Or perhaps, 'What is the maximum which consumers could have been persuaded to pay for the increase in travel which they chose when the price fell from p_1 to p_2?' Historians seeking to answer those questions

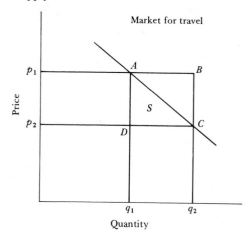

6.6 The effect of a price reduction

have attempted to measure the relevant consumers' surplus S. To do so, we need to know the shape of the relevant section of the demand curve, an inquiry that depends on the traditional skill of historians with incomplete information.[14] We should also, of course, have to account for any associated income change separately.

Supply curves

A supply curve has many parallels with a demand curve. It shows the amount of a good which people are willing to make available for sales at a given price level. It is again a relationship between prices and quantities. We must again define what good we are singling out for treatment, and whether we are concerned with an individual or a community. If we think of the marketing of possessions which have some value to the holder, we must see the supply curve too as dependent on incomes, tastes, and the prices of all other commodities. But this parallel is broken when we conceive the present holder as somebody who does not value the good itself but holds it for the express purpose of selling it. Then readiness to go on gathering the good for marketing depends less on income and other prices directly and more on the prospective profitability of dealing in the particular good with which we are concerned.

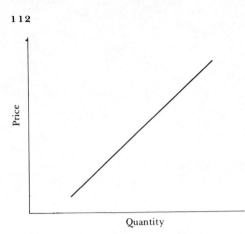

6.7 The supply curve

'Gathering the good' is used with deliberate vagueness. We might be thinking of a marketing operation, whereby the good is literally gathered from one source and distributed to another. Or we might be thinking of manufacturing in which materials are acquired, processed by the employment of factors of production into a different commodity, and then sold to the final consumer. In this latter case we see more clearly that supply is a function of entrepreneurship, the techniques of production and the relative price of labour and capital, all of which will affect the amount of output and its composition. We see the link between the supply curve of an individual good and the determinants of output discussed in Chapter 3.

In any case it is intuitively plausible that the supply curve will slope upwards to the right[15] as in Fig. 6.7. A rise in price of the relevant good X with other prices constant will make the holder of it more willing to sell since the opportunity cost of not doing so has increased; it is likely to make the purely commercial supplier foresee greater profits from gathering or producing X, even perhaps to the extent of switching resources from the production of other goods. These intuitive considerations are usually sufficient for historians; an upward slope for supply curves can be derived from other assumptions, and because of their general importance we shall turn to them presently.

We can define an elasticity of supply or, more specifically, an own-price elasticity of supply in a manner precisely parallel with our treatment of demand;

$$e_s = \frac{\Delta q/q}{\Delta p/p}$$

(no negative sign is required to avoid clumsy negatives since p and q vary in the same direction in an upward-sloping supply curve). It is again a measure of responsiveness, this time of willingness to supply the market in response to changes in price. This time, however, an elasticity of 1 simply defines a kind of average responsiveness; in the case of straight line supply curves it denotes any which pass through the origin. (See Fig. 6.8) An elasticity greater than 1 indicates that supply responds more substantially to price increases; in the linear case it denotes an intersection with the vertical axis at a price greater than zero and this is readily assimilated (even more logically than in the case of demand curves) into a curve more nearly horizontal than the middle of the range of curves with $e_s = 1$. Conversely, an elasticity of less than 1 indicates a more nearly vertical curve with an intersection with the vertical axis at less than zero price. Any entirely vertical curve has an elasticity of zero, and any horizontal line has an infinitely large elasticity of supply.

Supply elasticities too have been used in historical studies. It has often been alleged that some farmers show no respon-

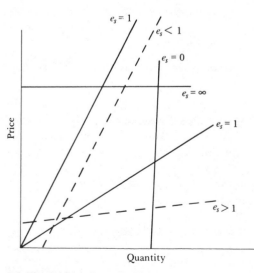

6.8 Elasticities of supply

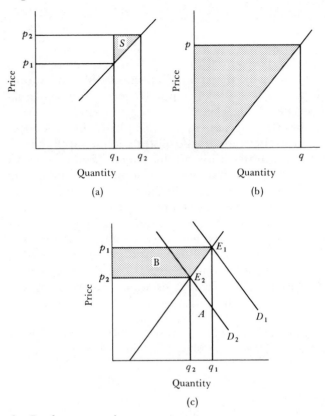

(a)

(b)

(c)

6.9 Producers' surplus

siveness to the different prices of particular crops; they are peasants acting as they and their forefathers have always done. This
is equivalent to asserting that the elasticities of supply of the particular crop are zero. Various historians have measured elasticities, normally finding that such assertions are at least grossly exaggerated.[16]

We can construct a *producers' surplus* analagous to the consumers' surplus of a demand curve. In part (a) of Fig. 6.9 a price
change from p_1 to p_2 stimulates an increase in quantity supplied
from q_1 to q_2. The additional quantity is sold at the price p_2 so
that the total revenue sellers gain from the additional output is
$p_2(q_2 - q_1)$. But we can observe from the supply curve that if the

price change were made in small steps, suppliers could have been induced to make the same increase in quantity at a lower price for all but the last step. Because the price change is made at once, the revenue from the additional output has a surplus associated with it, the triangle S in part (a) of the diagram. As in the case of consumers' surplus, we can extend this from a change in price to any price-quantity point as in part (b) of Fig. 6.9. We note that the concept again depends on the divisibility of the good in question, and paralleling the requirement for consumers' surplus that income effects should be negligible, we need this time to be sure that the price change is not associated with such a change in the relative profitability of the good that the position of the whole supply curve is shifted.

We can go one step further in the case of the supply curve. If we think of a willing seller, one not having an emotional attachment to the good but seeking an income from gathering and selling it, then we might conceive of the supply curve as showing the cost of increasing the quantity supplied to the market. What then is to be made of the producers' surplus? It shows the receipts of the supplier over and above the cost he incurs; it is natural to associate this amount with his particular skills or knowledge and to refer to it as a 'rent' by analogy with the terminology of Chapter 3. Consistent with the concept of quasi rent introduced there, rent is greater in the case of an inelastic curve than of an elastic one.

The usefulness of this concept is shown in part (c) of Fig. 6.9. We think of Britain supplying industrial goods to other countries in the nineteenth century. As other countries industrialise the demand for British goods declines from D_1 to D_2. The price of British goods declines from p_1 to p_2, and the quantity supplied falls from q_1 to q_2. (We explain the significance of the intersection of demand and supply curves in the next section; for the moment, these statements can be taken simply as assumptions.) How should we describe the effect of foreign industrialisation on British suppliers? Their total revenue, price multiplied by quantity, has fallen from the rectangle $0p_1E_1q_1$ to the rectangle $0p_2E_2q_2$ and the difference can be divided into the two areas marked A and B. If we consider the supply curve to show the cost of supplying goods, then the area A measures the resources formerly used for producing exports but which, after the fall in demand for those goods, are available for some other use such as supplying a different good to the home market. The area *B*, however, measures the producers' surplus associated with the former exports, the rent which Britain obtained from particular qualities for which the foreign market was prepared to pay but for which there can be no certainty that an equivalent rent is available in any other occupation. Thus the decline in rent may be used to measure the impact of the loss of the foreign market. When this is done in the case of nineteenth-century Britain, the apparent effect of foreign industrialisation is smaller than might be expected.[17] Of course, before this is treated as a historical result, the assumptions employed should be carefully checked. For example, resources used for exports have to be equally valuable in producing for the home market, and the measure of loss is concerned only with a once-for-all transfer between foreign and domestic markets. But we do have a beginning to a more precise formulation of a familiar historical question.

There is a further point to be made about the supply curve. It is sometimes useful to think of it as depending on time, this being no more than an instance of the general point that it is not always possible to ignore the time needed for production to take place. We can think of a market for a perishable commodity in which there is a rise in price. There is no possibility of an immediate response by producers, and so the first effect is simply a rise in their receipts with no change in the quantity supplied. But *in the short run* some measures can be taken to increase the supply of the commodity and *in the long run* assets can be accumulated so that output is further increased. We thus have a family of supply curves, very short run, short run, and long run, with increasing elasticity. (See Fig. 6.10.)

The relationship between the periods so defined and calendar time varies from case to case, depending most on the ease with which additional factors of production can be accumulated and used. The classic example in the economic literature is the response of a shore-based fishing industry to a rise in demand for fish. In the very short run the catch cannot be increased at all, and the existing fishermen simply receive higher prices for the unchanged catch. In the short run fishermen can spend more time at sea and arrange relief crews for greater utilisation of the existing fleet; the use of more labour gives some elasticity to the

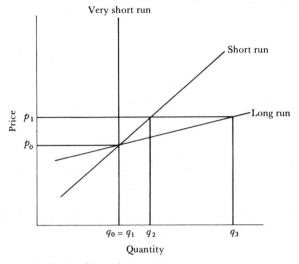

6.10 Periods of supply

supply curve. In the long run the fishing fleet itself can be increased, so giving more elasticity still. The very short run is little more than a day, the short run depends on the availability of labour, and the long run on the time needed to build fishing boats. A more significant historical example is the growth of the market in frozen meat in Britain in the late nineteenth century. The innovation of refrigeration markedly raised the price of sheep in countries such as New Zealand. The immediate response was simply that sheep previously consigned to boiling down for tallow or literally abandoned were supplied for freezing. In the short run sheep were diverted from wool growing to meat freezing (in the sense that they were killed younger) and labour and capital were effectively transferred from one product to another. In the long run more labour was trained in the shepherding skills needed for meat production, flocks of different sheep breeds were built up, and capital was invested in the pasture formation and farm building needed for more intensive farming.[18] Each of these periods was longer in calendar time than in the case of fish, and this time the periods do not correspond one-to-one to the ability to acquire more of a particular factor of production. It is still the accumulation and use of fac-

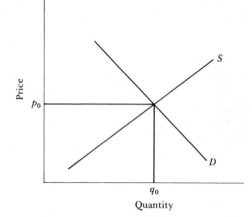

6.11 Equilibrium of supply and demand

tors of production which determine the increasing elasticity of
supply. Note too the link to the quasi rents of Chapter 3 as calendar time permits the reduction of producers' surplus.

Market clearing

An upward-sloping supply curve and a downward-sloping demand curve determine a unique price and quantity pairing, $p_0 q_0$
in Fig. 6.11, at which the desire for a good in the market and
willingness to sell it can be satisfied simultaneously. If such a
position were reached, neither buyers nor sellers would seek to
change the market price or quantity; the market would be in
equilibrium.[19]

The existence of an equilibrium does not guarantee that the
market will reach it; further conditions about the behaviour of
buyers and sellers are needed for that to be assured. In some
cases market behaviour might mean that equilibrium will be
reached very quickly and maintained; in some cases a market
might never reach equilibrium.

The simplest example of the former is where buyers both can
and do respond very quickly to changes in price. We might think
of an example where the sellers have a store of the commodity
and the supply curve results from careful calculations about the

relative attractiveness of retaining the store and selling from it. The market itself is organised along the lines of a stock exchange so that buyers and sellers can readily communicate their willingness to deal at various prices. Then if the price begins above p_0 (in Fig. 6.11), the holders of the commodity can make it known that they are willing to sell more than is demanded at that price. This will provide a signal to buyers to offer a lower price, and their bids will be met by willing sellers. The price therefore falls, and this continues until it reaches p_0 when q_0 will be sold. Conversely, if the price should begin below p_0, the willingness of buyers to offer more brings more goods into the market, and the reverse process drives the price and quantity to equilibrium levels. If the market is efficient, in a technical rather than economic sense, equilibrium prices will be established quickly, and price and quantity changes will indicate a change in the underlying demand and supply curves.

The conditions for this equilibrium to occur might appear rather stringent, but a modern stock exchange does come close to fulfilling them. So does a commodity[20] exchange where the sellers are dealers rather than farmers (and where transactions between dealers and farmers need separate consideration). Even the markets for the produce of some natural resources, such as an oil well not controlled by an oil processor, might not be far from the appropriate conditions.

At the other extreme we can construct an only slightly unrealistic model where equilibrium will never be reached. Consider a group of farmers producing a particular product. The amount of their output depends entirely on the area they think it worthwhile to plant in that crop. Once it is harvested, it is sold on the market and none is carried over; the harvest years are quite distinct. Farmers decide on the planting for the subsequent year according to the price received this year. In Fig. 6.12 the sloping 'supply curve' in each of the diagrams in part (a) shows the amount of land which will be planted (and therefore, by construction, the amount of the crop which will be produced) in the subsequent year according to the price received this year. The higher is this year's price, the greater the acreage which will be planted, and the more that will be produced next year. Once the harvest is gathered, the supply curve for this year, echoing the very short run of the preceding section, is simply a vertical line,

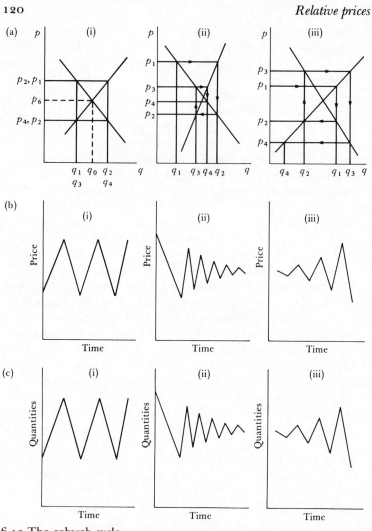

6.12 The cobweb cycle

inasmuch as supply can no longer be influenced by price. We assume an unchanged demand curve (of the conventional kind) throughout. Then if we start with a particular harvest, q_1 and assume that the very short-term market clears instantaneously like those just discussed, the market price will be p_1. The response of the farmers will be such that in the next year the quantity produced will be q_2 (determined by the intersection of the horizontal through p_1 and the supply curve). That year's price will be p_2, and so on. In none of the three diagrams of part (a) of Fig. 6.12 will the stable equilibrium point of $p_0 q_0$ be reached. Parts (b) and (c) of the diagram plot, for each of the combinations of demand and supply curves of part (a), the course of prices and quantities against time. We see that the diagrams of part (a) produce respectively regular cycles of prices and quantities, a convergent cycle (which would still take an infinite time to reach $p_0 q_0$), and a divergent cycle.

None of these pure cases is found in practice although most farm economists believe that the 'cobweb' does occur in part in many farm products. The pure cases are inappropriate because farmers learn the folly of tying production entirely to the current ruling price, harvests and the annual planting are not the same, and farmers are supplemented by dealers, who smooth the fluctuations by buying for store when prices are low and selling when the prices are high. If the farm economists are correct, then the perishability of farm produce restricts the activities of dealers, and farmers judge future prices too much by those ruling now. More generally, the cobweb is useful for showing how expectations can affect the use of prices as an incentive or signal to suppliers, it shows in a crude way how it is possible to move from static supply and demand diagrams to a sequence of such diagrams set in calendar time, and it shows that instantaneous adjustment to equilibrium need not be true of all markets nor assumed in all economic theory.

We can construct an intermediate case by considering a producer who 'makes' a price rather than 'takes' what a market sets. Casual empirical inquiry will reveal many manufacturers who set the price for a particular commodity by calculating (with more or less accuracy) what it costs to produce and adding on a conventional 'markup' for profit. In some countries it is even more obvious that importers set or make the prices of the goods they import in exactly the same way. Both the manufacturer and the importer then consider only whether they can sell the quantity on which their calculations are based at the price they arrive at. If they think they can, the product is manufactured or imported. If they think they cannot, or if experience shows that an optimistic view of the prospects is ill-founded, the manufacture or importation of the product is not undertaken or is terminated.

In such a case the supply schedule does not exist in the mind of the manufacturer or trader (although it is usual for some demand curve to be conceived). But it is still possible to determine to some extent whether the price which has been set is an equilibrium one. If it is not, the order book of the supplier will increase as customers cannot be satisfied, or stocks of the good will accumulate as output exceeds demand at the fixed price. In the latter case, as already explained, unless the manufacturer or importer can revise his calculations, production of the good ceases. The former case is more interesting. Unsatisfied demand obviously means that opportunities for profit are being missed, and if the supplier is sufficiently anxious to increase his income, he will seek elimination of the missed opportunities. If he can increase his output without affecting his costs per unit, the situation is equivalent to a market with a horizontal supply curve. If the increased output actually lowers unit costs, the supply curve is downward sloping (at least temporarily), and if increased output necessarily incurs more expensive supplies, then the supply curve is the conventional kind. All of these supply curves are implied rather than observed; supply depends on the reaction of producers to the available evidence of disequilibrium in the market. Whether the market price will come to equal, or approximate, the equilibrium price depends on the reaction of the producer to such evidence. That is, the market clearing process will necessarily be more drawn out in time, and probably more approximate, than the first case we discussed. But employment of the basic notions of supply and demand is not ruled out when the market is of a kind where prices are made; whether or not such markets are 'cleared' is an empirical question of producers' responses.

Historians have certainly used the supply and demand apparatus, and in so doing have implied that market clearing occurred within an acceptable approximation. To explore this further, we need some acquaintance with the *identification problem*. The historical record provides pairs of observations of price and quantity. It does not immediately reveal the demand and supply curves. Figure 6.13 shows a set of observations, each marked by an *X*, of the kind that we can find in the usual documentary

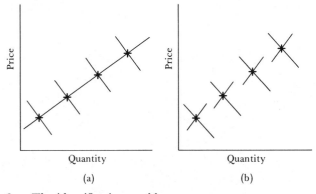

(a)   (b)

6.13 The identification problem

sources. As the two parts of the diagram show, these are compatible with two quite different sets of supply and demand diagrams. In part (a) the observations are explained by rising demand curves while the supply curve remains unchanged; in part (b) both the demand and supply curve have moved. We need other evidence to discriminate between these possibilities, to 'identify' the appropriate historical explanation. If, for example, we knew that the demand curve had a constant elasticity and that the supply curve shifted at a certain rate because of productivity increases, then we could explain the observations.

But to do so, it is still necessary to assume that what we observe are equilibrium prices. If the marked points on the diagram cannot be assumed to be equilibrium points, then the identification problem may be insuperable. Many historical studies assume at least implicitly that market clearing was sufficiently rapid for observed pairings of price and quantity to be taken as equilibrium points. For example, in dealing with the market for pig iron in the United States in the nineteenth century, Fogel and Engermann [21] assumed that the number of firms competing against each other and run by businessmen anxious not to miss opportunities for profit ensured that the market would be cleared quickly and that they could proceed to identify the demand and supply curves. They were then able to go on and consider the impact of the tariff by looking at its effect on supply and demand.

On the other hand, historians might be equally interested by a

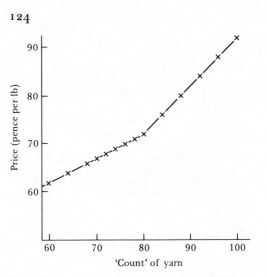

6.14 Cotton yarn prices in Manchester, 1804

situation in which market clearing does not take place. In Manchester in 1804 the price of cotton yarn was related to its fineness or 'count' as shown in Fig. 6.14. Up to a count of 80 the price in pence per pound increased by 1 for every increase of 2 units in the count; for greater fineness the price increased by one penny for each unit increase in the count. What is interesting about this is the evidence that these prices made the higher counts carry a greater profit margin while also making them harder to sell than the lower counts.[22] With the aid of the supply and demand apparatus we can interpret this as a case where convention prevented the market from clearing. Equilibrium required a fall in the price of high counts relative to low, but the conventional belief that higher quality, fine spinning deserved certain price differentials prevented the attainment of equilibrium. What might otherwise be left as a puzzling ambiguity in the evidence is much better understood as a failure of market clearing.

Theory of the firm

Economic theory has a particular construction or set of assumptions which permits a very much sharper definition of some of the issues with which we have been dealing in the preceding sec-

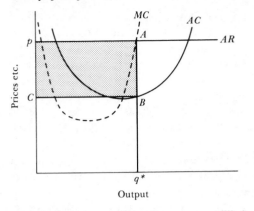

6.15 Perfect competition: short-run equilibrium

tions. This is what is known as the 'theory of the firm' but which would be better called 'the logic of profit maximisation'. Historians will often feel that the assumptions are too unrealistic to permit them to make much use of the theory, but its terminology is useful, it does facilitate understanding of some of the issues we have been discussing, and it is often useful in an indirect fashion. It is best to approach this topic in an abstract manner, and it helps if it is not thought of as describing the behaviour of real business firms.

We begin by imagining an industry in which a large number of independent firms produce the same commodity X, and each of those firms not only aims at but achieves the maximum profit available to it. There is no barrier to new firms beginning to produce X too, and knowledge of how it is produced is readily available. These assumptions define *perfect competition*.

The position of an individual firm in such an industry can be represented as in Fig. 6.15. Because there is a large number of competing firms, none can individually influence the price at which X is sold; for each firm the average revenue or price which it can receive for a unit of X is fixed and is represented by the horizontal average revenue curve AR. The cost of producing a unit of output, average cost, is shown by AC; it is assumed to fall over some output range but eventually to rise with increasing output levels. The intuitive basis for this assumption is that after some level of output, each firm can increase output only by incurring higher input costs such as raised wage rates to attract labour from the production of other commodities. For convenience we conceive of AC as including a 'normal profit', the minimum needed to keep the firm in the production of X.

From AC we can derive another curve which shows the additional cost of producing an additional unit of output and is therefore labelled 'marginal cost' MC. The relationship of MC to AC is entirely one of mathematics. It is intuitively clear that when the cost of producing an additional unit is falling, the average cost must be falling; that when the average cost is falling, the cost of an additional unit must be below the average of those already produced; and that when the average cost is rising, the cost of an additional unit must be greater than the average of those already produced. This is sufficient to establish that MC must cut AC at the minimum point of the AC curve and must be rising and above AC to the right of that minimum point.

We can then establish quickly that profit maximisation is achieved at the level of output, $q*$ in the diagram. This is the output level at which the marginal cost of output is equal to the price of X (not, it should be noted the point where average cost is at a minimum). A mathematically rigorous proof is readily available, but it is sufficient to experiment with the diagram and notice that an increase in output beyond $q*$ will incur more cost for the additional units (shown by MC) than can be recovered from their sale price; profit will therefore be reduced. A reduction of output below $q*$ means that some units of output will not be produced for which the costs of production are less than receipts; profits would again be reduced. Hence $q*$ is the profit maximising position and, by assumption, that is the output produced by the firm.

We now observe that in this structure the supply curve for X must indeed be upwards sloping to the right; we can improve on the intuitive explanation given earlier for more general cases. The supply curve is the sum of the supply curves of the individual firms. But these are simply the MC curves to the right of the intersection with AC curves. Variations of price appear to each firm as a movement of the whole AR line; the corresponding quantity changes obviously follow from the intersection with the MC curve. For prices below the minimum AC level supply is zero, since the normal profit needed to keep the firm producing X cannot be earned.

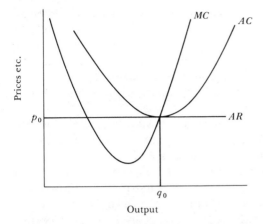

6.16 Perfect competition: long-run equilibrium

We have not yet exhausted even the more obvious implications of the set of assumptions with which we started. In Fig. 6.15 the firm is earning more than the normal level of profit – as shown by the shaded rectangle. But there is freedom of entry into the industry and the opportunity for such extra profits will attract more competitors. With a stable demand curve for X this will necessarily lower the price of the good. Competition by new entrants will continue until each firm reaches the situation shown in Fig. 6.16 where only normal profits are being received. (If for some reason one firm has higher costs than the others, it will leave the industry; the market will then be shared among the remainder but new entrants continue until all firms are equally efficient and all in the position of Fig. 6.16.)

We again notice that in the particular conditions assumed here, the notions of an earlier discussion can be given more rigour. Consider an increase of demand when an industry is composed of firms in a situation such as that of Fig. 6.16. In the short run the increase in supply is the aggregation of movements along the MC curves; the short-run supply curve lies upward to the right. But with an unchanged level of normal profit, the transition from Fig. 6.15 to Fig. 6.16 is begun again. The long-run supply curve is therefore perfectly elastic, a horizontal line. If new entrants have to be attracted from other industries, the economy-wide level of normal profit may be raised. The transition from Fig. 6.15 to Fig. 6.16 will therefore be complicated by a rise in the *AC* curve; fewer new entrants would be attracted, but the long-run supply curve would still be more elastic than the short-run curve. Similarly, if for technical reasons the expansion of the industry encountered diminishing returns to one of its factors of production, the long-run *AC* curve would rise, but we would still expect long-run supply to be more elastic than that of the short run.

The possibility of new entrants is obviously crucial, and it is natural to connect the extra profits of the short run, as in Fig. 6.15 again, with the temporary shortage of resources while new entrants are drawn into the production of *X*. Hence, we think of them as rents as in Chapter 3. Furthermore, if we think of the long-run supply curve being horizontal, which as we have just seen is equivalent to assuming no change in the level of normal profit throughout the economy as new entrants are recruited, and that the production of *X* does not encounter diminishing returns, we can identify the producers' surplus of the short-run supply curve with economic rents. Again, in the specific conditions of perfect competition, a much clearer statement is possible than is generally the case. To our earlier example of the fall of demand for Britain's exports, we can now add that if British domestic industry were approximately perfectly competitive, then the resources shifted to production for the home market would be unable to earn rents there, at least in the long run, and the fall in producers' surplus would measure the decline in Britain's income caused by the change in the export market. Perfect competition in Britain's domestic industry is not the only way in which such a result can be derived, but something such as perfect competition is needed before this deduction can be made.

The logic of profit maximisation is rich in theoretical links. We will expound only one more. So far we have employed assumptions to prevent the actions of any one firm from having any effect on the equilibrium price. We can give some idea of the importance of this by looking at the opposite extreme, where one firm controls the whole output of the commodity *X*. The price received by the firm is then shown by the demand curve for the industry; the *AR* curve is downward sloping to the right as in Fig. 6.17. To this average revenue curve we can construct a marginal revenue curve *MR*, which is related to the *AR* curve in exactly the way *MC* is related to *AC*. It shows the additional reve-

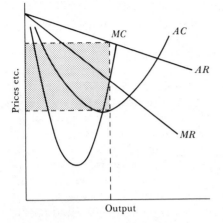

6.17 Monopoly equilibrium

nue from an extra unit of output, and if the *AR* curve is downward sloping, then the *MR* curve must lie below it and slope even more steeply.[23] We assume the same *AC* curve, and therefore the same *MC* curve as before. By the same logic as we employed above, profits are maximised where $MR = MC$; more output will incur more cost than the revenue it produces, less output sacrifices some profit. But the price of this output is shown by the *AR* curve, while the average cost is shown by *AC*. The firm therefore earns the extra profits shown by the shaded area in the diagram. This time, the firm controls the output of *X;* new entry is not possible and therefore in both the short and long run, the existence of such excess profits can persist. This is what economists mean by monopoly and monopoly profits. Control over the product is crucial, not mere size of the firm.

In the absence of monopoly power (in the strict economists' sense) the price of *X* in the long run equals the minimum average cost of its production. Changes in price in successive long-run equilibria must therefore result from changes in long-run costs of production, shifts of the *AC* curve, resulting from the discovery of new resources or improvements in technology. There is therefore a close link between changes in price and changes in productivity in the sense of Chapter 3. But this is not true in the presence of monopoly power (which need not be the pure kind of monopoly discussed above); the long-run equili-

brium is not at the minimum of the *AC* curve, and changes in
price may reflect changes in the degree of monopoly power as
well as productivity change. Historians have to be able to discriminate between occasions when they can and cannot use
prices as an indicator of productivity. Precisely the same is true
of the use of economics in other contexts. The logic of perfect
competition is rich in political implications too. Perfect competition produces the most economical use of resources, and there is
therefore no need for government intervention in the economy.
These results will not interest a government which thinks it is in
control of an economy not characterised by perfect competition
(or which is not interested only in the most economical use of
resources). In such arguments, historical or political, it is the
decision on whether or not the assumptions of the logic can be
admitted, whether or not perfect competition is an acceptable
approximation, which is the crucial step; thereafter, the implic-
tions follow inexorably.

Indirect uses of the logic are sometimes valuable. Given some
information on the costs of producing *X* by two different processes, we can deduce what profit-maximising firms would have
done. We can compare this with what firms actually did, and
perhaps even calculate what their decisions meant in terms of
forgone output.[24] No assumption that perfect competition char-
acterises the economy is involved. This greatly increases the historical fields in which the logic is helpful.

But the main use of the theory of the firm is simply to show
'pure' forms of the concepts of competition, economic rents, and
upward-sloping supply curves. Because the pure set of assumptions permits certain conclusions to be drawn, it must not be
thought that those conclusions follow only from that set of assumptions. Perfect competition guarantees market clearing, but
market clearing will also occur in other circumstances. Perfect
competition guarantees that rents will be short-lived, but they
may be short-lived even when there are only a few producers or
potential producers of a commodity. And so on. It may be remarked that the possibility of new entrants into the production
of a particular commodity is probably greater in a large economy like that of the United States than it is in a small economy,
and this may account at least in part for the greater willingness
of American economists to accept the assumptions of perfect

competition for empirical work. They are not prohibited from doing so by the existence of large firms in the American economy since it is the possibility of new entrants which is important. The difference between the American and British economies was somewhat less in the nineteenth century when free trade widened the geographical area from which new entrants to British markets could be drawn.

7

International economics

Introduction

Many economic ideas have been formed or developed in the course of thinking about trade between two or more countries. Some of them are equally applicable to trade between regions of a country, but it is still convenient to expound them as part of the theory of international trade. Others link directly to politics and patriotism in that they are joined to the concept of a sovereign state; policy measures have always loomed large in international economics.

In the early 1960s after some major theoretical advances in the preceding decade, it was common to think of trade theory (as economists often refer to the theory of international trade) as a somewhat sterile branch of economics. Since then, a new line of development linking international economics especially to monetary theory has made it one of the most lively fields of inquiry. Even though this has brought international economics more directly into contact with historical studies, we must be highly selective in what we deal with here.

Comparative advantage

Any consideration of international economics must start with the notion of comparative advantage, a very simple idea which has far-reaching implications. Figure 7.1 shows the production possibilities curves of each of two countries, both of which can produce either commodity X or commodity Y or some combination of them. By using its resources entirely for the production of X, country A can produce and consume the quantity A_x; by using its resources entirely for Y, it can produce and consume

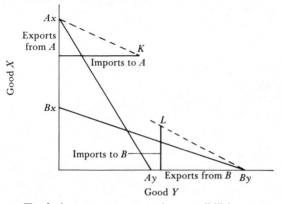

7.1 Trade increases consumption possibilities

A_y; by dividing its resources between the two goods, it can independently produce and consume anywhere along the $A_x A_y$ boundary. Similarly, country B can produce and consume at any point on the $B_x B_y$ boundary. So far, this is merely revision of the production possibilities curve introduced much earlier.

The diagram clearly implies that country A is somehow better at producing X and country B at producing Y. If trade between the two countries is possible, and the relative price of X and Y is established as shown by the dotted line in the diagram, then A can use its resources to produce X, so producing A_x, and then export some of that in return for imports of Y. The amount of Y received in exchange for exports of X is determined by the relative price, and one possible exchange is shown in the diagram. If country B uses all its resources for Y, it produces B_y. Its imports must equal the exports of country A and its exports must equal the imports of A. Hence its exports and imports, also shown in the diagram, are determined at the same time as those of A. The interesting result of this analysis is that the points showing the combination of X and Y consumed in each of the countries, K for country A and L for country B, are outside their respective production possibilities curves. Trade enlarges the consumption possibilities.

This is a case where each country has an advantage in the production of one of the two commodities, a case sometimes known as one of *absolute advantage*. Figure 7.2 shows an impor-

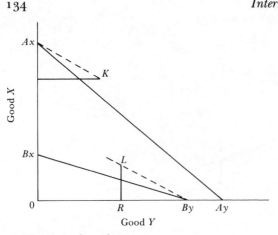

7.2 Comparative advantage

tant extension of the argument. Country *A* is 'better' at producing both of the commodities, but by precisely the same argument
both countries can consume outside their own production possibilities curve if trade between them is permitted and relative
prices are established along the dotted line as before.

This might at first seem paradoxical, but it is really very simple. As the production possibilities curves are drawn in Fig. 7.2,
country *A* has an advantage in the production of both *X* and *Y*,
but its advantage is greater in the case of *X* than in that of *Y*; it
has a 'comparative advantage' in *X*. Similarly, while *B* is disadvantaged in both *X* and *Y*, it is more so in *X* than in *Y* so that it
has a comparative advantage in *Y*. The best possible use of the
resources of *A* and *B* jointly is therefore for *A* to produce *X* and
B to produce *Y*. What we are seeing is a process of specialisation
so that the resources of the two countries considered as a unit
are used as efficiently as possible. Although comparative advantage was developed to discuss trade between countries, it is
merely a more rigorous demonstration of the older notion that
specialisation of resources in their best available use permits a
greater total output. Trade theorists sometimes emphasize the
point that trade produces gains even if neither country can
change its production to benefit from specialisation. That is certainly so; the simple reflection that both parties to a voluntary
exchange must at least not lose thereby is enough to give the essence of the argument. But it is the link to specialisation that

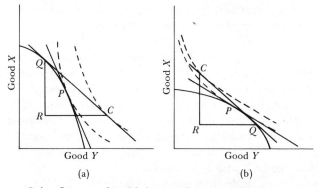

7.3 Gains from trade with incomplete specialisation

makes the availability of trade important for economic historians (and in most other contexts).

In the examples so far, maximum output is attained by the complete specialisation of each of the countries in one of the two goods. That is an implication of the production possibilities curves having been drawn as straight lines, which, as will be recalled from Chapter 2, implies that the factors of production are all equally useful in producing either of the two goods. If some resources are less productive when used for one good than when used for the other – for example, if more and more of X has to be given up for the same increment of Y as resources are increasingly concentrated on the latter – then the production possibilities curves will be shaped as in Fig. 7.3. Some experiments with the placing of exports and imports quantities on such a curve will probably satisfy the reader that in such a case specialisation remains incomplete but that 'gains from trade' are still available.

This can be shown with a little more rigour by using the device of an indifference curve introduced in the last chapter. We have to make explicit what was evaded there, that while the notion of an indifference curve poses few problems in the context of an individual consumer, it is by no means so obvious that a community can make consistent choices. But it is the idea of community indifference curves being stable over time which gives most concern and we will want to draw only lightly on the notion at all, let alone on that assumption.

The indifference curves are shown by dotted lines in Fig. 7.3.

If we·consider either country *A* or country *B* in isolation, it is clear that for both the preferred point of production and consumption (which in the absence of trade must be the same) is at *P;* no higher indifference curve is attainable, and all other points of the production possibilities curve lie on lower indifference curves. At *P* an internal price ratio shown by the slope of the tangent to the production possibilities curve at that point will be efficient[1] in that it shows both the relative cost of increasing production of one commodity in terms of the other, and also the relative prices at which consumers will choose to consume exactly the amounts of *X* and *Y* produced.

The possibility of trade, however, markedly changes the picture. If the international relative price of *X* and *Y* is established as shown by the line *QC* in either part of Fig. 7.3, the two lines being parallel, then producers in both countries will want to move to the point marked *Q,* so that prices remain equal to the relative costs of production. Consumers, however, will want to move to the points marked *C,* to reach the highest indifference curve encountered by the line *QC.* As the diagrams are drawn, this can be achieved – the exports from country *A* of *X* equalling the imports of *X* by *B,* and the imports of *Y* by *A* equalling the exports of that commodity from *B.* What we see, again, is the process of each country specialising in the commodity in which it has a comparative advantage and with the demand conditions in each country determining points of production and consumption so as to take advantage of international trade.

In both Figs. 7.2 and 7.3 the international price ratio was produced out of a hat. Inspection of the diagrams will show that there are gains from trade for both countries if the international price line lies between the two domestic price lines determined in the absence of trade. Only in such circumstances does the cost of obtaining the good in which the country is (comparatively) disadvantaged become cheaper through trade than through using its own resources. This sets limits to a range of international price lines within which gains from trade are available, but we have said nothing about the 'best' price ratio within this range. In Fig. 7.4 at the international price shown by line A_0, the country produces and consumes at $P_0;$ it cannot reach a higher indifference curve through trade. If international trade is possible with relative prices as shown by the line A_1, the preferred

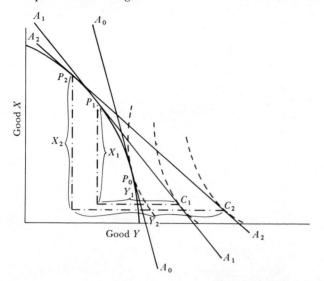

7.4 Desired exports and international relative prices

consumption point is C_1 while the preferred production point is P_1; the country therefore offers exports of X_1 in return for imports of Y_1. Similarly, an international price ratio shown by A_2 induces an offer to export X_2 so as to produce at P_2 and consume at C_2. By extending this analysis, we can derive a schedule[2] showing how the amount of X which this country wishes to exchange for Y through trade varies with changes in the international price ratio.[3] For the other country the exportable good will be Y, and the amount which it wishes to export will also change in response to the international price ratio. Given the usual forms of the production possibilities and indifference curves, the quantities offered by the two countries will vary in the opposite direction as the international price is changed; exports of X will be stimulated as the international price moves in favour of X, and conversely. There will then be one price at which the exports of X offered by country A will equal the exports of Y offered by B when these are converted to a common denominator by the international price. Both countries can then produce efficiently in that the international price curve will be tangential to the production possibilities curve, while consumers in both countries obtain quantities so that the international price just

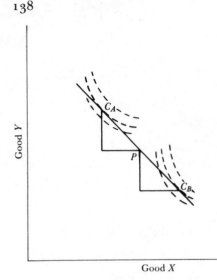

Good Y

Good X

7.5 Demand as a basis for trade

equals the relative valuations of the two goods along the relevant indifference curve. That is, we reach the posttrade situation portrayed in Fig. 7.3. Whether or not the particular international price which permits this will be reached depends on the same kind of market-clearing considerations as we discussed in the context of supply and demand analysis in the preceding chapter.

This might seem to take us a long way down the road towards purely abstract reasoning. In fact, it is but a step on the long journey which is readily available in the voluminous literature of the theory of international trade. As we have presented it, trade depends mostly on national productivities in the production of particular commodities. There is a line of thought whereby the productivities of factors can be traced back to their relative availability and so to all the issues introduced in Chapter 3. This integration was part of what we referred to earlier as the major advance of the 1950s although those developments rested heavily on earlier work.

We have introduced some demand elements, and to remove any lingering suspicions that trade is entirely a matter of relative costs, we pursue one extension. In Fig. 7.5 two countries have a common production possibilities curve but markedly different demand conditions, shown by the two sets of indifference curves. As shown trade can again provide gains for both countries. Both countries produce at *P*, but trade enables both to reach a higher indifference curve (higher among their separate sets) and consume at C_A and C_B respectively. In effect, trade is used to overcome the diminishing returns which each country would experience if it tried to produce mostly the good for which its consumers have a more intensive demand.

Trade is about more than relative production costs, but the core idea is comparative advantage. And this is used very directly in historical studies. It is to comparative advantage that historians turn when they seek to explain why from the late eighteenth century, Britain imported corn and exported cotton textiles. From such an immediate application of the concept, it is easy to move towards almost metaphorical uses. The concentration of Britain on services associated with international shipping and insurance in the late nineteenth century at the expense of manufacturing looks rather different when it is seen in the light of Britain's comparative advantage shifting as industry grew in countries such as Germany and the United States. The starting point of trade theory enables us to be more specific than our earlier suggestion that any decline of industry has to be seen in the context of changes in income as a whole. Again, remembering that comparative advantage is concerned with specialisation within a combined economic unit rather than necessarily with trade between countries, we can point to its use in explaining the growth of industries in some regions while others continued to concentrate on agriculture.[4]

Tariffs

The main economic argument against interference with trade follows more or less directly from the discussion of the preceding section of this chapter. Trade permits greater specialisation, and therefore a greater world income, taking into consideration the relative values which people place on the various commodities in individual countries. A really happy result requires that economies operate near their production possibilities curves, that prices reflect resource costs accurately and so on. Even if the qualifications are neglected, the transition to the political slogan

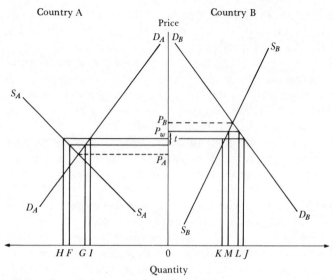

Country A   Country B

7.6 Supply and demand adapted to trade

that free trade is desirable will often seem simplistic to historians; what government has ever been interested solely in maximum income or entirely accepted community preferences as
beyond government influence? The objection is right, but so
equally is the economist's response that many historians have
been insufficiently sensitive to the complex effects of tariffs and
other impediments to trade. Any of Figs. 7.2 to 7.4 can be used
to deduce that an impediment to trade essentially makes one
good more expensive than it need be and that this is equivalent
to making total income less than that which is attainable. Some
of the ways in which this occurs and some of the complexities involved can also be approached through an adaptation of the
supply and demand apparatus of the preceding chapter.

In Fig. 7.6 we consider a single commodity X, which can be
produced in both of two countries A and B. The diagram shows
the demand and supply curves for X in each of A and B, but for
convenience of drawing, the quantity axis for country A is reversed; the same price axis will then serve for both countries.
If trade between the countries is not possible, then the intersections of the demand and supply curve for each country show
that the equilibrium prices will be different and, subject to the

discussion of market clearing in Chapter 6, the countries will have different market prices as well. These two prices, P_A and P_B, depend entirely on the demand and supply curves for each country. As the diagram is drawn, the demand curves are approximately the same (remembering that the direction of the quantity axis is reversed for country A), but the supply curves imply that the commodity X is cheaper to produce in A. At any given price more of X is supplied in A than in B.

If we now envisage trade taking place with no impediments at all – no transport costs as well as no tariffs or other barriers – there is a price P_w between P_A and P_B at which both countries can again reach equilibrium but with A exporting X to B. For at P_w supply in A is shown by the supply curve to be the length $0H$, while demand is shown by the demand curve to be only $0I$; the difference HI has to be marketed outside the country if equilibrium is to be attained. At the same price supply in B is only $0K$ while demand is $0J$ and therefore JK has to be obtained from another country. For any price between P_A and P_B, A has to find an export market for some quantity of X while B has to find some imports. P_w is the unique price at which the gap between the demand and supply in both countries is equal in size, that is, at which the exports of A and the imports of B are equal. (There is such a price if the demand and supply curves all have the 'usual' shape; they need not be linear as, for convenience, they are drawn in the diagram.)

It is apparent even before we introduce the topic of tariffs that trade between countries has complex effects. Comparing the no-trade and free-trade positions in Fig. 7.6, producers in A clearly gain; they have a bigger market to supply. But consumers in A lose in that trade makes them face a higher price, the world price rather than their original domestic price. The opposite is true for country B. And this, of course, looks at only one commodity; trade in other commodities might have partly offsetting influences. Furthermore, if a commodity is important enough to have a substantial effect on total income in either country, the income effects (changing the supply and demand curves) may outweigh the price effects which are visible in the diagram.

The one commodity diagram, however, does permit us to see the immediate effects of the imposition of a tariff on imports of that commodity into B. A tariff simply means that a gap is imposed between the price of the commodity in the two countries, so that it is higher in the importing country than it is in the exporter. The consumer of imports pays both the price received by the exporter and a tax. In Fig. 7.6 the gap is shown as t. Equilibrium is now found with exports of only FG from country A, still, of course, equal to the imports LM into B. Compared with the free-trade position, home supply expands by KM, demand falls by LJ, and tariff revenue increases by the product of LM and t. In appropriate circumstances we could quantify more precisely in terms of producers' and consumers' surpluses, the production and consumption effect of the tariff, and we would add an effect on customs revenue. The tariff imposed by B also has production and consumption effects in A; supply diminishes by FH and demand increases by GI. There is nothing comparable with the revenue effect, although if the limitation is not a tariff but an order of some kind restricting imports to LM, then the government of B collects no revenue, imports in B might sell at some nonequilibrium price or the exporters in A and their agents in B can divide some monopoly rent among themselves; the gap between the supply price in A and the equilibrium price in B is essentially 'up for grabs'. We might say that the suppliers in A are then given a chance to participate in the revenue effect in B. The comparison of tariffs and nontariff barriers like analysis of either alone is much more complex than often realised.

The relative size of the effects of a tariff on A and B depends on the shape of the supply and demand curves in the two countries. We will not explore all possibilities, but the general picture will be clear if the reader manipulates the diagram and satisfies himself that if the demand curves are similar, the greater the degree to which the slope of the supply curve in A exceeds the slope of the supply curve in B, the greater the portion of the cost of the tariff which falls on A. The reason is clear; A will bear most of the cost if its producers do not respond greatly to the loss of some part of their total market. This should be read carefully; the more responsive producers will respond most to a tariff, but the national cost depends on what else happens – producers of X in A 'lose' but if they become producers of some other commodity, the tariff may eventually be more of a burden to B than to A (even though it is unlikely that country A loses nothing at all).

We will not follow this shift from immediate to more indirect effects of a tariff very far but we must at least ask how *B* pays for its imports, and what impact a tariff has there. We start from the free trade situation with *A* exporting *X* to *B*, and assume that there is another commodity *Y*, which B exports to *A*, and that under free trade, world prices are such that the costs of these flows are exactly balanced. What then happens when *B* imposes a tariff on its imports? Trade becomes unbalanced as the flow of *X* from *A* to *B* is reduced – in both price and quantity. Can *A* ensure a return to balance by imposing a tariff on the goods it imports from *B*? It is possible, but determination of the tariff rate to be applied is complex. We might think of the two commodities being such that the demand curves for both are similar in the two countries but it is surely straining luck to postulate that the excess slope of the supply curve for one commodity in *A* is precisely equal to the excess slope of the supply curve for the other commodity in *B*. If it is not, equal tariffs will not have equal effects. Analysis of retaliatory tariffs is not simple even while we maintain the assumption that the total income of both countries is not significantly affected at all by the imposition of tariffs.

In particular, it may well be possible for one country to impose a tariff such that more of the cost of it falls on the exporter of another country than is the case with the tariffs which that trading partner has available to it. It may then be in the interests of a country to use tariffs rather than participate in maximum international specialisation even though world income as a whole is thereby reduced. A major interest of this for historians is that Britain in the nineteenth century may have been a case in point. For some time Britain supplied a large part of the world trade in manufactured goods, and its customers had little option but to buy from Britain. The agricultural commodities which they exported to Britain in return were probably characterised by supply curves with little slope. In such circumstances, the 'optimal tariff' for Britain alone might well have been nonzero. Ironically, the period when this was possible was also that in which British governments were most committed to free trade. When tariffs were reconsidered from the late nineteenth century, Britain's position in the world economy was no longer such as to permit her to gain from using tariffs to manipulate her own terms of trade, the ratio of her export prices to the prices of her imports.[5]

In any case we have been pursuing a line of argument which neglects the income effects of trade. Britain's income benefited not only from the exchange of one kind of commodity against another, but from the technical progress achieved in the agriculture of such temperate-region countries as the United States, Australia, and New Zealand and this progress might have been frustrated had a British tariff slowed down the growth of that agriculture. Britain would have suffered had she not been able to expand her provision of international services to such countries; this is the comparative advantage argument of another kind which we have encountered before, directing attention to specialisation within Britain. And Britain would have lost even more directly had the nineteenth century reduction in international transport costs been slowed down (since this raised world income by freeing resources from transport for other uses).[6] Consequently, the terms of trade argument for a tariff suggests not that free trade was a mistaken policy, but that the gains from free trade to Britain came in less direct ways than the simple effects of abiding by comparative advantage in an elementary textbook manner.

Two further aspects of tariffs are worth development here; both are concerned with the production effects. The first is the infant-industry argument, a valid objection to the notion that world income is maximised by the absence of impediments to specialisation and one which illustrates the possible importance of moving from the static analysis we have been concerned with to an explicit consideration of time. We can again draw on Fig. 7.6 and begin by noting that we have taken the supply curves as given (except for mention of possible income effects). If they shifted differentially for the two countries, for whatever reason, the importer-exporter positions of A and B could be reversed. Furthermore, consider the possibility that B has the potential to become a cheaper supplier of X than A is but that this depends on B having experience of an increased level of production – a level above $0K$ in Fig. 7.6. Then in a regime of free trade, B's supply curve remains stationary and it never becomes an exporter of X. But given a tariff, its producers can expand their output, the supply curve is moved to the right, and B may eventually become an exporter of X. The tariff provides an environment in which an infant industry is nurtured. It permits B to gain from a latent comparative advantage which would be unattainable without some assistance to the industry.

This argument is of historical importance because it has been used so often as an argument for tariffs rather than because there are clear historical examples of infant industries that have been nurtured into successful competitors in world markets. There are many more examples of infants of many years' standing still unable to survive without protection. Furthermore, the logic of the infant industry argument is incomplete. Why should the assistance be given in the form of a tariff? That obviously imposes costs on the consumers of X but the eventual gains will be to the community of B generally. It might be more equitable to subsidise the infant industry directly, reducing the costs of the domestic suppliers by a cash payment, so that they can expand their output and begin the process by which the supply curve moves and enables the industry to survive without subsidies. The infant industry argument assumes implicitly that there are some constitutional or financial barriers to more direct government assistance towards achievement of a potential comparative advantage. It is what has come to be known as a 'second best' argument as opposed to the first best policy of operating directly on a potential gain.

The second aspect of the production effect is the recognition that not all imports are for final use. An imported good may be used as an input to a domestic industry. A tariff on his output enables a producer to sell at a higher price, but his gain will be less if he requires an imported component which is also subject to a tariff; his *effective protection* will be less. We have to turn away from the one-commodity consideration of Fig. 7.6, but the core idea of effective protection is illustrated in Fig. 7.7. Column (a) shows a producer facing a world price P_w. The imposition of a tariff on his product raises the domestic price to $P_w(1+t)$, and the reward available to domestic factors of production is raised accordingly. But in column (b) the producer uses an imported component and it too is subjected to a tariff. The gain available to the producer depends on all of the tariff rate on his output, the tariff rate on his inputs, and the proportion of the final selling price which is available for distribution as income to do-

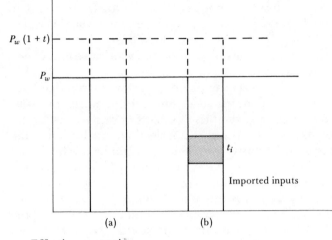

7.7 Effective protection

mestic factors of production. If we represent these as t_j, t_i, and $(1 - \Sigma a_i)$ respectively, (the a_i being analogous to input – output coefficients, each showing the proportion of the value of the product composed of one of the components), then the proportionate gain in domestic income made available by the tariff system as a whole can be shown to be

$$e = -\ \frac{t_j - \Sigma a_i t_i}{1 - \Sigma a_i}$$

where e denotes the rate of effective protection.[7]

This is still a partial analysis since it takes no account of the possibility that as a result of the tariffs the relative quantities of different components used in production will be changed. An input subjected to a heavy tariff may be replaced to some extent by one on which a lighter tariff is charged or even by a domestic factor of production. The advantage of the concept of effective protection is that it shows the need to consider producers' gains in the light of the entire tariff system and of the relative size of imported components to domestic value added; it does not provide a complete measure of the effects of protection.

The theory of effective protection, for which we have given only the starting point, is a creation of the 1960s. There is no reason why we should not reconsider the protective effects of earlier tariff systems in the light of it. Perhaps equally interesting to historians are the indications that contemporaries were aware of its essentials in an intuitive fashion very much earlier. Any producer would know that his business was affected by tariffs on inputs as well as those on outputs, and probably that the impact of tariffs depended on the relative importance of imported inputs. In the case of the United States the tariff structure became more coherent as the nineteenth century progressed in the sense that a ranking of industries by the size of the tariff rates of their outputs becomes more similar to a ranking by effective protection rates. Despite the apparently random bargaining in the political process by which tariff rates were fixed, the tariff rates on outputs which were used by contemporaries as indicators of levels of protection came to indicate also the relative effective protection accorded to individual industries, the outcome in which producers were interested.[8] Contemporary comments can occasionally be found to show that awareness of effective protection ideas had reached lobbyists for industries long before an academic theory of effective protection was created.[9] It is not known whether the same was true of the famous European tariffs of the later nineteenth century, but the British tariff of the 1930s looks more sensible in the light of effective protection than many commentators have assumed.[10]

Balance of payments

So far, we have followed various lines of thought that begin from the question of what goods a country exports and what goods it imports. Another set of concepts and linkages between variables proceeds from considering the relationship between the total of goods and services exported balanced against the total of goods and services imported.

This can be set out in a balance of payments statement that takes something like the following form.

Exports of merchandise:
        − Imports of merchandise
        = Balance of trade

+ Net balance of payments for services
= Balance of payments on current account
Financed by:
   Long-term capital transactions
+ Short-term capital transactions
+ Changes in international monetary reserves
= Balance of payments on capital account

The current account and capital account balances must be equal in size, although as the pluses and minuses may be reversed as long as they are consistent within each account, some countries' accounts show the balances as opposite in sign. This basic pattern is subject to many variations. Each item may be subdivided by commodity in the case of merchandise transactions and by particular service in the case of nonmerchandise current account transactions, and government items are often separated from private. Some countries exclude the monetary changes from the capital account so that the balances in the current and capital accounts differ by the amount of such changes rather than equate. Some countries admit that their recording cannot satisfy the simplicity of the ideal and include an item for 'errors and omissions', which may be of a substantial amount; the short-term capital movements in particular are hard to trace as they may reflect the net credit flows resulting from a difference in the speed with which import bills are paid and export receipts received. (Capital 'transactions' which arise in this way are known as 'leads and lags'.) Some countries produce different accounts, one recording only receipts and payments in foreign currency and known by a name such as 'overseas exchange transactions' accounts, while another attempts to date the transactions according to the movement of the good or service rather than by the resulting cash settlement and to include transactions which are not followed promptly by a cash settlement. The clearest example of such a transaction is 'unremitted profit', profits earned in country A, attributable to residents of country B because they own the profit-earning assets, but retained in A rather than remitted to the owners. They are included in a balance of payments account concerned with rights to income but excluded from an account of monetary transactions only. Consequently, the notion of balance of payments is one that requires exegesis.

The main lines of economic thinking, however, begin from a given balance of payments and ask how this is brought to an equilibrium position in the sense that all parties to it regard it as an acceptable continuing state of affairs. The earliest line culminated in analysis of the gold standard.

Adherence to the gold standard meant that a country fixed the value of its domestic currency, the pound sterling or the United States dollar, for example, in terms of gold and freely allowed transactions in gold between countries. In the pure case the domestic currency itself included a substantial element of gold coins. Then most transactions between two countries would be offset. Exporters would become entitled to payments in foreign currency but would sell their rights and obtain domestic currency from importers who needed foreign currency to pay their overseas suppliers. (There is no need to distinguish between goods and services here.) If we abstract from capital movements for the time being, any imbalance between exports and imports could not be so offset. There was, however, an alternative means of international payment because gold was acceptable in either country. The essence of the gold standard was that any such gold flows would remain small. A country with an import surplus would be tending to lose gold; its currency supply would therefore be falling. In line with the quantity theory of money discussed in Chapter 5, its price level would tend to fall. Its exports would therefore become cheaper in their markets, while imports would become more expensive relative to home production. In the country with an export surplus, the opposite process would occur, reinforcing the change in the relative prices of exports and imports for both countries. The price changes would induce volume changes in exports and imports for both countries, so that the imbalance of exports and imports would tend to disappear. Thus the 'price-specie' mechanism would automatically tend to remove any disequilibrium in the balance of payments and there would be no need for large flows of gold.

Allowing for capital transactions adds two elements to this picture. First, if residents of one country want to invest in the other what residents of that country want to borrow, the equilibrium balance of payments need not be zero. Importers will be able to acquire foreign currency not only to the extent of exports but also to that of foreign loans. The price-specie mechanism will begin to operate at the balance determined by the capital market. Secondly, a further instrument by which equilibrium can be attained is the rate of interest. In the deficit country, a rise in the rate of interest attracts foreign lenders; the resulting capital flow means that there is less pressure to remove the excess of imports. Furthermore, the rise in interest rates can be expected to diminish the demand for at least some commodities in the home market, contributing both to a reduced demand for imports and strengthening the price-specie mechanism in reducing the prices of domestic products relative to imports. (The greater profitability of exports following the change in price levels would be expected to offset any effect of interest rate increases on export industries.)

An alternative set of causes towards balance of payments equilibrium is postulated by the modern monetary approach. It assumes that direct arbitrage – buying cheap and selling dear whenever an opportunity arises – is sufficiently strong to ensure price equality in trading partners, and that there is a strong desired relationship between money stocks and expenditure levels. We consider a country beginning in external balance but then experiencing a rise in the price of its exports. Arbitrage guarantees that the price of exportable goods in the home market will also rise. That will make them less attractive to consumers, but the increased export receipts will feed money stocks. The level of expenditure relative to money stocks will therefore fall, and to return it to the desired relationship, expenditure on goods other than exportables must rise. The increase in exports therefore results in both a rise of expenditure and a switch away from exportables. This can be expected to produce a rise in expenditure on imports, whether by an increase in their price or their volume or both. The desired relationship of expenditure to money stocks can be maintained only when the balance of payments returns to zero.[11]

These simple ideas really amount to little more than finding links between economies sufficiently powerful to ensure that they operate as a single entity within which there can be no long-standing payments disequilibria. The extent to which they describe the international economy in any period is a historical question which has attracted a great deal of attention. Most inquiry has related to the late nineteenth century, and the question often takes the form of why the gold standard could not be reestablished after the First World War. A great deal of insight follows from posing the question in this way. The removal of gold coinage so that gold shipments had to be in the form of larger transactions in gold bars through central banks, while intended simply as a means of economising on gold, removed much of the freedom of individual agents on which both of the arguments previously outlined rest. The reluctance of governments to allow the balance of payments to determine changes in domestic incomes, or in the level of domestic money stocks, was an even more substantial impediment to the equilibriating mechanism of either the older or the modern theoretical analysis.

Historical inquiry has shown, however, that the simple theory does not produce a complete answer. Price changes were not always in the direction implied by the price-specie mechanism, nor did interest rates respond to balance of payments changes in the way predicted. On the other hand, arbitrage was not as efficient as some writers have argued or assumed, and the idea of a strongly desired constant relationship between money stocks and expenditures seems more plausible in some countries than others. Furthermore, some things which were emphasized by contemporaries such as the financial preeminence of London which enabled the Bank of England to spread any needed adjustments over the incomes of countries other than Britain through their ability to borrow in London as well as through the prices they received for their exports, have not been convincingly refuted. The simple ideas surrounding the balance of payments are a useful starting point for analysis of the historical position and not a ready-made description of it. But then, that is typical of economic theory.

The basic ideas of changes in relative prices and in interest rates as a means of removing balance of payments disequilibria can also be taken over into quite different institutional settings. When gold is not an essentially international currency, the relative values of two currencies may be fixed by an officially determined exchange rate. (Such rates are sometimes stated in terms of gold, but this is a historical relic of the gold standard era, and any numeraire would serve as well. Indeed, the United States dollar is used more commonly than gold.) The natural question to ask, then, is whether a change in the fixed exchange rate can be expected to remove disequilibrium in the balance of payments.

Again, there are several lines of analysis available, and it is a historical exercise to choose one with appropriate assumptions for any empirical work. The traditional analysis proceeds from price changes. A change from say £1 = $4 to £1 = $3 (the approximate figures of the sterling devaluation of 1949) enables the exporters of products from Britain to the United States to lower the dollar prices of their goods while continuing to receive the same sterling receipts. Whether export receipts rise depends on the elasticity of demand in the United States for British exports. If that elasticity is more than 1, then sterling receipts rise, and so on, exactly in line with the discussion of elasticities in Chapter 6. But the devaluation also means that the United States exporter to Britain has to raise his sterling price to maintain his dollar receipts. Whether Britain's import bill falls depends on the elasticity of demand for imports in Britain; if it is less than 1, import payments may rise despite the devaluation.

The immediate effect of a devaluation on the trade balance therefore depends on the elasticities of demand for exports and imports, and more intensive reasoning of this kind would produce the so-called Marshall–Lerner conditions that the trade balance improves, is unchanged, or deteriorates according to whether the sum of the elasticities of demand for exports and imports is greater, equal to, or less than 1. This concerns only the immediate impact, since it takes no account of income changes or of the supply elasticities in any of the industries concerned with exports or imports.

The basic set of ideas from which this *elasticities approach* to the balance of payments develops is simply the supply and demand analysis of the preceding chapter applied to international problems. The same can be done for the multiplier concept of Chapter 4, and this leads to the *absorptions approach* to the balance of payments. It will be recalled that we were able to show that

$$Y = C + I + (X - M)$$

where Y is income, C is consumption, I is domestic investment and $(X - M)$, exports minus imports, is a simplification of the balance of payments. It follows immediately that the balance of payments can be affected by any policy (or for that matter any other economic mechanism) which changes $(Y - C - I)$. Governments are usually more concerned about a deficit in the balance of payments than a surplus, and a deficit can be reduced by anything which raises Y leaving C and I unchanged, by anything which reduces C leaving Y and I unchanged, or by numerous other permutations of these variables. British governments of the 1960s frequently tried to use exhortation and credit controls of various kinds to change the consumption function and maintain autonomous investment in precisely this manner.

Although we do not propose to follow this analysis further, it is worth remarking that devaluation is not necessarily undertaken in an endeavour to remove a balance of payments deficit. A devaluation which succeeds in raising $(X - M)$ without markedly affecting C or I raises equilibrium income whether $(X - M)$ is negative or not, and may be undertaken for that purpose. The New Zealand devaluation of 1933 is a clear historical example of this.[12] In that case the government wished to raise X, since farm incomes were tied to export receipts and increased farm incomes could be expected to generate higher nonfarm incomes in a multiplier process. More common is government concern to reduce M, shifting the burden of adjustment on to the suppliers of imports. This is the essence of 'beggar-my-neighbour' policies, a feature of the international economy of the 1930s with which the action of the New Zealand government is often confused.

The modern monetary approach to the balance of payments attempts to combine the focus on prices of the elasticities approach and that on income adjustments of the absorptions approach. Its assumptions of effective price arbitraging between countries and a constant relationship between the money stock and total expenditure imply that a balance of payments deficit puts expenditures under pressure (since the deficit results in a loss of international reserves and therefore of the money stock) unless, of course, there is an offsetting feeding of the money stock by a means such as government expenditure exceeding government revenue. Devaluation raises export prices in domestic currency and arbitrage ensures that the prices of exportables rise in the home market too. The immediate effect will therefore be a decline in the ratio of money stock to expenditure, and there will therefore be increased restraint on consumption to restore the desired relationship. This will lower import payments as they share the decline of expenditure, although there is likely to be some lag before this becomes apparent. The increased export receipts (in domestic currency) and the decreased import payments permit the return of money and expenditure to the desired relationship without a continued loss of reserves, that is, with the balance of payments deficit removed. This analysis has the interesting feature of offering an explanation of the lag of import payments behind devaluation which was observed in the 1960s. It has been employed in reappraising devaluations in the past, especially in the 1930s, and may be expected to become more common in such studies.

Capital exports

The concern of economists with external balance leads them into many questions of economic policy formation. These questions are mostly restricted to the twentieth century because if earlier they were recognised at all, they were seldom seen as calling for government action. Historians have, however, been concerned with some questions about the role of capital exports, especially in the context of the British economy between 1870 and 1914.

Foreign investment is too often discussed as though it is simply a claimant on a pool of resources (or, worse, money) on which domestic investment is the only other claimant.[13] Foreign investment and domestic investment are treated as direct substitutes, insulated from the rest of the economy. We can see that there are at least other dimensions to foreign investment by returning to our outline balance of payments account. A country accumulating assets abroad must have a positive balance of payments on current account. The form of these assets or of titles to their ownership is shown by the items of the capital account. A positive balance of payments on current account must be accompanied by an accumulation of some combination of increased monetary reserves, short-term assets, and long-term assets (counting reduction of outstanding liabilities as an accumulation of assets).

In the case of Britain the accumulation of current account surpluses has been estimated by Imlah, although there are some doubts about his precise figures.[14] The capital account reconstruction is much less complete, although there are various estimates based on the records of issues of overseas securities on the London capital market,[15] which can be regarded as approximate measures of long-term capital movements. The question which arises is what mechanism guarantees that these two aspects of foreign lending are consistent?

The first answer must be that short-term capital movements and changes in monetary reserves can take care of some of the discrepancy. But they could not be expected to accommodate a large and continuing difference. Then the process of adjustment must follow from some mechanism such as those we described above. In the case of Britain between 1870 and 1914 the (historically corrected) gold standard mechanism can be invoked.

Consider first the case of an excess of exports over imports which was larger than the amount people were willing to purchase of foreign securities. The total of monetary reserves would tend to rise beyond what the Bank of England considered desirable. There would then be reason for English interest rates to fall (thereby making foreign securities more attractive); we would expect too that a rise in Britain's export prices would make its goods less competitive.[16] We would expect forces on both long-term investment and on the excess of X over M tending to bring them into equilibrium.

In the opposite case where people wished to purchase foreign securities beyond the level of the current account surplus, pressure on the reserves would lead to higher interest rates in Britain thereby discouraging foreign borrowers, while the price effect would encourage exports rather than imports. Again, $(X - M)$ and capital exports would tend to return to equilibrium.

It will be noticed that it is $(X - M)$ and the prices of English goods and securities which play a key role in this analysis. In historical accounts it is the idea of switching from foreign to domestic investment which receives most attention. A reduction in foreign investment requires a reduction of exports or an increase in imports or some combination of them. Neither of these is readily translated into an increase in domestic investment, especially when it is appreciated that British imports were predominantly foodstuffs. The most likely effect of smaller exports is a decline in investment in manufacturing, and increased imports would mean more food rather than more home investment. It is possible to think of some links to home investment but imagination is required. In the capital market it is easy to think of people switching from foreign securities to domestic, but that must be followed through the balance of payments to its effect on transactions in goods and services; and inasmuch as the most likely effect is a reduction of exports, the switch between securities is likely to be self-defeating.

The case is even more complicated when we notice that the British current account from 1870 to 1914 included receipts of dividends and interest on earlier investment, receipts which from about 1875 onwards exceeded the net balance of the account overall. This would obviously have made any reduction in foreign borrowing even more difficult. It can indeed be calculated that simply to restrain foreign investment to its 1870 level, about a 10 percent cut in all exports from 1870 to 1914 was required (unless British people renounced their interest and dividends). It would surely be strange to sacrifice the British export industries in order to achieve a higher level of domestic investment.

This is merely the start to any historical appraisal of the role of capital exports in the late nineteenth-century British economy, but it is enough to show the value of elementary balance of payments theory in linking together what might otherwise be treated inappropriately as quite disparate subjects.[17]

8

Growth

Growth and history

Because historians naturally focus on change over time, it might at first appear that the theory of economic growth is the area of economics on which they could draw most fruitfully. It is, after all, the product of economists' thinking about economies in the course of change and changes imply some element of time. Those who have been convinced by our repeated argument that historians have to use economic ideas in the construction of historical arguments rather than accept ready-made conclusions will not be surprised to learn that such expectations will be disappointed. The theory of economic growth has many merits as a system of logical thinking, but it does not provide completed descriptions of historical developments. Indeed, it does not readily provide concepts useful to historians although this is partly attributable to the relatively 'advanced' nature of the theory; useful insights can be gained from it, but most require more than a preliminary knowledge of the subject.

The theory of growth has followed several paths. Two particular foci of attention are the problems of low income countries, and the implications of maximum and optimal growth rates in richer ones. These are sometimes distinguished as the areas of development economics and growth economics respectively, a distinction which corresponds only in part with a terminology which reserves *growth* for problems of income change while using *development* for the wider changes in institutions and attitudes that often accompany increases in wealth.[1] Here we draw freely on the literature, crossing these boundaries in our search for those ideas which have been of most value to historians.

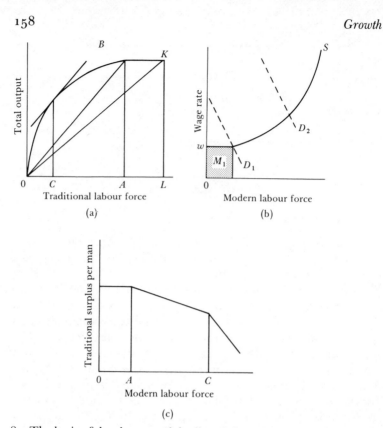

8.1 The basis of developmental duality. Adapted from J. C. H. Fei and G. Ranis, *Development of the Labor Surplus Economy* (Homewood, Ill.: Irwin, 1964)

Labor surplus

We start with a group of ideas usually thought to belong to development economics. In a poor country we can think of a traditional sector of the economy which has difficulty in providing sufficient jobs for all available workers to be employed with positive marginal products. Workers are retained, by custom, even though the additional labour they provide makes no contribution to the total product. This is shown in part (a) of Fig. 8.1. Total product does not increase as the labour force expands beyond A; those workers represented by AL, where L denotes the total available number of labourers, have zero marginal productivity.

We have deliberately spoken of a 'traditional' sector in a poor economy. The discussion is often presented in terms of the agricultural sector, but studies of poor economies in the present day and in earlier times, including England before the late eighteenth century, have shown that near-peasant communities engage in many activities other than farming. Food is usually the most important output, but by no means the only one. Whether or not there is labour with a zero marginal productivity in traditional activities is an empirical judgment and one that requires a considerable sensitivity. Members of a community who appear to be making no contribution to output may well be engaged in activities which are regarded as important by the community in question, even though their value is not apparent to our eyes. On the other hand, many communities have found it possible to maintain traditional outputs with less labour when alternative opportunities for income creation are perceived.

In practice, we would expect the labour involved in producing the maximum possible output of the traditional sector to be shared among all available labourers, but we can recognise the existence of 'surplus labour' in that the same output could be reached with fewer labourers. If there is no alternative use of labour, then the total output must be shared among the total labour force. The average wage, total output divided by total labourers, is shown in part (a) of Fig. 8.1 as the slope of the line AK. If an opportunity for other employment is introduced, a 'modern' sector employing labourers for wages, it could be expected to recruit up to AL workers at little more than the wage established in the traditional sector, and this would not decrease the total traditional output. In part (b) of Fig. 8.1 the traditional wage is translated and shown as w, and the supply curve of labour facing the modern industrialist is a horizontal line at that level of wages for a labour force up to the equivalent of AL workers in part (a). (It would be more realistic to allow a slightly higher level of wages than in the traditional sector to allow for costs of movement, but the simplification does no harm to the argument.)

A modern industry with the demand for labour D_1 would therefore be an undoubted advantage to the economy. It adds a total modern output shown by the shaded area M_1 without reducing traditional output at all. If the workers in it continue to have their share of traditional product, all of the modern output is available for investment and therefore rapid growth should be possible. What could stand in its way? There are two possibilities, one 'administrative' and one 'distributional', even if we rule out any lack of demand for the products of the modern sector. The administrative problem is that of retaining access for the modern workers to the traditional output which they would have obtained had they remained in the traditional sector. The 'traditional surplus', the output of the traditional sector which in the absence of a modern sector would be the wages of effectively unemployed workers, is shown in part (c) of the diagram. For a transfer of up to AL workers to modern industry it is simply the number of modern workers multiplied by the traditional wage. (For this particular purpose there are advantages in thinking of the traditional sector as entirely food producing and looking at the means of transferring food to workers in modern industry.)

The distributional question is related but concentrates on ownership and terms of exchange. We might expect those workers who remain in the traditional sector to question the right to any part of 'their' produce of workers who have left for employment in modern industry. They could see an opportunity to raise the traditional sector wage level to the slope of the line $0B$ in part (a) of the diagram. This would raise the level of w in part (b) and frustrate the whole process. The possibility of apparently 'free' growth would be removed.

If these problems are resolved, we can expect the output of the modern industry to constitute an 'investible surplus', so that the modern activity can expand quickly. Its demand curve for labour shifts to something like D_2 in part (b) of the diagram. While the supply curve for labour cannot remain horizontal, it can be expected to be elastic. In the traditional sector those workers between C and A in part (a) of the diagram, while not having a zero effect on total traditional output, still have a marginal product less than the average product of the labour needed to produce the maximum total output. (The latter, it will be remembered, is shown by the slope of the line $0B$. The marginal product of labour is shown by the slope of the tangent to the total product curve at any point. The tangent at point C is parallel to $0B$, and therefore it is the point at which the marginal product of labour is equal to the average product of the labour force needed to produce maximum total output.) For this reason some writers refer to all the workers beyond *C*, and not only those beyond *A*, as being in 'disguised unemployment' or 'underemployment', and while *A* is sometimes called the 'excess' point, *C* is termed the 'commercialisation' point. Many labels are possible, but what is significant is that it is only as labour in the traditional sector is drawn down below *C* that modern industry faces a commercialised traditional activity in the sense that wages equal marginal productivities, and the two sectors are in the same position as if producers of two commodities were in competition for labour. In part (c) of the diagram the available traditional surplus per modern worker falls after the transfer of *AL* workers from the traditional sector, but it falls even more sharply after *C* is reached, inasmuch as there is no longer any justification at all for preventing wage rises in the traditional sector.

We can use this diagram as a heuristic starting point for many analytical problems. What happens if technical change occurs in the traditional sector? Can we establish prices such that the transfer of workers occurs voluntarily and the output of the modern industry feeds consumption as well as investment? And so on. Once the starting point is grasped, the possible developments are legion.[2] So are the historical applications. One of the most obvious is to the movement of workers from agriculture to industry in the Soviet Union in the 1930s. More generally, one of the most frequently observed features of modern growth is a decline in the proportion of the labour force engaged in agriculture, the so-called movement away from agriculture, and it is easy to interpret this in the light of the differential productivities of labour in two sectors, which is the core of the construct under discussion here.[3]

Direct application to British economic history might seem to be confined to a remote past, but the ideas expounded here are frequently employed in discussion of the mechanics of growth in the eighteenth century. That British agriculture had been commercialised in the preceding centuries and intermingled so thoroughly with rural industry meant that no hard and fast barriers existed between industry and agriculture, or rural and urban activity, vastly assisting the changes of the Industrial Revolution. The differences between eighteenth-century Britain and the kind of economy envisaged in the preceding discussion

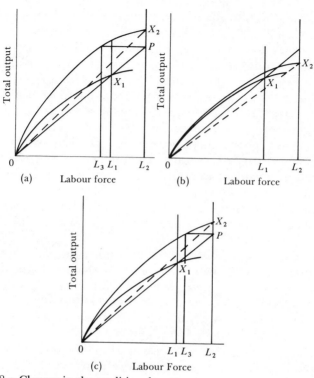

8.2 Change in the traditional sector

are central to the familiar question of why Britain was the first country to industrialise.[4] This illustrates very neatly the way in which we conceive imaginative thought to be needed to relate economic ideas to the problems of history.

A slight extension of the model introduced here has been used quite directly in connection with eighteenth-century England.[5] Each of the parts of Fig. 8.2 correspond to the traditional sector as in part (a) of Fig. 8.1. However, the labour force is growing, from L_1 to L_2 in each of the parts of Fig. 8.2, and at the same time the traditional activity is experiencing technical change so that the curve relating total output to labour input is shifted from the curve $0X_1$ to the curve $0X_2$ in each case. The effect of these two changes together obviously depends on the relative strength of the technical change and the diminishing returns to labour, the latter being represented by the curvature of the total product curves. By remembering that per capita output is shown by the slope of the straight lines $0X_1$ and $0X_2$ before and after the dual effects of technical change and diminishing returns, it is easy to see that parts (a) and (c) illustrate cases where the effects of technical change outweigh the diminishing returns, while in part (b) the reverse is true and per capita output is reduced.

There is, however, a difference between parts (a) and (c). Assume that the society in question is content with the per capita level of traditional output with which it begins. Then because technical change outweighs diminishing returns to labour, it can afford to divert some of its labour to a nontraditional activity exactly as we discussed earlier.[6] The level of output needed to maintain a constant per capita availability of traditional activity is shown by the point P in either of parts (a) and (c) where the line $0X_1$ intersects the vertical line at the increased labour force L_2. This can be produced in either of these diagrams with a labour force of L_3, and the difference between L_2 and L_3 can be diverted to a modern activity. But now we see a difference between parts (a) and (c). In the former the effect of technical change is so strong that the labour force in the traditional activity can be reduced; L_3 is less than L_1. In the latter while technical change outweighs the effect of diminishing returns and per capita consumption of the traditional output can be maintained with a declining proportion of the total labour force, the number of workers in the traditional sector has to be increased; L_3 is greater than L_1.

This can be related to the familiar question of enclosure and the supply of labour to industry in eighteenth-century England. Old notions of enclosure commissioners as a capitalist press-gang have been discredited, but it is possible to take the debunking too far. Equating enclosure with technical progress in rural activity for the purpose of this argument, it is known that the rural labour force continued to increase during enclosure. In terms of Fig. 8.2 we are concerned with a situation as in part (c), not as in part (a). But there is still a manner of speaking in which the technical change (= enclosure) permits a movement of labour from the countryside, since in its absence per capita consumption of the products of rural activity would have declined even if all the increasing labour force were retained in traditional activities.

As usual, there are points of a conventional historical kind to be explored before historical conclusions are advanced. We are aware that England imported corn in the late eighteenth century, and so it is necessary to check that the argument is not crippled when we distinguish between production and consumption of the traditional sector's output. (It isn't.) Even more important, the link between enclosure and technical change needs more than an assumed identification. But we have here the core of a conceptualisation of an old issue which is likely to avoid confusion and advance knowledge.

Analysis need not be limited to two sectors. The essence of the analysis is the simple point that the shift of resources from low-productivity to high-productivity uses raises the income level (and continuing shifts raise the rate of growth) of an economy as a whole. We might inquire, for example, how much the shift of labour from agriculture to activities such as services in the late Victorian economy contributed to the growth of the economy. The data are too frail to bear much weight, but they do suggest that in that case the growth of income per head in individual sectors was much more influential than the changing distribution of the labour force among them.[7]

Investment

The preceding section dealt essentially with a situation where different sectors were characterised by different productivities and looked on the shifting of resources from low to high productivity uses as the key element in changes of income. There are alternative lines of development beginning from the notion of a surplus available for investment, which lead to several somewhat ad hoc but useful growth mechanisms and to a fuller set of theoretical constructions known as neoclassical growth theories. They are so called because they incorporate the idea of savings providing a limit to investment as was common in the writings of pre-Keynesian or 'neoclassical' economists.

The simplest notion is that the rate of growth of income depends on the proportion of resources that is devoted to investment. The intuitive idea is that investment will be undertaken only if it provides a future output greater than the immediate cost in terms of resources reserved from current consumption. It seems natural to extend this to thinking of the rate of growth as directly dependent on the investment ratio; the greater the proportion of resources reserved for investment, the higher the resulting rate of growth.

It should be apparent immediately that this is much too simplistic an analysis. There must, after all, be some difficulties or limitations or we should all be enjoying unlimited rates of growth, and it requires very little historical or empirical sense to see that we are not and have not. Nevertheless, the notion that raising the investment ratio was the preeminent concern of growth formed a large part of many government policies in the 1950s and later, and uncritical concentration on the investment ratio was christened *growthmanship*.[8] Even now when it is more widely known that the records of growth in the richer countries show little correlation between investment ratios and growth rates,[9] when it is recognised that investment can take many forms among which housebuilding and transport (which are often among the largest claimants on investment) have effects on income quite different from investment in industrial plant and machinery and may reflect the geographial situations of different countries, many governments still give excessive attention to the investment ratio.

There are, however, more subtle ideas associated with it. One group concerns the need for a 'big push'. Arthur Lewis, whose early writings on growth did much to bring the investment ratio into prominence, spoke of a need to bring it from 5 percent of income to 10 percent (sometimes 12 percent)[10] and this might be read as postulating a critical minimum rather than an open-ended relationship between the investment ratio and the rate of growth. The intuitive basis of the 'big push' being needed can be seen in Fig. 8.1 simply by considering the need for a minimum acculation of resources in the modern sector to achieve a D curve at or beyond D_1, so that income is brought above the traditional level of wages w.

A different development of the simple investment-growth nexus looks directly at the limits on feasible growth paths. Resources devoted to investment are not available for consumption now, and it is certainly plausible to think of political constraints on present sacrifices for future benefits or, in poor countries, physical constraints in that food consumption has a minimum level consistent with survival. In Fig. 8.3 we show two paths of

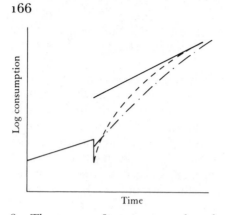

8.3 The traverse from one growth path to another

consumption growth at different compound growths (appearing as straight lines as the logarithm of consumption is plotted against time). For the present we leave uninvestigated the mechanism by which a higher rate of growth as well as level of consumption can be achieved except that it is assumed to have the following characteristics. A move from the lower to the higher path requires a diversion of resources to investment; and the greater the initial reduction of consumption, the more rapidly consumption subsequently moves to the higher path. Some resulting possibilities are shown by the dotted lines in the diagram. There are many traverses and what we have is essentially a choice of extent of present sacrifice paired with future gains. There is a substantial body of theory concerned with the selection of a 'best' traverse. Although this includes the case where the choice is essentially an aggregation of a large number of individual decisions, it is most easily comprehended as a choice of policies, and it is implied in many historical discussions such as that of the Soviet pattern of growth in the 1930s. Nevertheless, in English historiography, by far the most prominent example is indeed concerned with private decisions. This is the famous 'standard of living' controversy in the Industrial Revolution period. The debate ranges over many issues but a central one is the extent to which resources were diverted to investment and how the subsequent gains in consumption were distributed. (It is distribution which is the key since it is implausible to think that the investment which was undertaken did not lead to a higher consumption stream in total.[11])

The connection between investment and growth has so far been left as something of a 'black box' – more investment produces more income but precisely how is left as no more than an intuition. An early line of thinking to fill in the gap is associated with the names of Harrod and Domar, who developed some different but related models of growth from the Keynesian system of Chapter 4.

We showed there that if saving is a constant fraction of income, the multiplier process requires that $\Delta Y = 1/s \cdot \Delta I$, where s is the marginal propensity to save, and for equilibrium, $Y = 1/s \cdot I$. But investment is simply the change in the capital stock. If we now postulate a technical relationship connecting the increase in capital to increased income in the following period, so that x, the incremental output–capital ratio or $\Delta Y/I$, is constant, then we have a closed system defining an income path through time at which equilibrium is maintained. The two equations,

$$Y = 1/s \cdot I \qquad \Delta Y = x \cdot I$$

imply that $\Delta Y/Y = s \cdot x$ (and also that $\Delta I/I = s \cdot x$). Only along this path can ex ante savings and investment decisions continue to be satisfied.

It can readily be shown that this is an unstable equilibrium. For should $\Delta Y/Y$ happen to increase by more than $s \cdot x$, then savings is increased and so is the capital stock; the constant incremental output–capital ratio then ensures that Y must again increase by more than the former equilibrium rate. Similarly, any downward deviation of $\Delta Y/Y$ from $s \cdot x$ must result in a cumulative decline from the former path. It takes little empirical sense to know that cumulative upward or downward deviations in growth rates have not characterised many economies, so that we could not expect to use the equilibrium condition given here as a direct description of an economy. Rather the formulation must be regarded as a useful device for drawing attention to the dual character of investment, the driving force for income changes, while also creating capacity for the additional production which is simply another view of the same income.

For some time the incremental capital–output ratio itself seemed an important economic variable. It was prominent in many discussions of growth in the 1950s and 1960s and was employed in historical studies. Thus the lower incremental

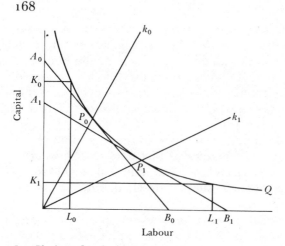

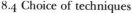

8.4 Choice of techniques

capital–output ratio of cotton textiles was used to explain the high growth rate attainable by Britain in the early nineteenth century.[12] The change in Britain's growth rate at about 1900 also was traced to changes in the incremental capital–output ratio rather than in the savings rate.[13] In both cases we gain useful insights into the historical problems, but we are immediately faced with the question of what determines the incremental capital–output ratio. Can we really think of it as a technical relationship? Do producers not have any choice over the techniques of production they use? And if we relate increased output entirely to new investment, what is being assumed about the capital stocks surviving from earlier periods?

To pursue some of these questions, it is convenient to use a framework which is the beginning of a great deal of thinking about the meaning of stability in a growing economy.[14] We employ a materialist conception of capital, and we think of investment very simply as the result of producers' decisions about the means by which output is to be obtained. Producers have a choice because we assume that any given level of output can be attained by a variety of combinations of labour and capital. In Fig. 8.4 the line labelled Q and known as an *isoquant* (equal quantity) joins all the combinations of labour and capital which can produce a given level of output. To take extreme cases, K_0 of capital and L_0 of labour, or K_1 of capital and L_1 of labour are both combinations which produce the same level of output. It will be noticed that the curve has the familiar property that as we move to combinations with more and more capital, greater increases of capital are required to compensate for the reduction of labour by a given amount. Similarly, as we move along the horizontal axis, more and more units of labour have to be included in a combination to permit a fixed reduction in the amount of capital used. The manager is faced with an infinite number of blueprints from which he can choose a particular combination of labour and capital, but the two factors are not perfect substitutes for each other.[15]

We assume that producers choose the least cost combination of labour and capital. The relative price of labour and capital is shown by a line such as $A_0 B_0$; £1 can buy $0A$ of capital or $0B$ of labour, or any combination along the line $A_0 B_0$.[16] Then by the usual reasoning, the least cost combination to produce the output Q is shown by the point P_0. The marginal output of a factor must equal the price of it, or else it would be worth purchasing more of a factor (if its marginal product exceeds its price) or profits could be increased by using less of a factor (if its marginal product was less than its price.)[17] The relative marginal product of one factor in terms of the other is given by the tangent to Q and this equals the relative prices of the factors at a point like P_0. If the relative price of labour and capital changes to $A_1 B_1$, then the least cost combination is given by P_1. It will be noticed that the illustrated change is of producers choosing a more labour intensive means of production in response to a relative cheapening of labour, and this is surely congenial to common sense.

We note that points such as P_0 and P_1 can be interpreted as the result of choosing a particular capital–labour ratio, k_0 in the case of P_0 and k_1 in the case of P_1, the choice being made to minimise production costs given the set of available blueprints and the relative price of labour and capital. It is the capital–labour ratio which plays the key role in the next part of the analysis; it is the variable on the horizontal axis in Fig. 8.5. We can notice too a distinction made in a useful piece of terminology. An increase in the capital stock may take two forms. It might be a matter only of equipping more labourers with the same amount of capital each; this is equivalent to a change in the scale on which Fig. 8.4 is drawn and is known as 'capital widening'. Alternatively, an expansion of the capital stock may take the form of increasing capital per man, a change in the capital–labour ratio. This is known as *capital deepening,* and if producers are choosing least-cost means of production, it must be associated with other changes in the economy such as a fall in the price of capital relative to labour. As is so often the case, these terms are used more loosely in everyday language; the technical terms are defined in relation to a given set of possible production blueprints, and although a manager choosing to change his capital–labour ratio may encounter techniques of production formerly unknown to him, no change in the range of blueprints available to the economy is involved.

Before we turn to Fig. 8.5, we need some further assumptions. We consider an economy with a production function such as we introduced in Chapter 3. It has constant returns to scale, so that if labour and capital both increase by a given proportion, output increases by the same proportion. It also has diminishing returns to each factor, so that an increase in either factor not matched by an equal increase in the other results in an increase of output but by a smaller percentage. We assume further that savings is a constant fraction of income. Finally, we are not concerned here with the Keynesian problem that ex ante investment may not equal ex post investment, and we assume that investment always equals savings.

We can now construct Fig. 8.5. We begin with the capital–labour ratio and construct first the schedule Y/K, the ratio of output to capital. As we move along the horizontal axis, the capital–labour ratio is increasing; capital must be increasing faster than labour. Because the production function has diminishing returns to capital, output must be increasing but by less than the increase in capital. Hence, the ratio of output to capital must be declining. This establishes that Y/K falls to the right as it is drawn.

By assumption, saving is a constant fraction of income, say sY. Investment equals savings, again by assumption, and investment is the increase in the capital stock. Therefore $\Delta K = sY$. Dividing both sides of this equation by K, we find $\Delta K/K = s \cdot Y/K$. That is, the proportional growth of the capital stock is equal to a constant times Y/K. Therefore, as we move along the horizontal axis, the

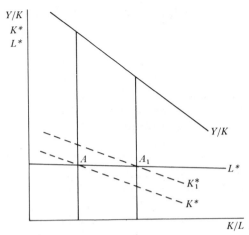

8.5 Neoclassical growth

proportionate growth of capital falls like Y/K. It is shown as K^* in the diagram. Finally, the growth of the labour force is taken to be unaffected by the capital–labour ratio; it is determined by the growth of population and participation rate. It therefore appears in the diagram as a straight line marked L^*.

We can immediately deduce that the only equilibrium point for an economy characterised by the assumptions we have made is at A. There the capital stock and labour force are growing at the same rate so that the capital–labour ratio can remain constant. And as Y/K will be stationary too, output must be growing at the same rate as labour and capital. (Alternatively, this can be deduced from the constant returns to scale of the production function.) To the right of A labour will grow more quickly than capital, and so the capital–labour ratio must return towards A. Conversely, to the left of A capital grows more rapidly than labour, and so the capital–labour ratio must increase towards A. (It will be remembered that these changes must be accompanied by changes in the relative price of labour and capital, and many textbooks show how these changes too can be portrayed in this diagram.)

Consider now an exogenous change in the savings rate. At any level of income more is saved and more is invested. Therefore for any level of the capital–labour ratio the growth of capital is faster. The change in the savings rate then appears in the diagram as the shift from $K*$ to $K*_1$. In the same way as before we establish that the new equilibrium point is A_1. Comparison of A and A_1 is interesting. Capital and labour are growing at the same rate as before, and by the same reasoning as we used earlier, income must be growing at the same rate too. The change in the savings rate has had no effect on the growth rate of the key variables. There are differences between A and A_1: that the ratio of output to capital is lower after the change in the savings rate is shown by the diagram, as is the higher level of the capital labour ratio. It can readily be deduced that the price of labour relative to capital must be higher, and it can be shown that provided the price of capital remains positive, output per man will be higher after the change in the savings rate.[18] In the terms of Fig. 8.3 we have a traverse during which income per head rises, but the upper rate of growth is equal to the earlier one; outside the traverse the lines of Fig. 8.3 are parallel, and eventually income, capital, and labour all return to the initial growth rate. We might say that the prices of labour and capital change so as to absorb the change in the savings rate leaving the growth path of the economy unchanged.

This result is so much at variance with common strongly held intuitive feelings about increased investment that it deserves further investigation. It will be noticed that it is quite independent of any problems in translating savings into investment; in this model all available savings are 'used'. But first, notice that investment is kept quite distinct from any change in technology in the sense that the range of blueprints available to producers remains the same. If Fig. 8.4 is interpreted as showing the unit isoquant, the combinations of labour and capital available for producing each unit of output, then the curve itself shifts as the whole technology of the economy changes. In Fig. 8.5 technical change in this sense raises the Y/K schedule. Still, one technical change will produce a change in output per head but leave the system constrained to a single equilibrium rate of growth; only continuing technical change will permanently raise the rate of growth. But we would be on one path towards an increasing rate of growth if for any reason a higher capital–labour ratio increased the likelihood of further technical change.[19] Second, although all the steps involved in this model are plausible, they combine to constitute a tightly constrained system in which it is not surprising that the rate of growth cannot change. Only the rate of growth of the labour force is left outside the system and it is assumed to be constant! There is no room in this construct for new products, for learning, or for any other force which might be expected to inject some dynamism into an economy. (In any case the traverse during which the rate of growth is increased might take a substantial period of calendar time.)

We have dealt with only the starting point of a theoretical literature which has its own appeal. But so far, the main lesson for historians is in the initial result that investment has to be considered with regard to both accumulation and technical change. Accumulation on its own need not lead to a continued change in the rate of growth, and simple growthmanship may be very misleading. We are led then to think about technical change.

There is, however, at least one place in the historical literature where the result we have developed has been employed directly. In the late nineteenth-century American economy there does appear to have been a rise in the savings ratio, and this was followed by an increase in output per man which was not continued into a new rate of growth of income.[20] The rise in the savings rate at about the time of the Civil War has not been explained entirely convincingly, although the growth of the financial system must at present rank as the best available candidate.[21] The response to increased savings does seem to follow the path of the preceding argument. These savings were absorbed by a change in the relative price of labour and capital; and American industry became more capital intensive, but the rate of growth rose only temporarily. For British historians both the theoretical argument and the American experience should engender caution before asserting that increased domestic investment would have generated a faster rate of growth in the late Victorian economy.

Technical change

If economic theory points decisively to the need to consider the role of technical change in growth, it does not take us far along the path to satisfying that need. It cannot be claimed that there is a large body of systematic knowledge about the nature and causes of technical change, and it can be observed that what exists is more the result of historical inquiry than of economic theory. We think here of Schmookler's work on patents, of the works of Jewkes and his collaborators on the role of the individual inventor, and of the recent attempts to summarise (and extend) the economics of innovation by Rosenberg and David.[22]

Economic theorists have provided some useful classificatory devices and some insights into particular parts of the origin and impact of innovations. The distinction between an *invention,* the discovery or construction of a new way of doing something – including a new product, and an *innovation,* the implementation of an invention into the production process, owes a great deal to Schumpeter, if indeed it did not originate with him.[23] It contributes to clarity of thought as long as it is not allowed to degenerate too readily into an artificial division between the inventor sitting in a garret and dreaming romantically while the clever hard-nosed businessman sits below and eagerly picks out all those inventions which have practical usefulness. Life and history have never been so tidy.

A second useful distinction is between disembodied and embodied technical change. Disembodied technical change is an improvement in production methods which can be introduced without any change in the capital being employed; embodied technical change is that which can be introduced only with a change in the capital stock being used. Disembodied technical change can be written as a quite separate term in the production function, $Y_t = A_t f(L_t, K_t)$. But the use of such a formulation in the presence of embodied technical change would lead to an underestimate of the contribution of capital to growth unless the issue is handled carefully and somewhat outside the apparent framework of analysis. This is the basis of many economists' criticisms of the *sources of growth* accounting associated especially with Denison but widely used in historical discussions.[24]

Sources of growth accounting begins from an equation such as

$$\Delta Y/Y = a \cdot \Delta K/K + b \cdot \Delta L/L + \Delta p/p \qquad a, b \text{ constants less than 1}$$

that is, the rate of growth of income is equal to the weighted sum of the growth rates of labour and capital plus the rate of productivity growth. We might say that the rate of growth of output is

Table 4. *Sources of growth in eighteenth-century England*

	Income growth dY/Y	Contribution of capital $(rK/Y)\,dK/K$	Contribution of labour $(wL/Y)\,dL/L$	Contribution of land $(zN/Y)\,dN/N$	Contribution of productivity change dp/p
1740–80	1.0	0.35 × 1.0	0.45 × 0.7	0.20 × 0.4	0.25
1780–1800	2.0	0.35 × 2.0	0.45 × 1.0	0.20 × 0.4	0.77

equal to the average growth of inputs plus a 'residual,' the latter being unexplained but believed to include technical change and any other reason for gains in productivity. We can be more specific if we believe certain assumptions to be acceptable. If we have a production function such as $Y_t = A_t f(K_t, L_t)$, that is, with only disembodied technical change, and furthermore if it has constant returns to scale and the markets for labour and capital are competitive so that wages and the interest rate equal the marginal product of labour and capital respectively, then it follows as a matter of mathematical logic alone that the rate of growth of output is determined by an equation such as that at the beginning of this paragraph; furthermore a and b are unambiguously the shares of capital and labour respectively in total income.[25] Given all the assumptions involved, the growth of income is equal to the sum of the growth rates of the inputs weighted by their shares in output, plus a residual which represents productivity gains, the shift in the production possibility curve over time.

Following such a procedure, Crafts presents Table 4 for eighteenth-century England. He distinguishes land as well as labour and capital; we have translated Crafts's notation into that used here and added N for land and z for its marginal productivity.[26] The table shows that of the increase by 100 percent in the rate of growth of income between the two periods distinguished, the increase in the rate of growth of capital weighted by its share of output was 35 percent (0.35 × 2 − 0.35 × 1 as a percentage of 2 − 1), and the increase in the rate of growth of labour weighted by its share of output was approximately 13 percent as much; it also shows that the rate of growth of land inputs did not change and that the change in the residual was 52 percent of the increase in the rate of growth of income.

It is when we want to take a further step and regard the terms in such an equation as showing the contributions to growth of capital, labour, and technical change that the distinction between embodied and disembodied technical change becomes important. For the terminology of 'contribution' suggests that the terms on the right-hand side of the equation are independent and, in particular, that the gains from technical progress are attainable independently of the course of $\Delta K/K$. Clearly, if some of the technical advances were available only because the growth of capital permitted the introduction of new kinds of machinery, the role of capital in growth would be underestimated by the calculation of the contribution of capital in Table 4. We might still want to distinguish the effect of accumulation from that of technical progress, but we can no longer proceed as though the results of the equation are self-evident. Until we perform the usual historical task in checking the appropriateness of particular assumptions, we should confine ourselves to describing p as the residual.

We consider only one possibility further. Crafts argues that scepticism as to the role of capital formation in the economic growth experienced in the eighteenth century should be reconsidered because the table shows it to have accounted for 35 percent of the acceleration which occurred. His case is understated; it should be strengthened to the extent that any of the rise in the residual p resulted from embodied technical progress.

Whether or not technical progress is embodied or disembodied in eighteenth-century Britain or elsewhere is a subject for empirical inquiry. There have been some documented examples of spectacular disembodied progress, but they have usually dealt with single factories rather than whole economies. We might still inquire how far embodied technical progress required an increase in the rate of growth of capital and how far it could be attained in the course of 'normal expansion' or even 'replacement investment', but we will not pursue those questions. Our interest is only in showing that the distinction between embodied and disembodied technical progress is important in trying to disentangle the roles of capital formation and technical progress in economic growth.

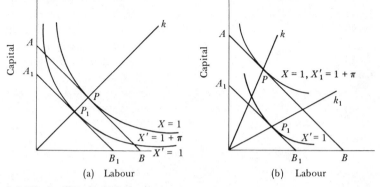

(a) Labour   (b) Labour

8.6 Kinds of technical change

Another set of distinctions made by economic theorists concerns the *factor bias* of innovations, their differential impact on the employment of labour and capital. These distinctions have not in fact contributed a great deal to historical inquiry, but the terminology seems such a natural one that it has been widely used by historians and it must now be understood.[27] There are already a number of examples of misunderstanding in the literature.

We begin again with the unit isoquant as in Fig. 8.6. As before the curve XX shows the combinations of labour and capital that can be used to produce a unit of output, while any straight line through the origin joins points at which increasing amounts of labour and capital are used but always in the same ratio; it shows a constant capital–labour ratio. Lines like AB again represent the relative price of labour and capital. In both parts (a) and (b) of the diagram cost-minimising producers first choose the capital–labour ratio k, and produce a unit of output by the combination of labour and capital P. Technical change can be represented by a shift of the unit isoquant to X_1; loosely speaking, technical change enables a smaller combination of labour and capital to produce a unit of output, or enables a combination previously required to produce one unit to produce more than a unit output, say $1 + \pi$. We notice a divergence between (a) and (b). In the former along the capital–labour ratio k, the relative price of labour and capital needed for producers to remain cost minimisers before and after the technical change remains the same. Cost minimisation at P_1 requires the same relative factor prices as at P_0. Each of the factors is, in a sense, affected equally by the technical change, so that the same combination of them is induced by the same factor prices. Such technical change is known as *Hicks neutral,* 'neutral' because of its limited impact on factor proportions and Hicks after its inventor to distinguish it from a different kind of neutrality yet to be introduced.

We should first check that technical change in part (b) of the diagram is not Hicks neutral. The isoquant shifts in such a way that cost-minimising producers must either change their capital–labour ratio or face different factor prices (or some combination of those). The diagram is drawn showing unchanged factor prices, and producers shift to a combination of factors in which labour is a bigger proportion. Such technical change is called *labour using* or *capital saving* (although it must be admitted that usage is less than perfectly uniform). A different change in the isoquant or, even simpler, a reversal of the L and K axes will illustrate capital-using or labour-saving technical change.

This notion can be developed into a study of what happens to wages, the interest rate, the shares of labour and capital in total product as growth proceeds, and so on. But the significance for historians is rather in showing how complex the recognition of capital-using or capital-saving technical change is going to be When the capital–labour ratio does change between two dates, we need to know a good deal about the shape of the unit isoquant or about the relative price of labour and capital before we can decide whether technical change has been biased one way or the other. That more capital is used is by no means sufficient.[28]

There is no reason why the Hicksian definition of neutrality should be the most useful one for all purposes, and it has a rival in Harrod neutrality. This alternative defines a neutral technical change as one which leaves the marginal product of capital unchanged at the same level of the capital–output ratio. We begin the construction of Fig. 8.7 as before. We observe that if the level of output is unity on the curve XX, then $0X$ must measure the capital–output ratio (K/X is necessarily $K/1 = K$). Consider now the technical change shown in the diagram, which shifts the isoquant to X_1X_1 but is accompanied by a change in relative factor prices from AB to AB_1. Cost-minimising producers move from P_0 to P_1. There is a change in the capital–labour ratio, but we notice

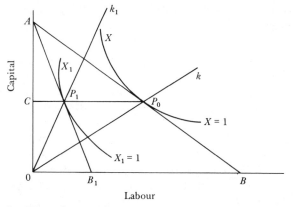

8.7 Harrod neutrality

that the capital–output ratio is unchanged. We note too that the price of capital has remained unchanged – the unit price is still $0A$ – although it has of course changed relative to the price of labour. Cost minimisation implies that the price of capital equals its marginal product and if the former is unchanged, so too must be the latter. Hence, the diagram shows technical change with a constant marginal product of capital at a given capital–output ratio; we have a case of Harrod neutrality. We could go on to define capital-saving and capital-using technical change in relation to this standard of neutrality.

This is a less natural definition of neutrality than that of Hicks. It gains importance because it can be shown that Harrod neutrality is equivalent to what is called *labour-augmenting* technical change. If we consider again the production function

$$Y_t = f(K_t, L_t)$$

and think of technical change such that with a given level of the capital stock, the same output can be produced with less labour, that is, that after the technical change, we can write

$$Y_t = f(K_t, qL_t) \quad \text{where } q \text{ is less than 1}$$

then it is natural to think of the technical change as labour augmenting. It makes each unit of labour 'worth as much' as $1/q$ units were 'worth' before the technical change. Such technical change is Harrod neutral. Proof of this is complicated, but the

essential idea can be grasped by noting that the change in Fig.
8.7 is essentially a shrinking of the L axis, while the K axis is
unchanged.[29]

Again, the definition of Harrod neutrality is significant for
historians mostly as a means for showing the complexity of influences on the factors of production in a technical change. It is
often tempting in historical circumstances to think of technical
progress as simply changing the scale of one of the factors of
production, thus assuming Harrod-neutral technical progress.
Crafts continues the table given earlier with alternative estimates for 1780–1800 of a growth in labour supplies of 1.6
rather than 1.0 and a consequential reduction in p to 0.5. Crafts
discusses this in terms of errors in the measurement of the labour input, thinking of increases in the hours of labour. But on
the assumption that much of the free time was involuntary, we
might interpret the manipulations as separating from p the effect of labour-augmenting technical progress, that which increased the effective growth of labour supplies. It will then be
obvious that in measuring the contribution of capital, we should
have to return to the distinction between embodied and disembodied technical change.

In one particular context the notion of factor bias in technical
change has entered economic history, but it has done so in a way
different from the usual conceptualisation of economists. In a
celebrated work already referred to, Habakkuk argued that labour scarcity in America relative to Britain promoted technical
change. The argument is a very subtle one, much more so than
has been realised by many commentators. One essential part of
the thesis can be represented in Fig. 8.8. We start by thinking of
the United States and Britain as producing by the same technology, that is, as operating on the same unit isoquant. Because of
different factor supplies, the relative price of labour and capital
differ between the two countries. Labour being scarce in
America, it is relatively dear there and relatively cheap in Britain; Britain operates on a lower capital–labour ratio. But then
Habakkuk departs from the standard economic analysis by postulating that technical progress is easier when entrepreneurs are
operating at the capital intensive end of the spectrum of available techniques. We may therefore find the United States bene-
fiting from technical change which is of no value to Britain as
only part of the unit isoquant is changed.

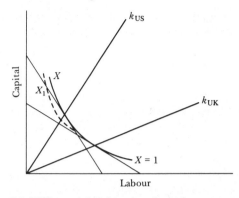

8.8 Differential induced technical progress

It can readily be seen that this raises many issues. There are questions as to whether Britain and the United States are reasonably portrayed as capital and labour scarce in this sense, and whether the picture would change significantly if more factors were distinguished (land, skilled, and unskilled labour, etc.); there is the observation that this is a partial equilibrium analysis which leads into the question of why the prices of labour and capital remain so different in the two economies, and so on. Perhaps most interesting is the question of why technical progress should be facilitated by operation at a particular capital–labour ratio. The economist's natural instinct is to say that for a cost-minimising producer both factors are always equally costly since they both produce their marginal products. Why should the fact that the capital–labour ratio is higher produce any greater effect in capital-saving innovations? Logically, this is unassailable, but the historian may respond that he is dealing with men rather than calculating machines. In an everday sense capital is more costly than labour, and it is not implausible to think of it being the everyday sense which corresponds to the degree of interest which a businessman will show in possible innovation.

Alternatively, we might think of technical progress as not only being embodied in new capital equipment but also as proceeding, at least in part, from the experience of using new techniques. This is known to economists as 'learning by doing' and has generated a substantial literature of its own. Although it began before the Habakkuk thesis was propounded, that thesis is interesting in revealing the value of economic concepts to his-

torical inquiry and also in showing that historians are wise not to
limit themselves to the motivations which come most naturally in
economics textbooks.[30]

Conclusion

Most of the thinking we have dealt with here has been drawn
from the tradition in which labour and capital are substitutable,
at least to a substantial degree, and in which capital and output
are both treated as though they were no more than variants of a
single homogeneous good. It would be unjust as well as inaccu-
rate to leave the impression that all economists have worked in
such a framework only, even though much has been done to determine just what degree of restrictiveness the mode of thinking
incurs. Our focus has been determined by what is useful to historians rather than by what is interesting to theoreticians.

Economists have worked on cases where capital goods, once in
place, could not readily be converted into output or into new
capital goods, and such *vintage capital* models have had a small
impact on economic history. It has long been suggested that the
slower growth of steel in Britain than in some other countries in
the late nineteenth century left Britain with an older vintage of
steel-making equipment and that this affected significantly the
productivity experience of the industry. Temin tried to quantify
the argument and suggested that the vintage capital effect might
indeed be significant.[31] But McCloskey has argued convincingly
that estimating errors make Temin's results grossly misleading,
that the extent of the difference in average age of the capital
stocks of the British and German industries could not have been
more than four years, altering hardly at all between 1900 and
1914, and that given the slow rate of technical progress being
achieved, such a gap could not have been significant in determining the relative productivity record of the two industries.[32] What
is interesting about this case is that it has been widely regarded
as a prime example of the vintage capital effect, and McCloskey's result suggests that it will often be an acceptable approximation to regard technical change as disembodied. We have to
be careful in speaking of capital's contribution to growth, but the
measurement of productivity will be little affected. The point is
that productivity gains can be expected to be distributed not

randomly across all net investment but concentrated on the net investment first undertaken (or in the expenditure concerned with maintaining the capital stock even when net investment is zero), so that the rate of growth of capital will have only a small effect on productivity.

Economists have begun to work on models which include features such as distinct construction and production phases and in which 'time' appears more as it does to historians. In our discussion time has been merely a dating device, since it is immaterial whether we think of a change from t_1 to t_2 or from t_2 to t_1. Anybody concerned with empirical events knows that the clock cannot be turned back and that what happens now may constrain the choices available tomorrow. It may freely be predicted that this work will make an impact on economic history before long. Indeed, the study of historical events was one of the stimuli behind recent developments such as those of Hicks.[33]

9

Government

Government in history and economics

For several reasons historians often concentrate on the activities of governments. The bureaucracies of central governments keep records, and raw materials are often available more readily for the historian of government than for any other units of activity. Political history is older than other specialised branches of history and usually forms a substantial component of the training of historians, so that it is natural to emphasize the plans and actions of governments. And the big social and political questions of any age are usually debated in the context of what alternatives were available to the government. For these and other reasons historians are commonly especially concerned with governments.

This is much less true for economists, if it is true at all. Many applied economists work in government service; many academic economists spend some time in government service and many more spend time in criticising government economic policies. But for the most part, all these activities require an application of the economic theory which is available for governmental and nongovernmental activities alike. Government in itself, quite properly, occupies only a small place in economics textbooks. This does not mean that economic theorists think governments unimportant and still less that governments are only large economic units which otherwise resemble private producers and consumers; it is only too obvious that governments in control of a central bank do not experience the liquidity constraints of private sector firms and households, and in raising revenue there is a much larger element of coercion available to governments than to the legal activities of individuals and companies.

What it does mean is that the 'economics of government' is spread through all branches of economics, income analysis, international economics, supply and demand analysis, and so on rather than constituting a specialised branch in itself.

Balanced budget multiplier

Economists do speak of the 'theory of public finance' or similar terms, and to illustrate the point that this is mostly 'standard' economics applied to a governmental setting, we expound one of its propositions. This is the *balanced budget multiplier* and it is an extension of the kind of income analysis presented in Chapter 4.

Consider an economy where we do not have to distinguish foreign trade, and where there is government whose expenditure is autonomously determined and which collects taxation by taking a proportion of all incomes. In the symbols of Chapter 4 government expenditure G equals $\overline{G}$, government receipts from taxation T equal tY, t being the tax rate and Y income. Investment is autonomous, $I = \overline{I}$, but saving is now determined as a constant fraction of posttax or disposable income. Taxation is tY so that disposable income is $(1-t)Y$. Thus saving is $(1-c)$ $(1-t)Y$, where c the marginal propensity to consume from disposable income.

We can now determine equilibrium income, in the sense of that level of income where planned savings equals planned investment, exactly as before.

$$Y = C + I + G \quad \text{and} \quad Y = C + S + T$$
$$C = c(1-t)Y \quad I, G \text{ exogenous}$$

Hence, in equilibrium $S + T = \overline{G} + \overline{I}$

$$(1-c)(1-t)Y + tY = \overline{G} + \overline{I}$$
$$Y(1 - c + ct) = \overline{G} + \overline{I}$$
$$Y = [1/(1 - c + ct)](\overline{G} + \overline{I})$$

It follows immediately that there is a multiplier effect associated with an increase in government expenditure, exactly analogous to the investment multiplier and equal to $1/(1 - c + ct)$. This will come as no surprise to those who followed the point made in Chapter 4 that multipliers are concerned with autonomous in-

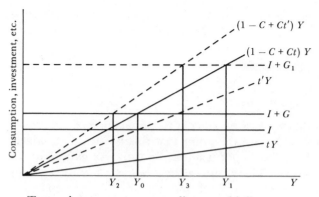

9.1 Tax and government expenditure multiplier

jections into the income stream rather than with investment. In Fig. 9.1 an increase in equilibrium income from Y_0 to Y_1 is associated with an increase in government spending from G to G_1, t and I being unchanged.

We have introduced government as more than a source of autonomous expenditures. It is apparent that equilibrium income will also be affected by a change in the tax rate, as it is by any other leakage from the income stream. Working out the size of the impact of changes in tax rates by other than elementary calculus is tedious, but it can be shown intuitively in Fig. 9.1. Equilibrium income is initially at Y_0, where $(1-c+ct)Y = \bar{I}+\bar{G}$. An increase in the tax rate from t to t_1 shifts the $(1-c+ct)Y$ line to $(1-c+ct_1)Y$ and reduces equilibrium income to Y_2 with I and G unchanged; t_1 greater than t increases the slope of the line referred to. It can be shown that the extent of the shift in equilibrium income is given by $\Delta Y/Y = c/(1-c+ct) \cdot \Delta t$, that is, it depends on both the marginal propensity to consume and the level of the tax rate as well as the change in the tax rate.[1] As those familiar with the great 'tax cut' debate in the United States in the 1960s may have realised, it works in either direction, the change in income moving in the opposite direction from the change in the tax rate.

We inquire next into the joint effect of an equal increase in government expenditure and in taxation, so that if the budget is balanced initially, it remains balanced after the change. We know that the increase in government expenditure increases income such that $\Delta Y = 1/(1-c+ct)\,\Delta G$. This will increase taxation revenue since taxes will be collected on the increase in income. The increase in revenue is $t \cdot \Delta Y$, that is, $t/(1 - c + ct) \, \Delta G$. But $t/(1 - c + ct)$ is less than 1, and so tax receipts will increase less than government expenditure, and in the absence of other measures the budget will become unbalanced.[2] There must therefore be an increase in the tax rate, and it must be such that tax receipts at the new level of income, $(t + \Delta t)(Y + \Delta Y)$ equals the new level of government expenditure $G + \Delta G$. That is, the increase in government expenditure must equal the increase in taxation receipts $(t + \Delta t)(Y + \Delta Y) - tY$. Ignoring $\Delta t \cdot \Delta Y$ as too small to matter, we deduce that the needed increase in the tax rate is given by

$$\Delta G = Y \cdot \Delta t + t \cdot \Delta Y$$

The increase in the tax rate will itself lower equilibrium income by $\Delta Y/Y = -c/(1 - c + ct) \, \Delta t$, so that the net effect on equilibrium income is given by

$$\Delta Y = 1/(1 - c + ct) \cdot \Delta G - c/(1 - c + ct) \cdot Y \cdot \Delta t \qquad (1)$$

where Δt is such that

$$\Delta G = Y \cdot \Delta t + t \cdot \Delta Y \qquad (2)$$

Only simple algebra is now required. Rearranging (1) gives

$$\Delta Y(1 - c + ct) = \Delta G - c \cdot Y \cdot \Delta t$$

and substituting for the last term from $(c \cdot Y \cdot \Delta t = c \cdot \Delta G - c \cdot t \cdot \Delta Y)$ as can be seen from (2), it follows that $\Delta Y = \Delta G$. That is, an equal increase in government expenditure and taxation receipts raises equilibrium income by approximately (remembering that we have ignored the small $\Delta Y \cdot \Delta t$ term) the same amount.

In terms of Fig. 9.1 we know that an increase in government expenditure from G to G_1 by itself raises equilibrium income from Y_0 to Y_1, while an increase in the tax rate from t to t_1 alone lowers equilibrium income from Y_0 to Y_2. The changes drawn in the diagram are chosen so that we start with a balanced budget $tY_0 = G$, and the combination of changes leaves the budget balanced. The equilibrium income when both the tax rate and government expenditure are raised is Y_3 and $t_1 Y_3 = G_1$. The gain in income between Y_0 and Y_3 is approximately equal to the amount by which government expenditure (and taxation receipts) is raised.

188 Government

The precise line of argument follows only from the particular assumptions employed here. But the result that an equal increase in government receipts and expenditure raises equilibrium income persists over a number of variations from these assumptions. It is essentially an implication of the way we treat government expenditure as an injection into the income stream without qualification, while taxation is only a partial withdrawal (changes being partially offset by changes in savings) so that the usual savings-related multiplier still operates on part of the injection.

The result would not occasion much theoretical interest were it not for the long tradition in which a balanced budget was thought of as 'neutral'. Some of the major political issues of the seventeenth and eighteenth centuries concerned restrictions on the powers of kings to raise taxation, or to command resources by extending the money supply. Limiting the king's expenditure to his receipts from either his own assets or taxation approved by a representative assembly was a major protection against arbitrary exactions. This was readily translated into a rule that budgets should be balanced, not so much an argument about economic effects as one based on public morality. The major assault on this attitude was the direct demonstration that equilibrium income might be increased by government expenditure and the gain in income judged to outweigh the violation of the balanced budget precept. But it was a minor additional breach in traditional thought to show that a balanced budget was no guarantee that the government was neutral in its effects on equilibrium income.

Our major concern is to draw attention to the fact that the balanced budget multiplier is merely an application of standard income analysis to particular aspects of government activities. It depends on a particular relationship between an income injection and an income withdrawal, and plausible links joining both government expenditure and taxation receipts to income satisfied that requirement. There is no concern with how government decides on tax rates, or on the allocation of government expenditure. Government is stripped to its bare bones, leaving a skeleton to which income analysis can be applied in an interesting way.

There are historical applications for the balanced budget multiplier. We can begin by thinking anew about the policy of British governments in the nineteenth century of restricting government expenditure so as to allow lower tax rates while maintaining a balanced budget. (Because customs duties were a significant part of government revenue, we should have to reformulate the analysis to provide for exports and imports explicitly, but the result still holds.) It is clearly fallacious to think that this necessarily produced a neutral relationship between the government and the economy. We would have to scrutinise all the other assumptions involved. Is it plausible to think of government expenditure as unrelated to other economic variables? It is not now that so much government expenditure is related to things like unemployment, but even in the nineteenth century it is possible that reduced government expenditure so affected the expectations of entrepreneurs that private investment was raised. (This is often argued in reverse for the United States in the 1930s, when Roosevelt's apparent budget deficit may have caused a reduction in private investment.)

The balanced budget multiplier is loosely related to another 'applied' concept which is now used quite widely. We have assumed previously that resources were freely available, so that changes in equilibrium income applied to real income. But as we noted in Chapter 4, equilibrium income might not be that at which labour was fully employed. There is a particular level of tax receipts associated with full employment. We can define a *full employment budget deficit or surplus* as that which would rule if a given level of government expenditure were combined with full employment. An actual deficit may then be described as a full employment surplus, meaning that but for the unemployment in the economy, the expenditure and tax policies would produce a surplus for the government. For assessing the economic effects of a particular fiscal stance, it has been useful to distinguish between these possibilities. Thus we referred to Roosevelt's 'apparent' budget deficit in the 1930s because it has been calculated that had full employment been attained the tax rates of his budgets would have produced a surplus; Roosevelt's policies did not include 'full employment deficits'.[3] This has been useful in assessing policies although it is obviously no more than a rough and ready tool of analysis.

Tax incidence

Historians usually think of governments and policies in broad generalisations rather than in detail, and we therefore began with a family of concepts related to income determination and the budget as a whole. But many operations of governments necessarily affect particular markets. It is to the concepts developed in relation to individual commodities, those introduced in Chapter 6, that we turn to illuminate the issues that arise. This strengthens the observation that what are often read simplistically as appropriate only to economic calculating machines can be useful in the analysis of much wider issues.

The previous section treated tax revenue as being derived from levies on income. But some taxes are imposed on specific commodities and some interesting conclusions can be drawn from analysis of them. We consider a particular commodity for which the market clears, as discussed in Chapter 6. We can therefore expect the market price to be the equilibrium price. In part (a) of Fig. 9.2 we begin with price P_0 and quantity Q_0. What happens when the government imposes a fixed tax on each item of the commodity sold? This is equivalent to imposing a wedge between the price received by the supplier and that paid by the purchaser, the difference being the government's levy. In part (a) of the diagram this is shown in the difference between P_1 and P_2, the government receiving as revenue the product of $P_1 - P_2$ and the quantity sold at the price paid by purchasers P_1. We notice that that quantity Q_1 is less than the initial quantity sold Q_0; the imposition of a tax affects both purchasers and suppliers. Indeed, it does not matter whether we think of the tax as an additional cost imposed on suppliers so affecting the supply curve, as shown by the difference between S_0 and S_1 in part (a) of the diagram, or as a charge on purchasers so that we conceive the demand curve as embodying demand for the product plus a willingness to pay a fee to the government for the right to enter the market. In the latter case we can distinguish the market for the good alone by subtracting the tax from the demand curve, as in part (b) of Fig. 9.2. However it is thought of, we move from equilibrium at P_0, Q_0 to an equilibrium quantity Q_1, a producers' price P_2, and a purchasers' price P_1.

This important point is often overlooked. A tax is a wedge be-

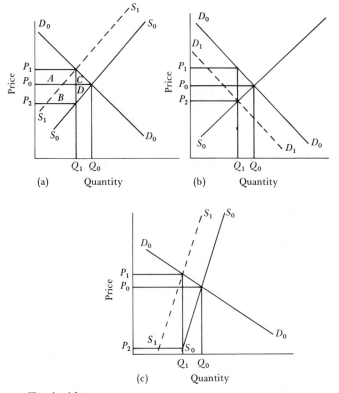

9.2 Tax incidence

tween the price paid and the price received, and the legal responsibility for transmitting tax receipts to the government is no
guide to the real incidence of the tax. If both suppliers and
purchasers can respond to the imposition of a tax, then they will
share the cost whoever the law says must pay it. The real force of
this observation comes when we think of certain rather unusual
commodities. The diagram might refer, for example, to the hir-
ing of labour. Legally, there seems to be a difference between an
employment tax imposed on employers and a tax collected from
the wages of workers. There may well be administrative differences (in enforcement systems for example), but contempla-
tion of parts (a) and (b) of the diagram should convince the
reader that there need be no economic difference at all.

This does not mean that suppliers and purchasers share equally in the cost of tax in all circumstances. In part (a) purchasers shift from Q_0 at price P_0 to Q_1 at price P_1. In the terms of consumers' surplus as discussed in Chapter 6, the cost of the tax to them is the loss of consumers' surplus of the areas marked A and C. Similarly, the cost to suppliers is the loss of producers' surplus of the areas B and D. In the diagram these appear to be about equal, but this depends on the shape of the curves. If we identify the equivalent areas in part (c) of the diagram, it is obvious that the tax 'burden' falls more on the suppliers than on the purchasers. The supply curve is much less elastic in part (c) than it is in part (a). If we experiment with demand curves of various slopes, we will find that the more horizontal the curve, the smaller the proportion of the cost of the tax paid by purchasers, and vice versa. We thereby reach the general proposition that the cost of the tax will be shared between purchasers and suppliers according to their ability to respond to it, as shown by the slopes of the supply and demand curves. This is congenial to common sense, but it must be remembered that this conclusion is unaffected by whether the government appears to impose a tax on purchasers or suppliers.[4]

There is yet another conclusion which can be derived from this simple application of demand and supply concepts to the issues of taxation. We can sum the cost of the tax to producers and purchasers in part (a) of the diagram to obtain $A + B + C + D$ as the cost to all parties. But the revenue to the government is $A + B$. The cost of the tax therefore exceeds the revenue to the government. The economic sense of this is that taxes produce a divergence between the prices seen by producers and those by consumers. If we can be sure that in the absence of taxes the economy would reach an equilibrium on the production possibilities curve at the highest available indifference curve, then a tax imposes a real cost on the community. Prices can no longer simultaneously measure the relative value of two commodities to consumers and the relative resource costs to the producers of the same two commodities. If we believe that an economy is not characterised by perfect competition, or that for some other reason it will not reach an optimal allocation of resources, then we will not believe that the general equilibrium effect of taxes is necessarily a social loss. The distribution of the cost of a tax on a particular commodity can still be analysed in a partial equilibrium framework (although producers' surplus may not be directly translatable into rents and national income, as we discussed in Chapter 6).

These ideas usually become important for historians in the course of references to the effect of taxes, often incidental to the main thread of an argument. A recent example where they are much more central to the historians' concern is a reappraisal of the relative effects of taxes in Britain and France in the eighteenth century.[5] Mathias and O'Brien have shown that the levels of taxes in Britain were not clearly lower than those of France, as has often been assumed, and that British taxes fell relatively heavily on items of general consumption. An unwary reader might think that the argument implies that taxes fell on the poorer sections of the community that consumed such goods. It will be clear from the foregoing analysis that such a conclusion requires an assessment of the elasticities of demand and supply for the taxed commodities, an assessment that Mathias and O'Brien are well aware is not yet possible.

Market failure

There is a sense in which the logic employed in economic theory casts a particular light on government activities and can easily be allowed to shade into particular political views. The assumptions of perfect competition imply that resources are allocated so that goods are produced to the maximum extent possible, given the relative values placed on them by society; consumers are faced with prices which accurately reflect the resource costs of particular commodities; free trade guarantees that a country gains as much as possible from international specialisation – whether or not other countries impose protection and provided only that monopoly gains are unavailable or rejected as immoral; and so on. What economic role is there for government? Should it not interfere in economic processes as little as possible?

The most obvious response to this line of thought is that economies are not always characterised by the assumptions of perfect competition. Indeed, the case may be reversed; the assumptions of perfect competition are so restrictive and unlikely to be fulfilled that there will always be an economic role for government.

But the influence of the original line of thinking is rather more subtle than that would suggest. The advantages of a competitive economy are so obvious that the role of government is seen to be to remove any barriers to the operation of competition. Thus a great deal of economic thinking about the role of government is in the context of 'market failure', of impediments to the operation of competitive markets which governments may be able to alleviate.

There are many possible forms of market failure. The oldest is probably the existence of monopolies,[6] and there is a long tradition of government intervention designed to make monopolies behave as much as possible like competitive firms.[7] British governments of the nineteenth century, often characterised in a rather loose fashion as committed to laissez faire, imposed various limitations on railways culminating in statutory price fixing and justified their actions in terms of the restriction of monopoly power. The succession of United States acts and commissions against trusts was in the same tradition. Indeed, adherence to the market failure philosophy in the United States is shown by the way the antitrust legislation usually emphasized the behaviour of business units rather than their mere size in deciding whether or not concentration was undesirable.

Market failure can take other forms too. One to which a great deal of attention is given nowadays is where producers and consumers of a product are substantially the same group. We cannot think of one set of people being represented in the demand curve while a different set of people making independent decisions are represented by the supply curve. The clearest examples relate to health and education. In the British Health Service the consumers of the product may well be the medical personnel who decide what the health needs of a member of the public are at the same time as they make decisions about their own incomes. We do not have a market with separate demand and supply curves which can be expected to result in appropriate decisions about the allocation of resources. (There may still be a case for using price barriers to deter frivolous claims on the health service, but that is a different argument.) Similarly, debates over the allocation of resources to education in line with market criteria are often bedevilled by ambiguity over who the consumers of education are. They may be thought of as the parents or as the children. In the case of the former there is attraction in the antipaternalist argument that people should be left to make their own decisions. But if it is children, and children cannot be relied on to make appropriate consumer choices, who should be given the responsibility of acting in their place? The choice of parents must rest on sociopolitical grounds and cannot be deduced from the logic of competitive markets alone; the choice of educators clearly gives the same people control of the demand and supply curves of the 'market.'

In the British context these two examples relate to areas which are substantially run by the government. But the questions apply equally to societies where the health care and education services have a much larger component of private enterprise, and they apply in cases where there is no government involvement at all.[8] Another kind of market failure lies in areas which by their nature must be government activities. The extreme case is of *pure public goods*, those where individual consumption makes no difference at all to the amount of the good available to other consumers. When the state organises defence, the security afforded an individual does not depend at all on the extent to which other people also benefit from the service provided. Each individual has an incentive to claim that his valuation of the service is zero and that, on market principles, he should not be asked to contribute to its cost. The resources used in defence cannot be paid for as though it were being provided by a competitive industry.

Pure public goods are rare, but the *free-rider* problem exists where a good is only in part a pure public good. Some consumers of the agents of law and order can be identified, those who use the police and courts because they have been the victim of a crime or a breach of the civil law. But the law and police exist to deter breaches of the criminal and civil codes as well as punish transgressors, and individuals may benefit from such deterrence even if they make no explicit calls on the police or courts. Costs are not allocated according to benefits if they are imposed entirely on the explicit users, but those who benefit only from the deterrent effects have an obvious incentive to act as free riders. The 'free-rider' issue arises in the private sector too, as soon as collective action is involved. Exactly parallel issues to those just discussed arise in the membership of trade unions or any other regulatory combination and in many other contexts.

Market failure would thus seem a sufficient ground for a wide range of government interventions in economic affairs.[9] There are, however, good reasons to be sceptical of the ability of governments to counter all the problems which arise. These reasons begin with simple doubts about the ability of a large government apparatus to deal with issues effectively. There is no logical reason why government organisations should differ from private enterprises of an equal size, but it may be found that individuals whose own income depends on the skill with which they use the resources under their control take greater care with them. This is an empirical question rather than one of economic logic; there are many inefficient private organisations, but the experience (documented by historians) of state regulatory agencies becoming trustees for the producers they are supposed to regulate rather than for the consumers of their products suggests that there is force to the argument.

More economically based is the reflection that if a society is characterised by more than one market imperfection, there is no guarantee that the removal of one imperfection will result in an overall improvement. To take a very simpleminded example, consider a country which could import a commodity from either of two sources *A* or *B*. It begins with a tariff against both, two market imperfections. *A* can produce the commodity more cheaply, and so initially the commodity is imported from there. The government is then converted to the idea that it should remove market imperfections and it negotiates a mutual reduction of tariffs with *B*, while agreement with *A* proves more difficult. The impediment to market-based trade with *B* is removed, and the differential tariff which results leads to imports from *B* rather than *A*. Removal of a market imperfection results in trade being shifted to a less efficient producer. The example is simpleminded since it really depends on changing the nature of an imperfection (from a tariff on a commodity to a tariff on the efficient producer of a commodity),[10] but it can be extended to more significant cases at the cost of more complex analysis. If a tariff means that prices do not give producers an incentive to maximise the social usefulness of resources, it might seem desirable to remove the tariff. But if the economy also has taxes that affect the consistency of prices and social costs, then we cannot be sure on the grounds of logic alone that removing the tariff will benefit the community. In any real-world economy the desirability of a specific government intervention to reduce market failure is obviously a complex matter. We might argue more directly that any government intervention may have unintended effects. This is best shown by a particular example, although it is really an obvious point and by no means restricted to governments. In the 1930s the New Zealand government wished to devalue the New Zealand pound relative to sterling. The banks doubted that the government's desired exchange rate could be maintained in the face of market pressures that would result if their anticipation of an excess of external receipts over payments were realised. They feared that they would accumulate sterling and suffer a capital loss when the government gave way and allowed the New Zealand pound to appreciate. The government resolved this problem by agreeing to buy sterling from the banks and hold it on its own account. It paid for the sterling by the issue of government securities bearing interest. This seems a perfectly sensible way to resolve a difficulty, but it had a quite unintended effect. The rate of interest agreed provided a floor below which the price of bank finance could not fall. Bank lending would have stimulated the demand for imports and reduced the accumulation of overseas assets,[11] but the banks had no incentive to offer finance at less than the interest paid by the government. There was no intent by the banks to subvert government hopes for a resurgence of private investment and the mechanisms involved were understood by few people in the 1930s, but an agreement made for one purpose had unintended and mostly unrecognised side effects.

Recognition that market failure may be widespread does not give unconditional theoretical support for government interventions in an economy. There is, however, a still more fundamental reason why government policies, whether active or restrained, cannot be deduced from the logic of competitive markets. There is simply no reason why political notions of justice should be satisfied by perfect competition, whether state repaired or not. Perfect competition implies that factor rewards equal their marginal products, and it is possible to argue that this is 'fair'. But that must be an additional argument; it can be derived from various individualistic definitions of justice, but some criterion of fairness must be introduced. Different notions of justice can be chosen, and they have different implications. We might, for example, say that a fair distribution of rewards is not one depending on an individual's marginal product but on the ratio of his product to some assessment of the skills with which he was endowed. Is it so obvious that a clever person who uses his natural intelligence only partially should be rewarded more than a less clever person who uses his limited endowment as much as possible even if the former has a higher marginal product? (Such a 'productivity' notion of fairness comes easily to a reader of economics.) Such questions cannot be answered by economics alone, but they have to be answered explicitly or implicitly, before it can be decided that the distribution of income resulting from perfect competition is desirable. (Equally, choice of a means of implementing a desired distribution of income may, and probably will, involve economic analysis of alternatives.) Political decisions cannot be avoided in deciding on economic policies.

Transaction costs

Some readers may think that the preceding section has less of the character of economic theory than of the philosophic reflection familiar in any historical analysis. There is some justification for such a view, but the section gives an accurate impression of the way in which economic concepts and theories can be used in a discussion of government activities while providing no description of them.

The literature of economic history provides another more specific example. One particular market failure which we refrained from introducing in the previous discussion is what economists refer to as *transactions costs*. A competitive market may be capable of reaching an appropriate set of decisions, but the cost of gathering all the individuals involved and persuading them of the rightness of the decisions may make the whole process prohibitively expensive. If transactions costs are reduced, a market solution previously ruled out as too costly may become practicable.

Economists usually exemplify the first of these propositions by pollution. If an industrial producer causes environmental damage, then the competitive market framework requires that he should compensate those who suffer. This restores them to their 'correct' income level, while the producer has to make his decisions about prices and quantities on the basis of the 'correct' social costs of his operations. But many individuals who each suffer only a little may be dissuaded from action by the cost of claiming damages from a single producer for whom it is worthwhile to employ expensive legal talent. The transactions costs of aligning private and social costs and benefits are too high. An appropriate remedy may be to use state power to impose a pollution tax on the producer so at least making him respond to the appropriate social costs.[12]

The most obvious historical example along these lines concerns the issue of enclosure in eighteenth-century England.[13] It has long been known that the open field system by which strips of land in each of several large fields were allotted to individual villagers could be explained by an inherent desire for equality or as a means of minimising the risk costs of failure of a particular crop because of local variations in soil and other natural conditions in part of the village's land.[14] Equally, it has been clear that technical progress in the eighteenth century (or earlier in many cases) could explain a decline in the risk of such localised failures. But why were eighteenth-century enclosures effected by parliamentary means? If the risk was known to have declined, should not a series of market transactions have made it possible for the land to be redistributed in a manner appropriate to the new situation? It was possible, and enclosure by agreement was indeed frequent. But the cost of such market transactions could be high (and might involve a variant of the free-rider problem, where an individual blocked agreement in the hope that he would be bribed to cooperate). The use of a parliamentary act to drive through the negotiations over details might appear worthwhile.

Analysis of enclosure in terms of transactions costs is no more than a first step towards a reappraisal of the enclosure movement. It takes no immediate account of the different chronology of enclosure in various parts of the country; it raises the question of whether new methods of agriculture remained technically compatible with small strips; it raises the question of whether parliamentary enclosure was really an evasion of negotiation between equals by a public-minded appeal to parliament to enable the costs of negotiation to be avoided in the interests of justice and speed, or whether some people such as tithe holders saw an opportunity to economise on the costs they incurred in collecting their traditional rights by having them capitalised into a compact agricultural holding.[15] But the idea of transactions costs certainly initiates a fruitful new approach to appraisal of enclosures.

Another historical example stretches the concept still further until the evolution of government seems to be simply an exercise in the choice of institutions so as to minimise the costs of government. Feudalism emerges as the rational choice of people who need protection and can find it only in the force available from a local lord. With the growth of a centralised power capable of preserving the most basic peace, and making available also a legal service for mediating disputes, the basic institutions of government could shift from a local warlord to the law of contract. The form of government is essentially a means of minimising transactions costs. This summary is to some extent a caricature of what many historians will see as a caricature of the complexity of history,[16] and if it were offered seriously as a complete explanation of major historical processes, such scepticism would be justified. But as a means of focusing attention on an important element in a major process, thereby making it easier to see how one part fits with another, the emphasis on diminishing transactions costs is well justified.

For our particular purposes it is also worth noting how the main force of the argument about transactions costs is better understood against the background of a competitive economy even if the latter is regarded as an unrealistic construction. To use a terminology likely to be more familiar to many historians, it is a useful 'ideal type'.

Objectives of policy

It would be wrong to think of government as no more than a device for minimising transactions costs irrespective of the purposes of the transactions as it is to think that governments must always intervene in economic affairs to maximise income irrespective of the distribution of that income. The objectives of government come from outside economics. So does analysis of the relationship between government policies and the interests of particular groups within the community. An economist might, however, reasonably express scepticism of too ready an identification of the 'public interest' with the interests of particular groups of producers; widely spread consumers often have no obvious spokesman while a tightly knit small group of producers does and the latter therefore has an advantage in debates over where the interest of the community as a whole lies.

A knowledge of economics sometimes assists in showing that measures adopted in pursuit of one objective of government economic policy may make it more difficult to achieve another objective. It is useful to remind governments that if they wish to pursue two objectives, they must, in general, possess and use two different instruments of policy, even if a dogmatic assertion of this precept assumes that governments have clear and specific objectives while casual empiricism soon indicates that governments are willing to compromise and aim only approximately at their declared objectives. Furthermore, we need to analyse the effects of government actions which may well differ from the objectives which led to those actions being undertaken.

For all these purposes, economists employ the standard tools of economic analysis. There is no special 'economics of government' for which historians should look.

History and economics again

An injustice to economics?

Economists may well complain that this book fails to do justice to their subject. We have ranged over economic theory, picking out those pieces which have been used by historians. In so doing, we have noted several places where the concerns of different pieces of economic theory come together; supply curves apply to a factor of production like labour as well as to an individual good, and the concerns of income generation and commodity exchange overlap in both monetary and international economics. But we have not been much concerned with the internal logic by which economic theory is advanced, an internal logic in which a large part is played by creating single frameworks to contain what were previously seen as theories about different topics.

The first response to any such complaints from economists must be that this book is both for historians and merely an introduction. Historians are well aware that they deal with material which also falls within the province of economists; they are less easily convinced that the more formal content of economics has anything to assist historical inquiry, and our object has been to remove such doubts (without arousing unrealistic expectations of what economic theory can contribute). Retention of interest must be a high priority in any missionary endeavour, and it is reason enough for concentrating on certain aspects even if this involves neglecting such interesting alternative themes as theoretical advance itself.

That this book is an introduction has two aspects. The theorising by which different aspects of economic theory are brought together requires a deeper knowledge of economic theory than can be conveyed in an introduction. A convincing exposition also often requires a more mathematical treatment than is appropriate for nearly all historians. Secondly, the value of such advanced theory, other than as part of a training in clear thinking, is mostly in facilitating conceptualisation of economic problems, in helping us to see an economy as a set of interrelationships. This we have tried to do as we expounded historical analyses employing economic theory, in a manner which might be primitive but which goes well beyond the standards of everyday journalism (and some more exalted places). This book alone does not confer a mastery of higher economic theory but use of its content in historical inquiry will induce an appreciation of the possible usefulness of more advanced theory and perhaps even a gradual acquisition of deeper economic understanding.

Our posture, however, is not entirely defensive. There is no doubt that major gains in economic theory come from bringing under a single umbrella what start as distinct conclusions; the unifying or generalising role of theory is important. But it would be easy to exaggerate the coherence of economic theory as a whole.

Many economists like to think of theoretical economics as proceeding in a 'scientific' way, because personal preferences and beliefs are subjugated and because its advance proceeds in the same way as scientific theories. For many people, not only economists, that means mostly the methods of theoretical physics with perhaps a little chemistry as well.

It is nowadays fashionable in the 'hard sciences' to think of theoretical advances in terms of the 'methodology of scientific research programmes'.[1] Briefly, this suggests that theoretical advances come in clusters, each one being identified as a 'scientific research programme'. A new hypothesis suggests a whole line of inquiry and if that explains a number of empirical observations that were not readily compatible with earlier hypotheses, the new research programme gains adherents and becomes orthodox belief. It may not explain all known facts, but even if these cannot be dismissed as erroneous or misunderstood, the research programme continues while minor adjustments are sought to render the anomalies compatible with the new theory. Over time, the central idea of the new programme, its positive heuristic, gathers an accretion of secondary hypotheses, the protective belt, so that the anomalous observations do not seem to contradict the overall theory. But if continued work on the programme should cease supplying explanations for new empirical knowledge, the field of inquiry becomes ripe for a new research programme.

This conceptualisation of theoretical advance has greatly enlivened methodological discussions. It has brought together what had become the nearly separate areas of tracing the chronology of theoretical advances and justifying the results of theoretical works. (It had become customary to think of the sources of hypotheses as irrelevant, and while this was – and is – appropriate when trying to show logically that a line of argument was consistent and compatible with empirical observation, it made it difficult to link one hypothesis with another.) The more recent approach has led to clarification of many notions such as the somewhat pejorative term, 'ad hoc', much employed by economists. Economists usually use this to mean something like 'produced out of a hat', or a *deus ex machina* justified by the results produced, but philosophers now find it useful to distinguish at least three meanings. An ad hoc hypothesis may be one explaining a particular observation but adding nothing to earlier hypotheses; or a hypothesis which explains an observation but has no implications for any observations other than that for whose explanation it was consciously formulated;[2] or a hypothesis which explains some observations, including perhaps new observations, but which is inconsistent with the positive heuristic of the prevailing research programme. The economists' use of the term is usually in the first of these senses but may overlap several of them.

Furthermore, the methodology outlined here has proved useful in explorations of specific cases of one scientific theory prevailing over another. It remains a conceptualisation or, in Lakatos's phrase, a 'rational reconstruction' rather than an established explanation of theoretical change – not only because historians of science are as unable as any other historians to reach finality but also because much can depend on the identification of what constitutes a specific scientific research programme. Major advances lead to subsidiary results, but a shift from one positive heuristic to another is never a simple matter of observation.

This is even more true of economic theory. It is possible in retrospect to identify some major shifts in the focus of attention of economic theorists, the marginalist revolution of the late nineteenth century and the Keynesian concentration on short-run aggregate changes in the 1930s being the most obvious examples. But these represent changes of question at least as much as superior explanations of the same observations. In physics we think, perhaps simplistically, of a hypothesis proposed to explain one observation which is shown to imply the existence of 'quarks', of this being followed by an empirical observation of quarks, and so on. 'Anomalies' are also found, and these are either fitted in or eventually a different hypothesis is constructed. We cannot think of analogous processes being as important in economics.[3] We think rather of the problem of short-run income determination giving way to means of stimulating economic growth in poor countries and of whether a 'steady state' of growth is compatible with various kinds of savings behaviours and technical change. Economics is simply less coherent than physical sciences even if the latter are less tidy than is realised by many laymen (and some scientists).

It has often been observed that economists have less control over their raw material than physicists, and even if the popular notion of scientists repeating experiments and ensuring that they isolate the effects of one change is exaggerated, there is a significant difference in this respect. The more important aspect is not that economists have to accept less accuracy in empirical observation, important though that is, but that what they observe is likely to vary in time and place. The savings behaviour of one economy can differ between periods; savings behaviour in two economies can be markedly different. The assumptions on which an appropriate theory should be based will therefore be different, depending on where it is to be used. A major advance in conceptualisation in one context may leave the earlier formulation as the better hypothesis in another. A switch from one positive heuristic to another will never be as complete as in the physical sciences.

By this indirect route we come back to the proposition that the coherence of economic theory is not of great relevance to those like historians who are concerned with explaining empirical observations. They must select those parts of the theory which can explain features of empirical reality with which they are concerned. It is advantageous to have as broad a knowledge of economics as possible, so as to increase the range of material which can be drawn on. But historians will still draw selectively, and treat economic theory as an available 'bag of tricks' rather than a coherent body of knowledge.

Economics in history

Because both economics and history are diverse fields, it is not easy to summarise the ways in which historians can benefit from economic theory. The previous chapters have illustrated gains of various kinds and these can be categorised under the following headings, which, however, should not be regarded as mutually exclusive: advantages of economic terminology, use of theoretical tautologies, the use of near-tautologies which have explanatory power, the revelation of oversimplification, and the employment of theory to relate what might otherwise appear as self-contained elements of an economy.

Mere terminology can be useful. We have already conceded that many complaints about jargon are justified even though we are nearly always tolerant of familiar jargon and critical of somebody else's shorthand expressions. A writer can convey his meaning to a reader more easily if both parties understand certain key words to have a precise meaning. *Investment* can extend to all kinds of transactions in everyday language, but its reservation for the more specific economic sense of the creation of an income-earning asset, the sacrificing of present consumption in expectation of greater future consumption, does a great deal to clarify historical issues too. For any individual in the eighteenth century the purchase of land might well be an investment. But for every purchaser of an established estate there must be a seller, and for the community as a whole the purchase of land is not an investment. It is therefore misleading to treat it as an alternative to financing new machinery or buildings. (This is especially so if we believe that land was sold only to meet debts incurred by consumption expenditure, so that we cannot see the purchase of land as enabling the seller to finance investment.) There are, of course, many reasons why we may be interested in the structure of land ownership in the eighteenth century; the point here is only that transactions in existing assets should not be confused with investment when we are concerned with the community as a whole, even though from the point of view of an individual, land might compete with other uses of surplus funds.[4] The point applies to all kinds of assets, such as existing buildings or company shares, but land is likely to loom large in historical studies.

In some cases the issue might be slightly different. In nineteenth-century New Zealand, for example (and to some extent the United States too), land ownership was concentrated in the hands of the government. Whether or not land purchases led to investment depended on the use the government made of the funds received from land sales. If they financed railway building, the land sales could be said to result in investment; if, however, they financed the day-to-day administrative expenses of the government, the land sales could not be related directly to investment. Some cases are less clear-cut. Government revenue financed assisted immigrants and it might be thought that this was similar to administrative expenses; the government paid transport costs for people, an item in the current account of the balance of payments not obviously related to investment. But if the relevant immigrants had particular skills, so that their arrival could be expected to raise per capita output for the economy as a whole, the fares paid by the government could be interpreted as an investment in the human capital invested in them.[5] It requires historical skills to evaluate these possibilities, but there is one common theme; whether or not the land sales can be directly related to investment depends crucially on what recipients of receipts from them did, and not on the transfer of ownership of the land itself. Adherence to economic terminology promotes the depth of historical thought and understanding.[6]

Perhaps the most common use of economic theory in history is the employment of tautologies[7] created in the former as frameworks for analysis in the latter. The relation of income to land, labour, and capital, and the explanation of relative prices and quantities by supply and demand are two most common examples. Much of economic theory is simply the working out of the implications of these conceptions and contributes to a fully controlled employment of them in particular settings, historical or not. We have explored both in this book, and repeat only that supply and demand analysis is far from a sterile preoccupation with unrealistic consumers and producers. If we are intrigued by the way in which English towns adopted street lighting in the seventeenth and eighteenth centuries, the dichotomy of supply and demand is the natural starting point.[8] Did the values placed by society or its decision makers on light increase? Did it become cheaper to provide lighting? And so on. Perhaps an even more striking example for historians is the usefulness of the same apparatus for understanding the disruption of the lead market when the dissolution of the monasteries involved a revaluation of ecclesiastical buildings; their roofs ceased to be a final product and became a natural resource mine with the textbook results of an increase in supply.[9]

The third use of economic theory which we distinguished is the employment of sets of assumptions and their implications which are still very simple but which have many fields of application. These are the constructs which open up fields of economic theorising, and which in retrospect come to appear self-evident but are a little further removed from tautology than the ideas we have just discussed. With sufficient understanding, they are recognised as means of giving depth to analysis, not mere artificial abstractions of interest to mathematicians rather than historians. Into this category fall the ideas of comparative advantage of Chapter 7 (which deepen understanding of specialisation) and the multiplier of Chapter 4 (which generates comprehension of the circular flow of income and so of the notion of an economy itself). Again, it is important not to be misled by the language in which they are usually introduced. The multiplier is most easily explained in the context of an economy without government operations or foreign trade, but this is for convenience of exposition only. The multiplier concept is a key to understanding the evolution of the British economy under the influence of the government's decision to separate sterling from the gold standard.[10]

Our next use of economic theory was expressed as the detection of oversimplification. That may seem paradoxical because many historians associate economic theory with oversimplified assumptions. The charge is mistaken, except that economic theory, like other scholarly tools, can be misapplied. A more sophisticated point is that empirical studies can reveal oversimplification in theoretical constructions. So they can, but the converse is also true. More generally, simplicity is desirable but oversimplification is misleading, and scholarly efforts of all kinds are properly devoted to locating where one turns into the other. Chapter 8 gave examples of how theory helps to locate oversimplification in common linkages of investment to growth and in terms like *labour saving* which are widely used by historians. It is often possible to show that while a historical observation might indeed result from some particular set of circumstances, it is also consistent with a quite different set and further work is needed to decide which was the case in history. For example, we can observe falling wheat yields in medieval England. This could be consistent with the existence of a Malthusian crisis, with wheat growing pressing against diminishing returns as population expanded. But it would be at best premature to deduce from the observation that such a situation existed. It might be that real incomes were rising and that the income elasticity of demand for meat exceeded that for cereals, so that farmers with an eye on market trends realised that the prospects for pastoral production were better than those for wheat farming. They therefore planted wheat on inferior land and reserved more fertile areas for grass on which cattle or sheep were raised. The wheat yields fell not because of any crisis but because of the growing prosperity of the community.[11] The direct linking of wheat yields to crisis is an oversimplification possibly leading to error. Economic theory, often as primitive as in this example, is useful in identifying and rectifying such slips in historical arguments.

Finally, we come to what might be regarded as the most glamorous use of theory, the value of links established and explored theoretically to relate different variables that enter a historical analysis. The equalities of marginal costs and prices in certain circumstances, and the dual relationships between prices and quantities in such contexts as the movement of productivity are only the most common of a wide range of theoretical relationships used in economic history even when we try to leave on one side as applied economics those studies concerned with very recent years. This use of economics is often associated with more technical writing, inasmuch as elucidation of links between variables is done most succinctly in mathematical language. It is difficult to think of any recent development in economic theory which is not likely to have some applicability to history. While such analysis requires more knowledge of economics than can be gained from one book, we have given examples of the significance of relating things which are often left distinct. Chapter 5 noted interconnections between institutions and aggregate income trends through the financial system, while Chapter 7 argued the importance of seeing capital exports in the context of an economy as a whole.[12]

Even if all this is accepted, we may still wonder whether there is anything which can be gained only from a knowledge of economics. The historical analyses still rely on the techniques of gathering empirical information together with the processes of standard logic. (They need not be in that order; some guide is needed to what empirical information should be sought.) There is validity in the suggestion that economics can be bypassed. But it is not of much substance. Any theoretical construct can be built again from first principles, but to do so wastes time and effort just as it does if a historian ignores all secondary sources and reproduces work on the primary materials.

There can be no doubt that our understanding of history has been advanced by writers using economic theory. (Increasingly, this is true also of other kinds of theory such as that of anthropology.[13]) Each individual step may be small, but our overall assessments of events like the Industrial Revolution or the course of the British economy in the late nineteenth century are now very different from what was orthodox before writers reexamined them in the light of economic theory. Each step needs assessment of the theory employed and examination of a more traditional kind, but no historian can ignore the modern advances and remain at the frontier of knowledge. Competence in economics can be acquired in many ways, and it is indispensable.

Historical periods

It may be objected that even if the example of the late Victorian economy is not unique, we have concentrated unduly on the recent past. It is true that the role of economic theory is more obvious in the history of the nineteenth and twentieth centuries than it is in earlier ages. Economic theory is mostly the creation of the nineteenth and twentieth centuries and many theoretical constructions have taken their course from a starting point of observation of an economy within that period.[14] Furthermore, in the last 200 years, economic questions, those things about which economists were speculating, have become more prominent in the public questions with which statesmen and politicians were concerned. The franchise, Ireland, and foreign policy, which dominated contemporary thought in the nineteenth century and so attracted the attention of historians, all gained a more substantial economic component than the equivalent issues of many earlier ages. The acceptance by governments from about the 1930s of responsibility for the course of the economy was merely another step, albeit an important one, in the same direction.

This does not imply that economic theory is useful only to the historian of the nineteenth and twentieth centuries. Economic questions of a modern kind can be asked about earlier periods. Economic change was proceeding in any period studied by historians and in those usually left to classicists and archaeologists. This is a sufficient reason for expecting economic theory to be useful, but even if change were not proceeding, a historian might be interested in the relationship of one variable to another. We have used several examples for the eighteenth century in the preceding chapters; we have made no conscious attempt to gain chronological spread or we would have referred to analysis of the trade of the Roman Empire in terms of comparative advantage.

Nevertheless, there are differences in the use of economics as we go backwards in time. We can certainly ask the same questions as we do of a more recent economy; it may be difficult to find the information needed to answer them, but there is no methodological difference. However, whereas those questions were asked by people living in the nineteenth and twentieth centuries, increasingly sharpened and deepened by theoretical thought but still of a kind that would be recognisable to contemporaries, this is less true in earlier ages. The notion of foreign trade and prices in *all* markets being linked would not have occurred to most people in the eighteenth century; the idea of governments being concerned with the course of aggregate income even when the latter term was (tediously) translated into more everyday language would not have been apparent either. Historians anxious to comprehend what was interesting to contemporaries will find less and less in common with economic theory as they deal with periods increasingly distant in time.

This does not mean that they can disregard economic theory with impunity. Our emphasis has consistently been that economic theory has to be used, and few historians are content with discovering what contemporaries were thinking about; they want to know how accurately contemporaries perceived what was going on around them. Any inquiry into economic change or balance of forces can benefit from economic theory when it is appropriately and selectively used. We study the processes of the labour market in the fourteenth century in exactly the way we study a modern market when we wonder whether it cleared efficiently. Clearly, it would be foolish to assume uncritically that in the fourteenth century a sudden reduction in the labour supply would be followed by a smooth rise in wages, but so it would be to assume that market prices always equal equilibrium prices in a modern economy. The speed and degree of market clearing can vary, as we discussed in Chapter 6. It would, of course, be equally foolish to assume uncritically that an imbalance in the supply and demand for labour at any time will not affect the level of wages.

These points are neatly illustrated in a recent study of the Hundred Years' War.[15] Bridbury argues forcefully and cogently that in the medieval economy, war was not a diversion but that its adventure and discipline were essential parts of political life. (We might wonder whether the difference in modern times is as great as he suggests.) But he goes on to deduce from that proposition that any attempt to use opportunity cost concepts in relation to the resources appropriated to the Hundred Years' War is misguided, and that deduction is incorrect. It would indeed be misguided to develop some arguments on the basis of such studies. We could not infer that if the decision makers had known what income they could derive from other uses of the resources devoted to the war, they either would, or should, have chosen a different use of them. But that is no reason why we should not enrich our knowledge of the historical event by inquiring how much the war cost, measuring that by what the resources used for war could have produced had they been used, for whatever reason, for other purposes. There is no conflict between such an inquiry and Bridbury's characterisation of medieval attitudes.

It is worth noting too that Bridbury employs economic theory in the course of his argument. He uses supply and demand concepts, such as we have introduced in Chapters 6, 7, and 9, in looking at the incidence of war costs and arguing that export taxes fell on foreigners and 'subsidies' on tenants or landowners. He rightly judges that the question of the clearing of medieval markets is not crucial to his argument, and the whole paper is an interesting demonstration of an intelligent drawing on those parts of theory which are relevant to his purposes.

Bridbury's interest is within what can be called economic history. The relevance of economics to 'mainstream' history before the nineteenth century is, however, easily demonstrated. We need to look only at the treatment of the early modern period by historians of such diverse viewpoints as Elton and Hill, noting first their explicit attention to economic phenomena and then the way in which their accounts in general are more easily understood with some elementary economics. We think especially of the price movements discussed by Elton and of the treatment of monopoly by Hill.[16] We can indeed follow these discussions without any economic theory, but depth of understanding follows from a greater acquaintance with the concepts on which they draw either implicitly or explicitly. It is depth of understanding which is the most important contribution of economic theory to historians.

Notice, finally, how the analysis of particular historical events often draws widely on economic theory. Bridbury's paper has been discussed in relation to both basic income and supply and demand concepts. Although we have looked for variety in the examples used throughout the book, we have often returned to the late Victorian economy and to the Industrial Revolution in order to show how many parts of theory combine in the exploration of particular historical problems. In the former, for example, we saw the need to see any part of the economy in the context of the whole in Chapter 3, the development of this in terms of income elasticities in Chapter 6, the intensification of this by considering specialisation in Chapter 7, the links between different aspects of capital exports in the same chapter, and the significance of investment in Chapter 8. Consideration of the Industrial Revolution is similarly spread through the book. Any major historical topic is likely to involve many aspects of theory and the historian needs an alertness to recognise them just as he needs alertness to appreciate the significance of documentary sources.

Conclusion

Historians need much more than a knowledge of economic theory, but they need to know some economics and the more they know the better equipped they are. They need to use economic theory rather than to expect any instant solutions.

Many historians doubt the value of economic theory. But it is difficult to think of one familiar with economics who does not find it useful; nor is it likely – at least not until economic theory becomes so well-known that its distinctive contribution is difficult to recognise.

Notes

Chapter 1

1. Joan Robinson and John Eatwell, *An Introduction to Modern Economics* (Maidenhead: McGraw-Hill, rev. ed., 1974).
2. P. A. Samuelson, *Economics*, numerous editions and adaptations to particular countries.
3. See especially John Hicks, *Economic Perspectives* (Oxford: Clarendon Press, 1977).
4. The methodological literature associated especially with I. Lakatos is discussed a little further in Chapter 10.
5. That this is not a farfetched example is shown by the study of the Hundred Years' War by A. R. Bridbury, which is discussed in Chapter 10.
6. One might think that other differences will also have an impact; there are, for example, national differences in importance attached to documentation and to the use of original sources.
7. W. H. B. Court, *Scarcity and Choice in History* (London: Arnold, 1970), p. 151.
8. L. Robbins, *An Essay on the Nature and Significance of Economic Science* (London: Macmillan, 1932).
9. A. Marshall, *Principles of Economics* (London: Macmillan, 8th ed., 1961), p. 1.
10. A. C. Pigou, *Economics of Welfare* (London: Macmillan, 4th ed., 1960), p. 11.
11. The basic notions are introduced in Chapter 7.
12. Introduced in Chapter 3.
13. For example, H. D. Henderson, *Supply and Demand* (Cambridge: Cambridge University Press, 1940), p. v.
14. The different meanings of rationality complicate efforts to find common ground between economics and psychology. Compare with T. Scitovsky, *The Joyless Economy* (Palo Alto: Stanford University Press, 1976). See also A. W. Coats, 'Economics and Psychology: the death and resurrection of a research programme', and H. A. Simon, 'From Substantive to Procedural Rationality', both in S. Latsis (ed.), *Method and Appraisal in Economics* (Cambridge: Cambridge University Press, 1976).

15. D. N. McCloskey and L. G. Sandberg, 'From Damnation to Redemption: Judgments on the late Victorian Entrepreneur', *Explorations in Economic History*, 9 (1971), pp. 89–108; L. G. Sandberg, Ch. 19 of R. C. Floud and D. N. McCloskey (eds.), *A New Economic History of Britain Since 1750* (Cambridge: Cambridge University Press, forthcoming).

16. There has recently been some revival of the terms *catallactics* and *plutology* for these constellations, and the terms are useful even if they are not readily committed to memory. They are merely names for strands in economic thinking, and while those strands play some role in the organisation of this book, the names are not at all important. For the revival of the terms, see J. R. Hicks, ' "Revolutions" in Economics' in S. Latsis (ed.), *Method and Appraisal in Economics*, and 'The Scope and Status of Welfare Economics', *Oxford Econ. Pap.*, N.S. 27 (1975), pp. 307–26.

17. This book is intended to be virtually self-contained, but readers may find some consolation in the fact that surveys of readers of professional economic journals nearly always produce the lament that too much mathematics is contained in them. We all sometimes wish that mathematical techniques remained static at the point reached in our own student days.

18. J. H. Clapham, 'Economic History as a Discipline', *Encyclopaedia of the Social Sciences*, Vol. V (New York: Macmillan, 1930), reprinted in F. Lane and J. Riemersma (eds.), *Enterprise and Secular Change* (London: Allen & Unwin, 1953), p. 416.

19. R. C. Floud, *An Introduction to Quantitative Methods for Historians* (London: Methuen, 1973).

20. R. C. Floud and D. N. McCloskey (eds.), *A New Economic History of Britain since 1750* (Cambridge University Press, forthcoming).

21. D. H. Aldcroft, *From Versailles to Wall Street*, (London: Allen Lane, 1976).

Chapter 2

1. Historians may well come across cases where misunderstanding of this simple definitional point has some political significance. The Douglas Credit movement of the 1930s, with political importance especially in Canada and New Zealand but also in other countries, began from a misconceived 'gap' between income and output.

2. For a useful discussion of the index number problem see R. C. Floud, *An Introduction to Quantitative Methods for Historians* (London: Methuen, 1973), pp. 118–24.

3. See Fig. 3.2.

4. Not all countries adhere to this convention.

5. The shape of the curve is not important for the argument here, but it is significant later, and the curvature shown in the diagram is readily explained. It follows from the likelihood that some of the

resources of the economy will be better suited to the production of one good than to the other. As the economy concentrates on producing *M* for example, the resources got by shifting them from the production of *W* will be increasingly ill-adapted to the production of *M*. That explains the curvature of *QP* as we move along the horizontal axis. A similar argument explains the curvature as we consider the economy choosing outputs of which *W* constitutes an increasing share and thus the curvature of *QP* as we move along the vertical axis. The shape of the production possibilities curve – 'convex as shown from above' or, what is the same thing, 'concave as viewed from the origin 0' – is a general expectation, not an invariable rule. We may well be concerned with a particular 'economy' in which all the resources are equally good at producing the relevant goods; the production possibility curve is then a straight line.

6. A movement towards the frontier is now sometimes referred to as a gain in *X* efficiency. This is actually a gross simplification of a distinction introduced by H. Leibenstein, who distinguished two classes of reasons why an economy might operate inside the production possibilities frontier: (1) Distortions which prevented people and firms from allocating resources to their most efficient possible use such as barriers to price movements; these matters, in Leibenstein's terminology, affect 'allocative' efficiency. (2) All other reasons, and these affect *X* efficiency. '*X*', the usual algebraic symbol for an 'unknown', quite deliberately reflects the more limited understanding that can be derived from orthodox economics.

7. We follow the general lines of the accounts most likely to be used by historians in C. H. Feinstein, *National Income, Expenditure and Output of the United Kingdom, 1855–1965* (Cambridge: Cambridge University Press, 1972). The best simple introduction to national income accounting is J. R. Hicks, *The Social Framework* (Oxford: Clarendon Press, 4th ed., 1971), Chapters XIV, XX, and XXI.

8. See also Chapter 9.

9. The reader will recall that the distinction between a final and an intermediate demand is not always self-evident.

10. Compare, for example, H. U. Faulkner, *American Economic History* (New York: Harper, 8th ed., 1960), p. 395 and L. Davis, R. A. Easterlin and W. N. Parker (eds.), *American Economic Growth* (New York: Harper & Row, 1972), p. 433.

11. G. N. von Tunzelmann, 'Britain's New Industries between the Wars: A New "Development Block"?', paper presented to Warwick cliometrics conference, January, 1978.

12. It is not only in historical studies that care is needed. It is common to compare the sales of large multinational companies with the income of poorer countries. This can be a useful scaling device, but it can be misleading if the difference between the income and the total sales of an economy is forgotten.

13. Namely, G. R. Hawke, *The Development of the British Economy*, (Auckland: Heinemann, 1970); C. K. Harley in Floud and McClos-

218 Notes to pp. 35–46

key, *New Economic History*. We return to this example later, but it would be a useful exercise for readers to use Table 2 to see if they can translate these statements into an input–output format.
14. S. Kuznets, *Modern Economic Growth* (New Haven: Yale University Press, 1966); C. H. Feinstein, *National Income and Expenditure of the United Kingdom* (Cambridge: Cambridge University Press, 1972); N. Butlin, *Australian Domestic Product, Investment and Foreign Borrowing* (Cambridge: Cambridge University Press, 1962).
15. See, for example, E. L. Jones and C. O'Grada in Floud and McCloskey, *New Economic History*.
16. See Chapter 8.

Chapter 3

1. We use *tautology* and *tautological* in the sense of self-evident truth rather than of unnecessary repetition. Economists might prefer the mathematical term *identity*, but that is less common and often thought to refer only to expressions involving mathematical symbols.
2. Readers should now be able to reconstruct the argument for themselves. As the extensive margin is moved, the income that a tenant farmer could gain by going on to land outside the margin must fall. Rent on all intramarginal land is therefore raised, as is the proportion of rent to total produce. (For readers accustomed to absorbing historical narrative before reflecting on it, this exemplifies an instance where the slower and more active reading style is often better suited to economics. The two styles do, of course, come together eventually.)
3. A. Fishlow, *American Railroads and the Transformation of the Ante-Bellum Economy* (Cambridge, Mass.: Harvard University Press, 1965), pp. 40–52; R. Fogel, *Railroads and American Economic Growth* (Baltimore: Johns Hopkins University Press, 1964), pp. 53–5, 214–16; P. K. O'Brien, *The New Economic History of the Railways* (London: Croom Helm, 1977) pp. 48, 107–9.
4. Recent and sophisticated studies do indicate that more narrowly conceived economic explanations may be more potent than has been thought. See P. H. Lindert, 'American Fertility Patterns since the Civil War', in R. D. Lee (ed.), *Population Patterns in the Past* (New York: Academic Press, 1977), pp. 229–76.
5. All these points can be found in any competent study of eighteenth-century English population history. A convenient theoretical source is H. Leibenstein, *Economic Backwardness and Economic Growth* (New York: Wiley, 1957), while J. Simon, *The Economics of Population* (Princeton: Princeton University Press, 1977), illustrates the way in which historical and theoretical treatments converge in this area.
6. This somewhat convoluted formulation is convenient here, and also serves to relate employment to the earlier discussion of opportunity cost. Notice the formal identity of the work–leisure choice with that between two goods.

7. It is more conventional to relate the supply of labour to the wage rate, but the essential points are unchanged. For reasons explained in Chapter 6, the price – the wage rate – is often put on the vertical axis and the labour supply on the horizontal. The backward bending curve then bends towards the vertical axis. Again, the argument is unaffected.

8. See, for example, E. K. Fisk, 'Planning in a Primitive Economy: From Pure Subsistence to the Production of a Market Surplus', *Econ. Rec.* 48 (June 1964), pp. 156–74.

9. M. A. Bienefeld, *Working Hours in British Industry: An Economic History* (London: Weidenfeld & Nicolson, 1972).

10. J. R. Hicks, *Economic Perspectives* (Oxford: Clarendon Press, 1977), Ch. VII.

11. See also the discussion of the stock exchange in the section, Non-bank financial institutions of Chapter 5.

12. L. Davis, 'The Investment Market, 1870–1914: The Evolution of a National Market,' *Jour. Econ. Hist.* 25 (1965) pp. 355–99; R. Sylla, 'American Banking and Growth in the Nineteenth Century: A Partial View of the Terrain', *Expl. in Econ. Hist.* 9 (1971–2) pp. 197–228; R. Sylla, 'Financial Intermediaries in Economic History; Quantitative Research on the Seminal Hypotheses of Lance Davis and Alexander Gerschenkron', in *Research in Economic History*, Supplement 1 (Greenwich, Conn.: J.A.I. Press, 1977).

13. L. S. Pressnell, *Country Banking in the Industrial Revolution* (Oxford: Clarendon Press, 1956).

14. For example, Rhodes Boyson, *The Ashworth Cotton Enterprise* (Oxford: Clarendon Press, 1970), pp. 18, 29ff. For a case where new entrants could be excluded, see D. C. Coleman, *Courtaulds: An Economic and Social History* (Oxford: Clarendon Press, 1969), Vol. II. Compare also F. Crouzet (ed.), *Capital Formation in the Industrial Revolution* (London: Methuen, 1972), pp. 195–203.

15. M. Palairet, 'Merchant Enterprise and the Development of the Plum-based Trades in Serbia, 1847–1911', *Econ. Hist. Rev.*, Sec. Ser., 30 (1977), p. 590.

16. This is the meaning of '*f*' in the following equation. It denotes a 'functional' relationship between the left-hand side of the equation and the variables within the brackets.

17. For nonmathematical readers it will be sufficient to read this as 'a particular form of relationship between income and the factors of labour and capital'. The same applies to the next equation in the text; α is a parameter, and in any particular case it will have a numerical value. It might be 0.5, for example, in which case $Y = L^{0.5} K^{0.5}$, or it might be 0.7, in which case $Y = L^{0.7} K^{0.3}$.

18. This is expressed intuitively rather than rigorously, since we have evaded the question of the units in which L and K (and Y) are measured.

19. The elasticity of substitution is a measure of the response in the use of labour and capital to the relative price of those factors. For present purpose it may be read as a measure of the flexibility with

which labour and capital can be interchanged. For the Cobb–Douglas function it is one so that the economy can respond 'fully' to a change in the relative prices of labour and capital, and it is this rather than the mere number of available combinations which is the important feature. Those who go on to more advanced texts will find it possible to rewrite this section much more rigorously.

20. Although only simple mathematics is involved, some readers will have to take the assertions of this section on trust. Those who insert some numbers in place of the algebraic symbols will readily verify the assertions, but then they will probably regard them as obvious anyway. The concept of returns to scale is so important to historians, however, that a reasonably precise statement of it is necessary.

21. R. Moorsteen and R. P. Powell *The Soviet Capital Stock, 1928–1962* (Homewood, Ill.: Irwin, 1966).

22. Σ (sigma) is a convenient symbol for 'the sum of'.

$$\sum_{i=1}^{n} Z_i = Z_1 + Z_2 + Z_3 + \cdots + Z_n \qquad \sum_{i=1}^{n} a_i b_i = a_1 b_1 + a_2 b_2 + \cdots + a_n b_n$$

Where there is no danger of confusion, the subscripts and superscripts are often omitted from the summation sign. Similarly, Δ (delta) is the conventional symbol for 'the change in'. Thus, $\Delta I = I_1 - I_0$

23. The reasons for this are explained in note 17 to Chapter 8.

24. See M. Abramovitz, *Resource and Output Trends in the United States since 1870* (New York: NBER, 1956).

25. M. Abramovitz and P. A. David, 'Reinterpreting Economic Growth: Parables and Realities', *Amer. Econ. Rev. Pap. & Proc.* 63 (May 1973), pp. 428–49.

26. A. Bergson and S. Kuznets, *Economic Trends in the Soviet Union* (Cambridge, Mass.: Harvard University Press, 1963); Moorsteen and Powell, *Soviet Capital Stock*.

27. R. C. Floud and D. N. McCloskey (eds.), *A New Economic History of Britain* (Cambridge: Cambridge University Press, forthcoming), Chapters 1, 4, 7, 10, 15, and 24.

28. D. H. Aldcroft, *From Versailles to Wall Street* (London: Allen Lane, 1976).

Chapter 4

1. J. M. Keynes, *General Theory of Employment, Interest and Money* (London: Macmillan, 1936).

2. J. R. T. Hughes, *Fluctuations in Trade, Industry and Finance* (Oxford: Clarendon Press, 1960).

3. A convenient exposition against which the reader can check this assertion is Michael Stewart, *The Jekyll and Hyde Years: Politics and Economic Policy since 1964* (London: Dent, 1977).

4. *Ex post* = after the event, realised; *ex ante* = before the event, anticipated, desired. Latin tags now part of the profession's jargon.
5. We use linear functions for simplicity. All that is required is that the marginal propensities to consume and save are each less than 1. The constants merely place the straight line functions on the graph. For example, in Fig. 4.1 C is positive when $Y = 0$; therefore a' is positive and a is negative.
6. Thomas in Floud and McCloskey.
7. As any series such as $1, a, a^2, a^3, \ldots$ is called. [Any student mathematical text will show that the sum of the first n terms is $(1 - a^n)$ $/(1 - a)$ and that this approaches $1/(1 - a)$ as the number of terms becomes infinitely large.] Then $\Delta Y = \Delta I \,(1 + c + c^2 + \ldots)$ and hence the earlier formula is immediately derived.
8. $\Delta Y = 1/[1 - c(1 - t) + m] \,\Delta A$. The marginal tax rate is t and other symbols are as before.
9. J. R. Hicks, *Contribution to the Theory of the Trade Cycle* (Oxford: Clarendon Press, 1950). We deal with a much simplified analysis here.
10. But see Thomas in Floud and McCloskey; and on late nineteenth-century America, J. G. Williamson, *Late Nineteenth-Century American Development: A General Equilibrium History* (Cambridge: Cambridge University Press, 1974).
11. For example, in Britain, A. D. Gayer, W. W. Rostow, and A. J. Schwartz, *The Growth and Fluctuations of the British Economy, 1790–1850,* (Hassocks: Harvester, 2nd ed., 1975); R. C. O. Matthews, *A Study in Trade Cycle History* (Cambridge: Cambridge University Press, 1954); J. R. T. Hughes, *Fluctuations;* Ford in Floud and McCloskey.
12. J. R. Meyer, 'An Input–Output Approach to Estimating British Industrial Production in the Nineteenth Century', in A. H. Conrad and J. R. Meyer, *Studies in Econometric History* (London: Chapman & Hall, 1965).
13. W. A. Sinclair, *The Process of Economic Growth in Australia,* (Melbourne: Cheshire, 1976); C. G. Simkin, *The Instability of a Dependent Economy* (Oxford: Clarendon Press, 1951); G. R. Hawke, 'The Government and the Depression of the 1930s in New Zealand', *Aust. Econ. Hist. Rev.* 13 (1973), pp. 72–95.
14. This is simply the first equation of the second section (multipliers) of this chapter, except that more of the aggregates of national income accounting are distinguished. Compare with Chapter 2 (measurement procedures and problems). Y is income as before, I domestic investment, G government expenditure, X exports, and M imports. Total output is then $Z = (C - M) + G + X;$ M is subtracted to obtain consumption expenditure on domestically produced goods and services. Note that the simple formulation $Y = C + I$ does not necessarily imply that there is no government and no foreign trade; it implies that there is no significant difference between consumption expenditure by governments and individuals

and no significant difference between domestic investment and foreign investment ($=X-M$).
15. The immediate reference is to an impressive paper presented by G. Toniolo to a St Antony's Oxford seminar, but the points apply to many standard histories.

Chapter 5

1. In the sense of Chapter 2, that is, after allowing for price changes.
2. Such a bank is usually known as a *central* or *reserve bank*. The Bank of England occupies this position in Britain, although because of its historical development it is not a 'pure' example.
3. We have here to concede one advantage of the orthodox exposition. Governments wish to control bank *lending*, but reserve requirements are almost invariably stated as a ratio of *deposits*. This reflects the historical origin of reserves as the banks' precaution against being asked to return deposits in a nonbank currency such as gold. Reserves (as the word suggests) were assets held for this purpose and it was against deposits that they were assessed. We make this concession without reluctance as a demonstration of the usefulness of historical knowledge for understanding commercial terminology and of the existence even in academic writing of an opportunity cost of departure from the status quo. (See Table 3 for an explanation of why reserves against deposits and ratios of lending are interchangeable.)
4. P. Temin, *The Jacksonian Economy* (New York: Norton, 1969).
5. At a different level the word *bank* is redolent of wealth and security to many people and is sometimes used in the name of what is clearly an NFI. Some countries prohibit this except for savings banks. But the name of a financial firm is no guide to its status in the terms of our analysis.
6. After Irving Fisher, an American economist of the early twentieth century who did much to develop this analysis.
7. P. H. Ramsey (ed.), *The Price Revolution in Sixteenth-Century England* (London: Methuen, 1971). See also D. D. Flynn, 'A New Perspective on the Spanish Price Revolution: The Monetary Approach to the Balance of Payments', *Expl. Econ. Hist.* 15 (1978) pp. 388–406.
8. Because of its development by economists in Cambridge, England.
9. See G. R. Hawke, 'Estimating Income from Monetary Data: Further Explorations', *Rev. Income and Wealth* 21 (1975), pp. 301–7.
10. For example, M. Friedman and A. J. Schwartz, *A Monetary History of the United States 1867–1960* (Princeton: Princeton University Press, 1963).
11. Hence 'Hicksian cross', from its inventor, J. R. Hicks, in a paper reprinted as Chapter 7 of *Critical Essays in Monetary Theory* (Oxford: Clarendon Press, 1967).

12. J. R. Hicks, *Economic Perspectives* (Oxford: Clarendon Press, 1977), Ch. III.

Chapter 6

1. It will be noticed that in partial equilibrium the change in the price of one good is a change in its relative price, since all other prices remain constant. The focus is in fact on changes in relative prices as contrasted with the attention given to inflation in monetary economics. The best historical study for showing how relative prices are the key to analysis of a major issue is probably G. Hueckel's Chapter 4 of Floud and McCloskey (eds.), *New Economic History of Britain since 1750*.

2. Readers with any mathematical knowledge at all will notice that although we have spoken of price influencing the quantity demanded we have placed p on the vertical axis and q on the horizontal. This departure from the usual convention of placing the independent variable on the horizontal axis and the dependent variable on the vertical is traditional in economics, although only in the context of supply and demand diagrams. It is a minor irritant, too well established to be displaced.

3. That the curve should be a straight line, on the other hand, is a specific additional assumption. It is usually convenient and unimportant for theoretical issues, but as the discussion of Fig. 6.3 shows, it can be significant in empirical analysis.

4. The quotation is from A. Marshall, *Principles of Economics* (8th ed., 1920), p. 132. The best known scepticism is in G. J. Stigler, *The Theory of Price* (New York: Macmillan, 1952), pp. 43–4. See also D. N. McCloskey, *The Applied Theory of Price* (forthcoming). The last of these is probably the best text for those who wish to take the topics of this chapter on to the next stage of analysis.

5. Readers should check their understanding of the concept by working out why these curves cannot intersect. (Consider the point of intersection; each of the combinations on one curve must be judged equally satisfactory as that at the point of intersection. But so must each of those points on the other curve. Therefore the consumer must be indifferent between a pair of points, one on each curve, and the two curves must coincide.)

6. Note (and explore) the formal similarity between a budget constraint and a production possibility curve where the relevant resource is all equally good for producing either of the two outputs. Compare with note 5 in Chapter 2.

7. Economic theorists would indeed define e as $(-dq/q)/(dp/p)$, where dq and dp are the infinitesimal increments of elementary calculus. Many texts recommend the use of the average of q_1 and q_2 and the average of p_1 and p_2. The economic sense of this is not clear, and for changes that are not small we prefer to go straight to more advanced techniques as described in the text.

8. D. Alexander, *Retailing in England during the Industrial Revolution* (London: Athlone Press, 1970), p. 17.

9. The mathematics is not difficult, but requires elementary differential calculus to establish that the curve of part (b) of Fig. 6.3 has an equation of the form $q = kp^\alpha$, where α is the elasticity of demand and k is a constant. Taking logs then gives two simple equations in a and α from which we can calculate that $k = 240$, $\alpha = -2$, approximately.

10. The elasticity may be exactly unity throughout the curve. Such unit elasticity curves have the form $p \cdot q = a$ constant; that is, total receipts are the same whatever pair of price and quantity is chosen. In the form used in the preceding note, the equation is $q = k \cdot p^{-1}$.

11. It is then easier to describe one of the features of a good for which the demand curve is likely to be stable – that it is a good with low cross-elasticities of demand.

12. It is worth remarking that the direct link between income and price is used implicitly by those historians who seek to use single commodities as indicators of income trends. The first equation of this chapter can be written as $q_x = f(p_x, Y)$, the quantity of a good demanded depends on its price and on income, tastes being subsumed into the form of the function. If we have price and quantity information and knowledge of the form of the function, then we can estimate income trends. For a most interesting and unusually explicit use of this procedure, see J. de Vries, 'Barges and Capitalism. Passenger Transportation in the Dutch Economy, 1632–1839', *A. A. G. Bijdragen* 21 (1978), pp. 33–398.

13. It is a regular triangle only if the demand curve is linear, but it would exist with a different shape for any normal demand curve.

14. The historical significance of the elasticity of demand in the context is well shown in R. W. Fogel, 'Notes on the Social Saving Controversy', *Jour. Econ. Hist.* 39 (March 1979), pp. 1–54.

15. Again, it takes an additional and convenient assumption to make the curve a straight line.

16. For example, C. O'Grada, 'Supply Responsiveness in Irish Agriculture during the Nineteenth Century', *Econ. Hist. Rev.*, Sec. Ser., 28 (1975), pp. 32–7.

17. D. N. McCloskey, 'Britain's Loss from Foreign Industrialization: A Provisional Estimate', *Expl. Econ. Hist.* 8 (1970–1), pp. 141–52.

18. Compare with R. Perren, *The Meat Trade in Britain, 1840–1914* (London: Routledge & Kegan Paul, 1978), Ch. 10.

19. It is possible for curves as described to produce multiple equilibria – for example, wavelike curves – but such curiosa have played no part in economic history.

20. This term is intended in the everyday sense of a farm product like wheat rather than in the usual economic usage of 'good or service'.

21. R. W. Fogel and S. L. Engermann, 'A Model of Exploration of Industrial Expansion during the Nineteenth Century: With an Application to the American Iron Industry', in Fogel and Engermann

(eds.), *The Reinterpretation of American Economic History* (New York: Harper & Row, 1971), pp. 148–62.

22. M. M. Edwards, *The Growth of the British Cotton Trade, 1780–1815* (Manchester: Manchester University Press, 1967), pp. 126–7.

23. In the case of linear curves the slope of the *MR* curve is exactly twice that of the *AR* curve, and its intersection with the horizontal axis is halfway between the origin and the intersection with the same axis of the *AR* curve. Some readers may be able to check that this is consistent with the assertion already made that a linear demand curve changes from being elastic to inelastic at the point halfway between its intersections with the vertical and horizontal axes. Many such geometrical properties can be developed, but historians can safely assume that they will be explained as they become relevant.

24. P. Lindert and K. Trace, 'Yardsticks for Victorian Entrepreneurs' in D. N. McCloskey (ed.), *Essays on a Mature Economy: Britain after 1840* (London: Methuen, 1971), pp. 239–84.

Chapter 7

1. It is a nice linguistic point whether this is the usual economic sense or that of everyday language. (Compare with Chapter 1.) The two meanings come together here.

2. International trade theory makes considerable use of this schedule and it is therefore convenient to give it a label, the *offer curve*.

3. Note the formal similarity between this argument and that by which indifference curves were related to downward-sloping demand curves in Fig. 6.2.

4. For example, E. L. Jones, 'Environment, Agriculture and Industrialization in Europe', *Agricultural History* 51 (July 1977), pp. 491–502; Jones in Floud and McCloskey.

5. McCloskey in Floud and McCloskey.

6. It may be as well to point out that while the simple analysis neglects transport costs, there is no problem in incorporating them. Indeed in Fig. 7.6 we might regard the gap between the equilibrium prices in the two countries as resulting from transport costs rather than from a tariff. This makes the term *natural protection* more readily understood; it should also make it clear how the terms of trade of each of a pair of countries can 'improve' when transport costs decline, as was the case in the later nineteenth century.

7. This formula uses the values of inputs and outputs at world or free-trade prices. In many cases it is more convenient to use the prices of inputs and outputs after they have been adjusted to the tariff; these appear more directly in the historical record. If the use of components is unchanged except that some cost more than others because of differential tariffs, then a'_i, the input coefficients in posttariff prices, equal $a_i (1+t_i)/(1+t_j)$ and the alternative formula for e is

$$e = -1 + \frac{1 - \Sigma a'_i}{[1/(1+t_j)] - \Sigma[a'_i/(1+t_i)]}$$

8. G. R. Hawke, 'The U.S. Tariff and Industrial Protection',*Econ. Hist. Rev.*, Sec. Ser., 28 (1975), pp. 84–99.
9. For example, D. C. Coleman, *Courtaulds, An Economic and Social History* (Oxford: Clarendon Press, 1969), Vol. II, p. 117.
10. Forrest Capie, 'The British Tariff and Industrial Protection in the 1930s',*Econ. Hist. Rev.*, Sec. Ser., 31 (1978), pp. 399–409; see also S. B. Webb, 'Tariff Protection for the Iron Industry, Cotton Textiles and Agriculture in Germany, 1879–1914',*Jahr National Statistik* 192 (1977), pp. 336–57; G. Toniolo, 'Effective Protection and Industrial Growth: The Case of Italian Engineering, 1893–1913',*Jour. European Econ. Hist.* 6 (1977), pp. 659–74.
11. Compare with D. N. McCloskey and J. R. Zecher, 'How the Gold Standard Worked, 1880–1913', in J. A. Frenkel and H. G. Johnson (eds.), *The Monetary Approach to the Balance of Payments* (London: Allen & Unwin, 1976).
12. G. R. Hawke, 'The Government and the Depression of the 1930s in New Zealand. An Essay towards a Revision',*Aust. Econ. Hist. Rev.* 13 (1973), pp. 72–95; cf. C. P. Kindleberger, *The World in Depression, 1929–1939* (London: Allen Lane, 1973), p. 191.
13. A full account would reinstate a partial justification for this in that the total of savings may be responsive to the interest rate.
14. A. H. Imlah,*Economic Elements in the Pax Britannica* (New York: Russell & Russell, 1969); C. K. Harley in Floud and McCloskey.
15. For example, M. Simon in A. R. Hall (ed.), *The Export of Capital* (London: Methuen, 1968), pp. 15–44.
16. Again, an alternative story is available if we believe that markets were efficiently arbitraged and people were aiming to maintain a constant relationship between money and expenditure.
17. Exactly the same is true of 'home' and 'foreign' investment in other contexts such as Holland in the eighteenth century; cf. P. G. M. Dickson, *The Financial Revolution in England* (London: Macmillan, 1967), pp. 332–3, 337.

Chapter 8

1. Compare with J. D. Gould, *Economic Growth in History* (London: Methuen, 1972), pp. 2–5.
2. See J. C. H. Fei and G. Ranis, *Development of the Labor Surplus Economy* (Homewood, Ill.: Irwin, 1964). Figure 8.1 is adapted from their p. 202 but really goes back at least to W. A. Lewis 'Economic Development with Unlimited Supplies of Labour', *Manchester School* 22 (May 1954), pp. 139–91.
3. We pass over as too obvious for comment historical studies of peasant societies. But see note 8 to Chapter 3, and C. Newbury, 'Imperial History or Development History: Some reflections on Pacific Labour Markets in the Nineteenth Century', paper read to section 26, ANZAAS, Auckland, 1979.

4. See M. J. Daunton, 'Towns and Economic Growth in Eighteenth-Century England', in P. Abrams and E. A. Wrigley (eds.), *Towns in Societies: Essays in Economic History and Historical Sociology* (Cambridge: Cambridge University Press, 1978), especially pp. 252–5.

5. Crafts in Floud and McCloskey.

6. This has the advantage of showing that the existence of zero marginal productivity in the traditional activity is not crucial to the main discussion of Fig. 8.1 either.

7. W. Ashworth, 'Changes in Industrial Structure', *Yorks Bulletin*, 17 (May 1965), pp. 61–74. A more systematic approach is possible using the data of P. Deane and W. A. Cole, *British Economic Growth, 1688–1959* (Cambridge: Cambridge University Press, 2nd ed., 1969), pp. 142, 166, and it is the result of such an exercise which is reported in the text.

8. C. Clark, *Growthmanship: A Study in the Mythology of Investment* (London: IEA, 2nd ed., 1962).

9. S. Kuznets, *Modern Economic Growth* (New Haven: Yale University Press, 1966).

10. W. A. Lewis, *A Theory of Economic Growth* (London: Allen & Unwin, 1955).

11. Compare with R. M. Hartwell and S. Engerman, 'Models of Immiserization: the theoretical basis of pessimism', in A. J. Taylor (ed.), *The Standard of Living in Britain in the Industrial Revolution* (London: Methuen, 1975), especially pp. 196–9; Engerman and O'Brien in Floud and McCloskey.

12. W. W. Rostow, *British Economy in the Nineteenth Century* (Oxford: Clarendon Press, 1948).

13. R. C. O. Matthews, 'Some Aspects of Post-war Growth in the British Economy in Relation to Historical Experience', in R. C. Floud (ed.), *Essays in Quantitative Economic History*, (Oxford: Clarendon Press, 1974), pp. 228–47.

14. This section is inevitably among the more difficult in this book. The final conclusion is however both significant and simple and some perseverence will be rewarded, even if detailed points of argument seem obscure at first reading.

15. Some readers may see that this can be extended towards the concept of elasticity of substitution introduced earlier.

16. Because the price of labour is the wage rate, while the price of capital can be thought of as a rental on machines, the line is often known as the wage-rental frontier.

17. It is from this condition that wages should equal the marginal product of labour, and similarly for other factors, together with the particular form of a Cobb – Douglas production function, that we can sometimes derive 'correct' weights for productivity indices as discussed in Chapter 3.

18. This can best be shown by an extension of the diagram, but some readers may be able to see that it depends on the increase in capital per man, outweighing the decrease in output per capital; by analogy

with our discussion of a demand curve, this depends on the elasticity of the *Y/K* schedule. The price of capital is to *Y/K* as any marginal curve is to an average and the statement in the text follows directly (cf. Chapter 6, note 23.)

19. This is one thread of the argument in H. J. Habakkuk, *American and British Technology in the Nineteenth Century: The Search for Labour Saving Inventions* (Cambridge: Cambridge University Press, 1962).

20. J. G. Williamson, *Late Nineteenth Century American Development: A General Equilibrium History* (Cambridge: Cambridge University Press, 1974).

21. L. E. Davis and R. E. Gallman, 'The Share of Savings and Investment in GNP during the Nineteenth Century in the U.S.A.' in F. C. Lane (ed.), *Fourth International Conference of Economic History* (Paris: Mouton, 1973), pp. 437–66.

22. J. Schmookler, *Invention and Economic Growth* (Cambridge, Mass: Harvard University, 1966); J. Jewkes, D. Sawers, and R. Stillerman, *The Sources of Invention* (London: Macmillan, 1958); N. Rosenberg, *Perspectives on Technology* (Cambridge: Cambridge University Press, 1976); P. A. David, *Technical Choice, Innovation and Economic Growth* (Cambridge: Cambridge University Press, 1975).

23. J. A. Schumpeter, *The Theory of Economic Development* (New York: Oxford University Press, 1961, originally published in German in 1911). Schumpeter is widely recognised as an especially historically minded economist.

24. For example, Crafts in Floud and McCloskey. The main Denison reference is E. F. Denison, *Why Growth Rates Differ* (Washington, D.C.: Brookings Institution, 1967).

25. *rK/Y* and *wL/Y*, where *r* is the interest rate, *w* the wage rate.

26. Note that land is treated as a factor of production which can grow, as is appropriate to eighteenth-century England. The usual distinction of only two factors is a matter of convenience only.

27. Again, this section is necessarily technical. Readers may skip it if they promise never to use terms like 'labour saving' and 'capital saving'. Even then, perseverance is rewarded, and few readers will be able to avoid authors who have not adopted this self-denying ordinance.

28. Compare, for example, T. S. Ashton, *An Economic History of England: the Eighteenth Century* (London: Methuen, 1955), pp. 108–13.

29. It can be shown that Hicks-neutral and Harrod-neutral technical change are equivalent if and only if the elasticity of substitution between capital and labour is 1. (Compare with Chapter 3.)

30. Much the best study in this area is David, *Technical Choice*, especially Ch. 1, but it is very difficult reading. See also P. Uselding, 'Studies of Technology in Economic History', in R. E. Gallman (ed.), *Recent Developments in the Study of Business and Economic History: Essays in Memory of Herman E. Kroos, Research in Economic History*, Supplement 1 (Greenwich, Conn: J. A. I. Press, 1977).

31. Peter Temin, 'The Relative Decline of the British Steel Industry,

1880–1913' in H. Rosovsky (ed.), *Industrialization in Two Systems* (New York: Wiley, 1966).
32. D. N. McCloskey, *Economic Maturity and Entrepreneurial Decline: British Iron and Steel, 1870–1914* (Cambridge, Mass: Harvard University Press, 1973), pp. 105–13.
33. J. R. Hicks, *Capital and Time* (Oxford: Clarendon Press, 1973); *Economic Perspectives* (Oxford: Clarendon Press, 1977). Compare with G. R. Hawke, *Railways and Economic Growth in England & Wales, 1840–1870* (Oxford: Clarendon Press, 1970), p. 365.

Chapter 9

1. We have $Y = 1(1 - c + ct) \cdot (G + I)$ and by elementary calculus $\Delta Y/\Delta t = [-c/(1 - c + ct)^2](G + I)$, which simply rearranges to the expression given in the text.
2. Note that t is less than 1 since not all income is appropriated in taxes; $1 - c$ is positive since c is the fraction of income consumed. Therefore $t(1 - c)$ is less than $(1 - c)$. Adding tc to both sides, t is less than $(1 - c + ct)$. Therefore $t/(1 - c + ct)$ is less than 1.
3. E. Cary Brown, 'Fiscal Policy in the Thirties: A Reappraisal', in R. W. Fogel and S. L. Engerman (eds.), *The Reinterpretation of American Economic History* (New York: Harper, 1971).
4. Readers may also be able to deduce that it is unaffected by whether the tax is specific (a fixed amount per unit of the commodity) or *ad valorem* (a percentage of the selling price). In Figure 9.2 the old and new curves are parallel in parts (a) and (b), so illustrating a specific tax. For an *ad valorem* tax the new and old schedules would diverge, but the argument would be essentially unaffected.
5. P. Mathias and P. K. O'Brien, 'Taxation in Britain and France, 1715–1810. A Comparison of the Social and Economic Incidence of Taxes Collected for the Central Governments', *Jour. European Econ. Hist.* 5 (Winter 1976), pp. 601–50.
6. Governments may either intentionally or unintentionally themselves create monopolies, but economic policy may still be to avoid 'market failure'. Governments, like any large and segmented organisation, often reach contradictory conclusions at the same time. Furthermore, governments might think that monopolies will be more likely to act as though they were competitive if they are owned by the state, although experience of nationalised industries does not give unqualified support for such a view.
7. To review this point, turn back briefly to the analysis of competitive and monopoly equilibria in Chapter 6.
8. For example, motor mechanics may control both the demand for and supply of motor vehicle repairs.
9. There is room embedded in this apparently innocuous statement for much more political debate. We have made no distinction between cases where a private market is possible but difficult and

those where the 'free-rider' phenomenon makes a private market impossible (or almost so). Holders of some political views would want to limit government action to only part of this spectrum of possibilities.

10. It is nevertheless an important result both in the context of 'second best' theory applied to customs unions and in the context of real world trade negotiations, where it is discussed in terms of trade diversion versus trade creation following reductions in tariffs and other barriers to trade.

11. To elucidate this argument, refer back to Chapter 5.

12. A first-best solution might well involve distributing the tax receipts so raised among the particular members of the public affected by the pollution. Compare with the earlier discussion of second-best policies.

13. D. N. McCloskey, 'The Economics of Enclosure: A Market Analysis' and 'The Persistence of English Open Fields' in E. L. Jones and W. Parker (eds.), *Economic Problems in European Agrarian History* (Princeton: Princeton University Press, 1975); D. N. McCloskey, 'English Open Fields as Behaviour Towards Risk' in P. Uselding (ed.), *Research in Economic History*, Vol. 1 (Greenwich: JAI Press, 1976), pp. 124–70; E. L. Jones in Floud and McCloskey.

14. Translating inchoate notions of variability into the technical language of risk and scrutinising the implications of risk influences against observed behaviour is the recent achievement of McCloskey.

15. E. L. Jones in Floud and McCloskey.

16. D. North and R. P. Thomas, *The Rise of the Western World* (Cambridge: Cambridge University Press, 1973). See also D. North and L. Davis, *Institutional Change and American Economic Growth* (Cambridge: Cambridge University Press, 1971); cf. J. R. Hicks, *The Theory of Economic History* (Oxford: Clarendon Press, 1969).

Chapter 10

1. Especially associated with Lakatos. See I. Lakatos, *Proofs and Refutations* (Cambridge: Cambridge University Press, 1976); I. Lakatos and A. Musgrave (eds.), *Criticism and the Growth of Knowledge* (Cambridge: Cambridge University Press, 1970); C. Howson (ed.), *Method and Appraisal in the Physical Sciences* (Cambridge: Cambridge University Press, 1976); S. Latsis (ed.), *Method and Appraisal in Economics* (Cambridge: Cambridge University Press, 1976).

2. This is what gives historians an enlarged role in understanding the evolution of science; to know whether something is ad hoc in this sense, one has to know what observation provoked the formulation of a hypothesis and what observations were unknown until it was formulated. Answering these questions requires the standard historical techniques.

3. Some examples do exist. The most famous is the Leontief paradox.

Chapter 7 can be used to deduce that a country will export goods it produces relatively cheaply, and this can be extended to the proposition that exports will be relatively intensive in the most abundant factor of production. But Leontief observed that U.S. imports were more intensive in capital than its exports while the U.S. is more abundant in capital than its trading partners. The theory of international trade was extended as this 'anomaly' was explored.

4. See Chapter 3, and J. V. Beckett, 'English Landownership in the Later Seventeenth and Eighteenth Centuries: The Debate and the Problems', *Econ. Hist. Rev.*, Sec. Ser., 30 (1977), pp. 567–81, especially 568, 569, 573, and 578–9. Compare with H. J. Habakkuk, 'English Landownership, 1680–1740',*Econ. Hist. Rev.* 10 (1939–40), pp. 1–17.

5. Compare with Chapter 3 (on human capital).

6. The same point arises in other disciplines. To a mathematician the 'difference' between 80 and 2 is clearly 78, the result of subtracting one number from the other. In ordinary language the difference may be that one number has two digits while the other has only one, or even that one consists only of curves while the other involves some straight segments. Deeper thinking is facilitated by precision, even at the expense of inviting misunderstanding by the uninitiated. Economists have more problems than mathematicians only because many people expect to be able to understand their language.

7. *Tautology* in the sense of Chapter 3, note 1. Anybody who thinks economists are always careless in their use of words, and anybody seeking some intellectual entertainment, should consult F. Machlup, *Essays on Economic Semantics* (Englewood Cliffs, N.J.: Prentice-Hall, 1963).

8. Malcolm Falkus, 'Lighting in the Dark Ages of English Economic History: Town Streets before the Industrial Revolution', Essay 12 in D. C. Coleman and A. H. John (eds.), *Trade, Government and Economy in Pre-Industrial England: Essays Presented to F. J. Fisher* (London: Weidenfeld & Nicolson, 1976).

9. Ian Blanchard, 'English Lead and the International Bullion Crisis of the 1550s', Essay 2 in Coleman and John, *Trade, Government and Economy.*

10. T. Thomas, in Floud and McCloskey.

11. M. Desai, 'A Malthusian Crisis in Medieval England: A Critique of the Postan–Titow Hypothesis', paper read at Cliometrics conference, University of Warwick, January, 1978. Much earlier, economic theory was significant in Postan's questioning of much recorded wisdom about the Middle Ages. Compare too the interpretation of increased labour supplies in the Industrial Revolution in Chapter 3 (on labour).

12. Readers willing to go on to 'New Economic History' might well start with C. H. Lee, *The Quantitative Approach to Economic History* (London: Martin Robertson, 1977).

13. For example, J. F. Goody, J. Thirsk, and E. P. Thompson (eds.), *Family and Inheritance: Rural Society in Western Europe, 1200–1800,* (New York: Cambridge University Press, 1976).

14. It is not always easy to locate such a starting point. The outstanding question of this kind is the motivation of the marginalist revolution of the 1870s onwards. It is usually regarded as a purely academic change, the discovery that it is possible to build economic theory on a foundation of exchange rather than of production, and this is at least a major part of the explanation. There may have been an element of observation in the more obvious role of fixed capital in the economy.

15. A. R. Bridbury, 'The Hundred Years' War: Costs and Profits', in Coleman and John, *Trade, Government and Economy,* pp. 80–95.

16. G. R. Elton, *England under the Tudors* (London: Methuen, 1955), especially Chapter IX; C. P. Hill, *The Century of Revolution* (Edinburgh: Nelson, 1961).

Index

Index

235

identification problem, 122
Imlah, A. H., 155
imputed rents, 20, 23
income, 16–36
  defined, 16
  equality of income and output,
    16–17, 34–5
  real and money, 22, 67, 75
  historical uses, 35–6
  and mortality, 44
  and fertility, 44–5
  long and short run determinants, 62
  and multiplier, real and monetary,
    67
  injections and leakages, 67–8,
    185–6, 208
  and demand curve, 98–100
  see also national income, prices
incremental capital output ratio, 167–8
index number problem, 22, 58
indifference curve, 102
  social, 135–6
industrial revolution, 36, 47, 52, 86,
    161–4, 166, 168, 175–6, 180, 193,
    199–200, 206–7, 210, 213–14
infant industry, 144–5
inflation, 78, 91–2
injections and leakages
  investment, 67–8
  monetary, 82–3, 93
  see also multiplier
innovation, 17, 174
  and factor bias, 177–82
input–output analysis, 7, 32–4, 55, 146
integration, vertical and horizontal, 31
interdependence, 12, 14, 16, 203, 211
  profits and share prices, 18, 50,
    89–90
  between individuals, 22, 24–5
  capital and product prices, 49
  interest, money and capital, 80, 97
  prices and quantities, 106
  capital exports and imports, 154–6
interest
  and money, 80, 93
  and balance of payments, 150
  see also production function
intermediate goods, 19, 145
international trade, 10, 12–13, 36, 74,
    86–7, 132–56
interwar Britain, 8, 34, 41, 62, 65, 66,
    71, 96–7, 147, 150–1, 208
invention and innovation, 174
investible surplus, 160, 164

investment, 17, 30, 206–7
  stocks, 23, 63
  and the multiplier, 63–8
  accelerator, 68–73
  induced, 70
  IS curve, 94–5
  and growth, 164–73, 209
  see also autonomous investment
isoquant, 168

Jewkes, J., 174
Jones, E. L., 60

Keynes, J. M., 7, 16, 62, 63
Kuznets, S., 6, 19, 36

labour, 37, 42–8, 191, 212
  supply of, 45–8, 180–2
labour augmenting, 179
labour saving, 178, 209
Lakatos, I., 204
land, 37, 38–42, 206–7
leads and lags, 148
learning by doing, 48, 181
legal tender, 77
Leontieff paradox, 230–1 n3
Lewis, W. Arthur, 165
liquidity, 80–1, 88
liquidity preference, 94
liquidity trap, 95–6
long run, 25, 44, 62, 116, 127–8

McCloskey, D. N., 15, 60, 182
margin, 38–9, 42, 51–2
  extensive and intensive, 39
marginal cost, 126
marginal equivalences, 227 n17
marginal propensities
  save and consume, 64
  import, 68
marginal revenue, 128–9
market clearing in international trade,
    138, 141
market failure, 193–8
markets, 19, 20, 118–24, 190–3, 212,
    213
Marshall, A., 101
Marshall–Lerner conditions, 152
materialist conception of capital, 48,
    50, 168
mathematics, 14, 209, 231 n6
Mathias, P., 193